ECOCRITICISM IN THE MODERNIST IMAGINATION

Although modernism has traditionally been considered an art of cities, *Ecocriticism in the Modernist Imagination* claims a significant role for modernist texts in shaping environmental consciousness. Analyzing both canonical and lesser-known works of three key figures – E.M. Forster, Virginia Woolf, and W.H. Auden – Sultzbach suggests how the signal techniques of modernism encourage readers to become more responsive to the animate world and nonhuman minds. Understanding the way these writers represent nature's agency becomes central to interpreting the power dynamics of empire and gender, as well as experiments with language and creativity. The book engages with the longer pastoral tradition in literature, but also introduces readers to the newly expanding field of ecocriticism, including philosophies of embodiment and matter, queer ecocriticism, and animal studies. What emerges is a picture of green modernism that reifies our burgeoning awareness of what it means to be human within a larger living community.

KELLY SULTZBACH is a professor at the University of Wisconsin, La Crosse. Her research explores modernist representations of the relationship between humans and the environment. Published and forthcoming work can be found in *A Cambridge Global History of Literature and the Environment*, *Understanding Merleau-Ponty Understanding Modernism*, and ASLE UK's *Green Letters: Studies in Ecocriticism*.

ECOCRITICISM IN THE MODERNIST IMAGINATION

Forster, Woolf, and Auden

KELLY SULTZBACH

CAMBRIDGE
UNIVERSITY PRESS

CAMBRIDGE
UNIVERSITY PRESS

One Liberty Plaza, 20th Floor, New York, NY 10006, USA

Cambridge University Press is part of the University of Cambridge.

It furthers the University's mission by disseminating knowledge in the pursuit of education, learning, and research at the highest international levels of excellence.

www.cambridge.org
Information on this title: www.cambridge.org/9781107161412

© Kelly Elizabeth Sultzbach 2016

First published 2016

Printed in the United Kingdom by Clays, St Ives plc

A catalogue record for this publication is available from the British Library.

Library of Congress Cataloging-in-Publication Data
Names: Sultzbach, Kelly, 1972- author.
Title: Ecocriticism in the modernist imagination : Forster, Woolf, and Auden / Kelly Elizabeth Sultzbach.
Description: New York : Cambridge University Press, 2016. | Includes bibliographical references and index.
Identifiers: LCCN 2016007898 | ISBN 9781107161412 (Hardback)
Subjects: LCSH: English fiction–20th century–History and criticism. | Nature in literature. | Ecology in literature. | Forster, E. M. (Edward Morgan), 1879-1970–Criticism and interpretation | Woolf, Virginia, 1882-1941–Criticism and interpretation. | Auden, W. H. (Wystan Hugh), 1907-1973–Criticism and interpretation.
Classification: LCC PR888.N36 S95 2016 | DDC 820.9/36–dc23 LC record available at https://lccn.loc.gov/2016007898

ISBN 978-1-107-16141-2 Hardback

Contents

Acknowledgments

This book would never have come into being without two very important mentors and friends, Louise (Molly) Westling and Paul Peppis. They were much more than dissertation advisors; they took me into their homes and through their challenging questions, formed the direction of my literary scholarship. Molly prodded me through some of my most frustrating moments of self-doubt about the project and championed my successes. I am deeply indebted to her scholarship and rigorous questioning. Evenings spent over dinner and wine with Molly and George Wickes' sustaining wit – indeed the affectionate energy of the whole furred and feathered family at Barber Drive – have been cherished times, undoubtedly to be renewed for years to come. Paul's passion for modernity and teaching continues to be the standard I set for myself. The intellectual counter-arguments he posed moved my work forward and were always matched with a kind, gracious spirit; his collegiality and belief in the work we do at a university brings out the best in everyone around him. I also am indebted to William Rossi and Ted Toadvine for their active participation in my dissertation process.

I am grateful to have been awarded a University of Oregon Humanities Center Fellowship, which gave me my first "office of my own" and sponsored my initial archival research on Virginia Woolf at Washington State University. Trevor Bond, the curator of WSU's wonderful collection drawn from the library of Virginia and Leonard Woolf, was particularly kind in assisting a novice archival scholar. The University of Wisconsin La Crosse's generous New Faculty Research Grant Award enabled me to complete archival research on W.H. Auden, while the cooperation and skillful suggestions of the staff at the Berg Collection in the New York Public Library made sure that time with the Auden material was full of happy surprises too. I am equally appreciative of the thoughtful emails and research suggestions of Edward Mendelson, who granted permission on behalf of the Estate of W.H. Auden to use some of Auden's unpublished material from the Berg Collection in this book. I also thank Wayne

Chapman and Clemson University Press for permission to reprint portions of "The Fertile Potential of Woolf's Environmental Ethic" related to Virginia Woolf's "A Sketch of the Past" and "Thunder at Wembley," originally published in *Woolf and the Art of Exploration: Selected Papers from the Fifteenth International Conference on Virginia Woolf* (2006), edited by Helen Southworth and Elisa Kay Sparks. As I gave conference papers that became the seeds for new chapters, the provocative questions and thoughtful feedback of fellow-presenters were deeply appreciated: at the Modernist Studies Association, I particularly benefited from the lively discussion of Jeff McCarthy and Anne Raine; the International Virginia Woolf Conference fosters an atmosphere that makes all new Woolfians feel warmly welcomed; and I thank the many keen friends and scholars who regularly attend the Association for the Study of Literature and the Environment, many of whom nurtured my fledgling interpretations.

The encouragement of Ray Ryan at Cambridge University Press was foundational to the completion of the more ambitious book manuscript. His faith kept me going and I will always be indebted to the patience he had for a four-four teaching load, which meant substantive revisions were a long time in coming. In the final stages of book production, assistant editors Rachel Cox and Helen Francis effortlessly made things hum along to the finish line. I am also exceedingly appreciative of the energy and detailed feedback provided by my anonymous Cambridge University Press reviewers.

Graduate school was a source of collegiality and joy thanks to my University of Oregon peers who have remained important friends. Mandolin Brassaw Swamy, in particular, with whom I shared an office and many a lavender-lemondrop cocktail when needed. I am grateful for an amazing group of compatriots, including: Michelle Kohler, Tiffany Beechy, Amanda Adams, Carter Soles, Kom Konyosy, Stephen Rust, Sarah Jacquette Ray, Teresa Coronado, Hannah Tracy, Stephanie Callan, Larissa Ennis, and Tamara Holloway.

I owe a huge debt of gratitude to my colleagues at the University of Wisconsin, La Crosse, who kept stimulating scholarly conversation churning, and would always ask about how the book was coming along in ways that kept it coming along: Lalita Pandit Hogan, Kimberly DeFazio, Rob Wilke, Kate Parker, David Hart, Gary Konas, Haixa Lan, Tom Pribek, Nabamita Dutta, and Tushar Das. I offer special thanks to Stephen Mann, Bill Barillas, and Sharon Jessee, all of whom generously read and reviewed material for me during a busy semester and offered keen insights. I am thankful for the friendship of Julie Wieskopf, who shared many weekend work-sessions, and put in an altruistic late night, helping me finish endnote formatting for the mere payment of pizza and wine. I also thank Adam Putz, who thoughtfully bought me Alexandra Harris's lovely book when I was in a writing rut, and played bowls with me at Monk's House. The epilogue of this book is dedicated to a group of UW-L students who continued to lead multiple literary hikes in our local marsh even after our environmental literature course was over: Zachary Allen, Ellen Brown, Sarah Mueller, Taylor Parrish, and Daniel Sheridan.

While they might be surprised to find themselves enumerated here, these acknowledgements wouldn't be complete without recognizing Fiona Lin Connolly-Smith and Kimberly Amrine. Fiona for cheering me on when I left a solid law career to romantically pursue a PhD in literature, sending brownies while I studied for my oral exams, paying for plane flights to visit her in New York during lean grad school years, and being the best friend any person could hope to have; and Kim for her unflagging support and long telephone calls whenever needed.

And, of course, most of all, *for my family*. They have always encouraged me to find beauty in the world and without their support this book would have been impossible. For my grandmother, Janet Somers Sultzbach, who had library books tucked away in cushions of the couch and made my childish opinions seem like thoughts that mattered. For my sister, April Sultzbach, whose love of "big books" is a sacred source of kinship and is passing that joy of reading along to my favorite niece, Sofia Rose Haftarski. For my talented mom, Gayle Macher Sultzbach, whose own deep well of artistic creativity has always been an inspiration to keep believing in this project and working with lines, be they in paint or words. And for my dad, Jon Sultzbach, who used to call owls when we were little and now that I'm grown up will probably be the first to read through every page of every chapter of this book, even though he has never read a single work by Forster or Woolf.

Introduction

The silence of the land went home to one's very heart – its mystery, its greatness, the amazing reality of its concealed life.... The smell of mud, of primeval mud, by Jove! was in my nostrils, the high stillness of the primeval forest was before my eyes ... All this was great, expectant, mute, while the man jabbered about himself. I wondered whether the stillness on the face of the immensity looking at us two were meant as an appeal or as a menace. What were we who had strayed in here? Could we handle that dumb thing, or would it handle us? I felt how big, how confoundedly big, was that thing that couldn't talk, and perhaps was deaf as well. What was in there?

But I couldn't. I could not tell her. It would have been too dark – too dark altogether ...

Joseph Conrad, Heart of Darkness

But the horses didn't want it – they swerved apart; the earth didn't want it, sending up rocks through which the riders must pass single file; ... the birds, the carrion, the Guest House, that came into view: they didn't want it, they said in their hundred voices, "No, not yet," and the sky said, "No, not there"

E.M. Forster, A Passage to India

And the stage was empty. Miss La Trobe leant against the tree, paralyzed. Her power had left her. Beads of perspiration broke on her forehead. Illusion had failed. 'This is death,' she murmured, 'death.' Then suddenly, as the illusion petered out, the cows took up the burden.... The cows annihilated the gap; bridged the distance; filled the emptiness and continued the emotion.

Virginia Woolf, Between the Acts

> Woken, I lay in the arms of my own warmth and listened
> To a storm enjoying its storminess in the winter dark
> Till my ear, as it can when half-asleep or half-sober,
> Set to work to unscramble interjectory uproar,

Construing its airy vowels and watery consonants
Into a love-speech indicative of a Proper Name.
W.H. Auden, "First Things First"

This book attempts to answer a problem posed by the ending of one of the first modernist novels, Joseph Conrad's *Heart of Darkness*. Marlow's final, broken, faltering conversation with Kurtz's beloved prompts one to wonder what it is that couldn't be said. What innate, unspoken, presences might palpitate underneath the horizon line of dash? What grows from those little black seeds of ellipses? Of course, it has to do with telling lies about national motives and hiding human brutality, but the presence of the Congo also inserts itself in the new, halting rhythms of their dialogue. Their hesitations recall the astounding immensity of the "silence of the land," its "smells" and its "concealed life" becoming a vivified force – a "face of immensity" whose "mute" stillness is powerful enough to reduce human conversation to merely ignorant "jabber." Marlow's new consciousness of nature's presence shakes him to the core, provoking a series of unanswered questions about human and nonhuman identity that ripple throughout modern literature. Marlow's experiences in the African wilderness transform his understanding of civilization, morality, and even his ability to use language.

Experiments with modern interiority delve into perceived realities that are difficult to articulate, more felt than understood, and subject to change. As the framing narrator listening to Marlow's story on the deck of the Nellie struggles to explain, meaning is often "not inside like a kernel but outside, enveloping the tale which brought it out only as a glow brings out a haze."[1]

The surrounding environment gains a new presence as modernism explores the boundaries of language and the possibilities of nonhuman lives that operate outside of human control. What emerges from some of the literature that follows Conrad is a sense of how the formal innovations of modernism construct humanity's understanding of itself within a fluctuating world of environmental actors – sentient others that are paradoxically both kin and alien to the individual characters encountering them. Although the modernist reactions to these new understandings of nature and the nonhuman varied – horror, hostility, and humility among them – the subjective voice of the nonhuman consistently asserts itself in distinctly new representations.

Modern British literature is concerned with all of these responses; a plurality of perspectives and viewpoints is typical for a period featuring a broadening expanse of authorial voices, a reason many scholars now refer to "modernisms" rather than "modernism." Today's ecocritical theoretical perspectives also contain a proliferating multitude of critical dialogues, as one can easily see in even a cursory perusal of Greg Garrard's *Ecocriticism*, currently in its second edition. In an effort to reflect some of that diversity, *Modernism in the Ecocritical Imagination* focuses on three canonical writers, E.M. Forster, Virginia Woolf, and W.H. Auden, who trace a chronological arc from the beginning to the end of the period, and integrates different types of ecocritical theory: primarily pastoral ideology, ecophenomenology, and animal studies, while considering how they also interact with queer ecocriticism, eco-Marxism, as well as posthumanism and ecomaterialism. Synthesizing these interrelated strains of ecocriticism demonstrates how modernisms' depictions of nature are complicated by the nexus of switches at the slippery exchanges of human, nature, and animal. Multiple nodes of modernist engagement with the environment emerge at junctures between not only human and animal, but also culture and nature, body and mind, as well as local and global identities. Accordingly, my project is designed to integrate a cluster of environmental inquiries into a larger picture of green literary modernism.

One issue Conrad's *Heart of Darkness* epitomizes is the presence of doubt within a modernist environmental consciousness. Thus, Thoreau's famous statement of a writer's duty to "speak a word *for* Nature"[2] becomes suspect. How does a human know what Nature would say? As Thomas Nagel famously queried in 1974, how do we know what it is like "for a *bat* to be a bat" and how do we attempt the endeavor without "deny[ing] the reality or logical significance of what we can never describe or understand"?[3] Modernists began to broach these questions by simply imagining that nonhuman agencies with individual perspectives existed. What would a stream of cow-consciousness or storm-consciousness look like and sound like? To what extent are writers who attempt to "speak a word" on Nature's behalf selflessly translating underrepresented perspectives and to what extent are they usurping the subjectivity of another to make it say what one might wish to hear? Are we making assumptions of "muteness" that belie the actual expressive, and sometimes even vocal, utterances of nature and the nonhuman, which we simply mistake as "mute" or "empty" due to our own ignorance for comprehending the cacophony of languages within it? Forster, Woolf, and Auden don't negate the need for such doubts; to the contrary, the way in which their writing consciously investigates the knotty problems of agency and representation exposes the ethical basis for such uncertainty. In a distinctly modernist maneuver, nature's voice is abstract, active, and not always readily interpretable by human characters.

As such, modernism is particularly relevant to contemporary discussions about defining "environmentalism." As Ursula Heise and Allison Carruth have defined this term, historically nature was understood and represented as either "essentially stable, harmonious, and in balance outside of human interference," or alternatively, as an apocalyptic "nature in decline." In contrast, during the last quarter century the environmental sciences and humanities have been "foregrounding instead the inherent dynamism and patterns of constant change that structure natural systems,"[4] undermining the binary reaction of harmony or loss with a more complex sense of humanity's own relevance as an actor in an environmental community. Our membership in the Earth's ecological community has ethical ramifications we are still attempting to conceptualize as we consider the global manifestations of humanity's role in the geological epoch of the Anthropocene. Donna Haraway's work has also attempted to trouble historical dualisms, reminding us that entrenched binaries about nature and technology create false divides: "Technophilias and technophobias vie with organophilias and organophobias, and taking sides is not left to chance. If one loves organic nature, to express a love of technology makes one suspect. If one finds cyborgs to be promising sorts of monsters, then one is an unreliable ally in the fight against the destruction of all things organic."[5] Many modernists were fracturing these environmental dualisms early on in ways that have sometimes escaped critical recognition. In part because the notion of modernity similarly suffers from a narrative that oversimplifies its "patterns of constant change" and fluctuation by relegating it to a singular movement away from one end of the binary, a Romantic foregrounding of organic nature, toward its opposite, the rise of an urban culture of detached aestheticism. Yet, when modernist texts are pressed through a sieve of ecocritical theoretical questions, they often offer startling representations of a more-than-human world that is in the midst of naming and breaking such binaries. A range of literary experiments depict the animate complexity of nonhuman agency and the spectrum of human reactions to what it means to be embedded within, rather than taking objective measurements outside of, the flotsam and jetsam of the creative, pulsating, flesh of the earth. Judith Paltin redefines the modernist shift to what she terms "anti-realism" – a stance traditionally associated with aesthete distancing from the physical world – by recasting it as an attempt to manifest the world's actual instability. Older, prepackaged ways of knowing the world were dismissed in favor of the destabilizing processes of flux offered by biology and physics. Paltin explains, "Modernist nature operates as an agile breaching force, exploding perceptual illusion and readerly comfort in a series of confrontational mimetic pulses"[6] Further, these aesthetic ruptures of expected meaning are not always celebratory; instead, they often *trouble* placating assurances of nature's capacity to offer humanity rapturous transcendence or a companionable mirror for our own emotions.

In a recent introductory anthology to environmental literature, Timothy Clark pinpoints a range of representational responses to nature which I argue Forster, Woolf, and Auden each illuminate. The first is a kind of feigning of environmental consciousness that is so reverent toward nature that it risks setting it up as an "other" that only has meaning in terms of how it reveals humanity's failings, thus producing what he terms "a romantic *humanism*."[7] Forster's early work begins in this register, using a kind of magical sense of nature's noble morality to critique the short-sightedness of human greed, as if holding out nature as a looking-glass for humanity's own reflection. Yet, his later work begins to acknowledge an increased sense of wonder and uncertainty, suggesting nature often exceeds the ability of humans to frame it with a handle. This second version of environmentalism Clark defines as "express[ing] the fact of an incalculable connection between bodies, human and nonhuman, across and within the biosphere,"[8] noting that "new terms emerge for the nature/culture we inhabit, or are, such as Morton's 'the mesh' or Stacy Alaimo's 'transcorporeality.'"[9] Indeed, several of the works by Forster, Woolf, and Auden seem to acknowledge what Karen Barad might term intra-action, or, as Stacey Alaimo describes it, nature inherently in the body already: "any creature, ecosystem, climatological pattern, ocean current – cannot be taken for granted as simply existing out there."[10] In this way Woolf's experiments with sketching the body's pulsating awareness of waves and particles that both reflect changing notions of science and record flashes of embodied knowledge, also stretch toward an intra-action of the material world. Her work tends to represent a self-already-material – made from the world and knowing itself as a component of the environment's meta-linguistic potential. For a modernist age that pondered the relevance of machine-made objects versus hand-crafted goods and grappled with conceptions of a molecular world teeming within what the human eye had previously seen only as a solid surface, ecocritical materialism is instructive. Drawing on Karen Barad and other experts in quantum physics, Serenella Iovino and Serpil Oppermann theorize the "dynamism inherent in materials of life encompassing a tremendously broad range of biological and material expressions that can admittedly generate complex narratives."[11] While the terms for these representations of humanity's relationship with nature may be new, modernist texts attest to the presence of this ideology within the literary imagination at the turn of the century. Third, Clark posits that the next questions for environmental literature might take a shape already suggested by Auden's representations of human animals, when he asks, "What, however, if one implication of the Anthropocene were that our immediate sense of what being a person is, its scale of reference, its intentional contours, must now also emerge as having become itself an 'environmental problem'?"[12] As an ecocritical reassessment of some of Auden's work reveals, the scale of a mountain and those who would wish to plant a flag on top of it, the contours of syntactic patterning in mineral coding, and even the impact of atomic discoveries themselves, were forcing the literary imagination to reconsider the oscillating scales of microcosm and macrocosm, from the microbes living in pockets of human skin to the blown-up oil holes humans were putting on the earth's body.

Moreover, these modernists do not always present us with ethical relationships to nature or the nonhuman that are necessarily positive models. My goal is not to provide a glossy patina of celebratory green over these works; I have no desire to obfuscate the very conflicted reactions to environmental relationships and human responsibility that make them so productively messy. Solipsism, racism, and desire for escapism are also literary responses that present themselves to the ecocritical questions this book poses. Yet it is the complexity of these human ideals and human failings that most provocatively reveal how we as a species continue to grapple with our scientific and emotional understandings of the more-than-human world. Those nasty bits we would wish to eradicate from our politics and from ourselves are important to understand as well, and shouldn't diminish the ecocritical importance of these works of literature. To the contrary, the problematized "Nature" of modernist works helps ecocritical theory resist its own didactic tendencies to only favor literature that seems to offer a "solution." In *Material Ecocriticism,* Hannes Bergthaller critiques older forms of environmental criticism that too often became distilled into all-encompassing views of equality and union with nature, warning that new ecocritical trends may purport to offer new ideas but risk following in some of those same time-worn ruts:

> It is especially important not to assimilate [ecomaterialism] too quickly into the "biocentric" worldview prevalent in much of contemporary ecocriticism, to simply replace "nature" with "matter" and leave the rest of the conceptual edifice undisturbed. This temptation is especially great because when they speak of their project, the new materialists sometimes do sound a

lot like deep ecologists: they recommend the new materialist thought as an antidote to the anthropocentric hubris that has brought on the ecological crisis; they argue that it instills a salutary humility and allows us to grasp the scope of our dependency on the material world.[13]

These recognitions are undoubtedly significant for promoting an empathetic impulse that generates a more humble sense of humanity's ethical place on a shared planet, but in its most self-aware practice, ecocritical analysis should also readily admit the limits of human knowledge and notice when demarcations, differences, and exclusions are also a valuable component of ecological representations. As a result, this book draws on a variety of theories while also acknowledging the perimeters of their usefulness, and analyzes what is ecocritically progressive about a text while still pointing out competing readings suggesting where social constructs of gender, race, or a desire for tidy resolution create ethical trapdoors. This maneuver is not meant to dilute the environmental importance of the literature of Forster, Woolf, and Auden, nor undermine the potency of ecocritical theory. Rather, a heightened attentiveness to the cracks and crevices, like the porosity of Auden's limestone landscapes, are the moments where the niches of our own desires and morality most reveal where we have yet to go to understand our role within a world we can never fully comprehend. The lacunae of fear, dislocation, and loneliness are the outer boundaries of our contact zone with the environment and our ability to represent it. The breaks have always been what makes modernism new; likewise, it is in the literary contradictions and the philosophical sink-holes, where, I argue, critics and readers can find the green literary imaginative territory most interesting to explore. As Louise Westling states in her seminal work, which reassesses the continued legacy of Maurice Merleau-Ponty in part by correcting misunderstandings of his ecophenomenology as an over-simplistic gesture of unification, "the relation of any creature to others within the flesh of the world is never fully realized or identical; this dehiscence or *écart* generates differentiation even as the intertwining of things and creatures ensures their kinship."[14] It is the recognition of fleshly boundaries of bodies that allows us to touch and wonder at something that we must then begin to dance with, akin to Donna Haraway's "natureculture"[15] – the back and forth exchange of companion species, which never fully become one, but create innovative relationships of communication because there is a mutual respect for the divide that creates the space for exchange.

Paradoxically, in the moments where modernist literature seems to be teetering on a dangerous pinnacle of anthropocentrism, it is often that very vantage point that reveals a new perspective from which to criticize systems of power constraining both human and nonhuman actors. Forster, Woolf, and Auden often use the animate environment to critique cultural assumptions about scientific hierarchies, political power, and traditional forms of knowledge, associating formal innovation and natural imagery with an effort to express a larger consciousness of a diverse world – at times simply reinscribing anthropocentrism, but in other works provocatively superseding human solipsism. The muddled dialectics within their work only strengthen the ecocritical potential of their varied responses.

As ecocriticism has expanded beyond its early roots in American realist nature writing – in part due to Lawrence Buell's inviting phrase "environmental unconscious," which acknowledges the formation of environmental values in texts that aren't overtly about the environment[16] – several ground-breaking publications have assessed how ecocritical theory enlivens our understanding of Renaissance, Romantic, and Victorian texts. Ken Hiltner has published two Renaissance studies: *Renaissance Ecology: Imagining Eden in Milton's England* (2008) and *What Else is Pastoral?: Renaissance Literature and the Environment* (2011) along with Robert Watson's *Back to Nature: The Green and the Real in the Late Renaissance* (2007); Romanticism's environmental inflections have been reassessed by Jonathan Bate's seminal *Romantic Ecology: Wordsworth and the Environmental Tradition* (1991) as well as Kevin Hutchings' *Romantic Ecologies and Colonial Cultures in the British Atlantic World 1770–1850* (2009); continuing the trajectory, John Parham's *Green Man Hopkins: Poetry and the Victorian Ecological Imagination* (2010) and Allen MacDuffie's *Victorian Literature, Energy, and the Ecological Imagination* (2014) have inaugurated similar inquiries into Victorian literature. The early twentieth century witnessed the advent of ecological science and some of its most salient literary themes revolve around place and human identity – for example, urban malaise, the legacy of Darwinism, concepts of home and colonial identity, the rise of mass tourism, and, most importantly, uncertainty about the status of language itself – making it ripe for a comprehensive study of how ecocriticism might intersect with these foundational modernist concerns. For every age, nature is a fertile subject of literary inspiration, but for each generation, the shifting perspective of new discoveries, the backward glance of nostalgia, and struggles within existing political frameworks pose different questions to the nonhuman world. In turn, each new set of cultural questions generates revised conceptions of how human beings value the natural world and define themselves within it.

Green modernism: Canonical themes and environmental questions

Testing boundaries has long been recognized as a defining attribute of modernism. To borrow Ezra Pound's famous phrasing, modern poets "make it new"[17] by "break[ing] the pentameter,"[18] resulting in formal ruptures that invite unspoken associative and imagist leaps of connectivity, expressing the roiling ambiguity of the age. Fiction writers prioritize what Forster terms "pattern and rhythm"[19] over linear plots and distort narrative objectivity with stream of consciousness techniques, or what Woolf describes as "life not as a series of gig-lamps symmetrically arranged" but "an incessant shower of innumerable atoms."[20] By 1962, Auden describes poems' "formal nature" as "a hymn to Natural Law and a gesture of astonishment at the greatest of all mysteries, the order of the universe."[21] If Conrad's *Heart of Darkness* was one of the first novels to make these breaches within modern language, its radically disjunctive form is bound up in astounding new conceptions of the self within nature and the nature within self. Marlow's shattering recognition that the wild – operating both externally and internally in the novel – would not conform to British hierarchical structures of commerce or expected codes of honor initiated the first pauses and stutters of modernism. For many modernists, prior representations did not satisfy a cultural imagination shocked by world war and theories of being from Darwin to Einstein that so forcefully decentered the stability of prior truths. As a result, mirrors that had served to reflect prior visions of earlier ages – the solipsistic transfiguration of nature's dizzying grandeur into a figure of the immortality of the poet's creative capacity, the gilded rhetoric of supreme religious transcendence, the figure of Nature as silent woman coyly revealing her secrets to the scientific touch of human knowledge – were broken. Of course, the modernists may not have been quite as unique as their canonized slogans profess, as has been shown by those who have offered productive complications of how environmental imagery was being deployed within prior eras. In a similar fashion, this project acknowledges the stereotypes regarding modernist treatments of nature, which often include an emphasis on the abstract rather than the physical; a preference for urban environments rather than rural ones; and troubling conflations of certain categories of classes and races of humans with a mute and inaccessible nature, even when those rustic or primitive relationships are ostensibly praised. Yet, akin to the works above, this book also unravels exceptions, twists, and other attitudes that simultaneously challenge or divert those stereotypes. Likewise, as other comprehensive environmental literary studies have shown how environmental consciousness necessarily impacts evolving attitudes that carry forth into other eras, this work aims to show how the modernist layers of thought build from earlier strata and provide the groundwork for existing ideology shaping twenty-first-century environmental consciousness.

I am not attempting to present Forster, Woolf, and Auden as "nature writers." Instead I examine how their representations of environmental forces and nonhuman characters inflect a wide array of recognized modernist themes, including interiority, instability, and concerns of empire. In the pages that follow, "modernism" is defined more by differences of degree in rhetorical experimentation and themes of disruption than by any strict chronological time period. John Marx has articulated a definition of modernism that parallels my own: "Although there is no end of discussion about exactly when modernity occurs or exactly what it entails, critics generally agree that one of its pivotal features is the emergence of systems and networks that reconfigured modes of communication and the lived experience of time and space."[22] This book finds a strain of modernism in which writers question the role of human characters within a larger environmental system or experiment with how nonhuman voices interrelate with human modes of communication.

Although *Heart of Darkness* shuttles between spaces as divergent as the Thames and the Congo, modernism's fragmented literary style has often been called "an art of cities," defined by "urban climates, and the ideas and campaigns, the new philosophies and politics that ran through them."[23] This book claims a more significant role for the nonhuman environment in modernism. My argument doesn't deny the influence of the metropolis, but it does suggest that the palpable sights and sounds of any sensory environment have just as great an impact on modern literature as the ideologies of urban intelligentsia. As other critics synthesizing the significance of the era have noted, "The novelists sought not to banish the outside world but to register it with a heightened precision."[24] Even modernism's most famous encounters with metropolitan space – Mrs. Dalloway contemplating the mists stretching between branches on her way through Regents Park to buy flowers, or Leopold Bloom fingering the lemon-scented soap in his pocket as he meditates on the lives of gelded horses eating from feedbags – are mediated by a new awareness of the surrounding environment. As Bonnie Kime Scott explains, "modernists also discovered the impossibility of rejecting the natural world, given powerful early memories of place and sensation, and the experimental satisfaction that comes with imaginative merger of human and non-human other," which she identifies as "one of the basic tropes of ecofeminism."[25] The fractures that result from modernist representations of the environment are fraught with a struggle to situate anthropocentric experience within a world of other beings. But modern artists begin to experiment with new voices for those imagined subjectivities in a form that is designed to cleave language from the security of traditional syntactical structures and play with the plasticity of its adaptability to other subjectivities; even trees, caves, snails, or cats. The hook of the interrogatives created by these gestures of empathy – without access to any language that is not always limited by the fact that it is bounded as human – pries open further productive crevices where wild things grow. Moreover, the dynamic ruptures modernism identifies in an emerging awareness of nonhuman networks are still molten today. Several modernist scholars have already offered productive inquiries into foundational ecocritical questions, including Carrie Rohman's *Stalking the Subject: Modernism and the Animal* (2009) and Philip Armstrong's *What Animals Mean in the Fiction of Modernity* (2008), as well as Christina Alt's new historicist work documenting how Virginia Woolf was influenced by natural history and modernist life sciences in *Virginia Woolf and the Study of Nature* (2010), and Bonnie Kime Scott's ecofeminist approach to Woolf, *In the Hollow of the Wave: Virginia Woolf and the Modernist Uses of Nature* (2012), all of which this book draws on and puts in conversation with one another against the backdrop of pastoral theorists such as Terry Gifford and Raymond Williams, ecophenomenologist philosopher Maurice Merleau-Ponty, forays into eco-Marxism with John Bellamy Foster and Rob Nixon, and the animal studies work of Cary Wolfe and Donna Haraway, as well as material ecocritics, Serenella Iovino, Serpil Oppermann, and Stacey Alaimo.

The queer identity of all three of these writers also suggests, even when it is not at the forefront of their work, representations of homosexual and bisexual perspectives offer unique insight into ecocritical ethics. Although Catriona Mortimer-Sandilands and Bruce Erickson's *Queer Ecologies* takes contemporary American literature as its primary focus, they refer to Forster's *Maurice* to remind us that "rural spaces in particular have served, in a wide range of literatures, as places of freedom for male homoerotic encounters,"[26] underscoring what is at stake in expanding our definitions of both "natural" places and "natural" sexualities. Writing about *Maurice*, Paul Peppis adds a British twist to the significance of green spaces, noting, "*Maurice*'s evocation of a mythical greenwood as a refuge of homosexual outlaws, akin to the refuge of Robin Hood and his class-crossing homosocial band, offers an English alternative to the common modernist route of exile to France or Italy, a space of homosexual outlawry and class-crossing homosex."[27] However, the green space may not have been as equally liberating for modernist lesbians, whom Peppis suggests were not as well represented in science or literature as male homosexuals.[28] In that regard, Woolf's prose is more likely to use techniques of aligning sexuality with an embodied appreciation of nature's ability to create alternative moments of ecstasy and passion, rather than a specific type of green space. Additionally, for a modernist era typically known for its contemplations on loss and mortality, the questions Erickson and Mortimer-Sandilands pose about silence and grief within the queer community are salient to English depictions of queer modernity too: "What might it look like to take seriously the fact that nature is currently ungrievable, and that the melancholy natures with which we are surrounded are a desperate attempt to hold onto something that we don't even know how to talk about grieving? Here, queer culture has a lot to teach."[29] Considered from this perspective, Auden's "Amor Loci," about an abandoned mining landscape that teaches him to "imagine a Love / that, however often smeared, / shrugged at, / abandoned / by a frivolous worlding, / does not abandon?" poignantly implicates a personal grief for places we love, even through their own forms of aging and death.

In addition to its fascination with urban place and feelings of loss or ennui, which this book will expand to the liminal categories of rural and colonial space as well, modernist uncertainty has been traditionally understood as being influenced by England's imperialism and two world wars. These encounters with foreign terrains and unfamiliar people strike at the very heart of what it means to be in a relationship, often violent, with a larger world. The darkness Conrad finds in that heart foregrounds British imperialism's brutal treatment of fellow humans. While this project is based on the fact that *all* humans are animals, it also recognizes that literature has frequently used images of bestiality as a way to derogate and ostracize people on the basis of race and ethnicity. Edward Said's account, in *Culture and Imperialism*, that British colonialists determined people native to other countries "deserved to be ruled" because "'they' were not like 'us'"[30] traces an inherent prejudice of exclusion within British culture; these same assumptions underlie anxieties about human relations with nature and the nonhuman. Work on postcolonial ecocriticism in wide-ranging anthologies such as *Postcolonial Ecocriticism: Literature, Animals, Environment* (Huggan and Tiffin, 2010), *Postcolonial Ecologies: Literatures of the Environment* (DeLoughrey and Handley, 2011), and

Postcolonial Green: Environmental Politics and World Narratives (Bonnie Roos and Alex Hunt, 2010) suggest a common ground that might further both fields of study. Indeed, in modern British literature the environment is recast as a kind of "other" that British culture attempted to contain when nature did not conduct itself as a benign entity in concert with Anglo-European hegemonic order. Yet, as Said points out, efforts to subjugate other lives can have the unintended effect of promoting productive resistance.[31] Similarly, Forster, Woolf, and Auden often use the animate environment to critique cultural assumptions about hierarchies, political power, and traditional forms of knowledge.

An ecocritical analysis of these issues also puts this work in dialogue with questions about how rural and metropolitan identity is influenced by the global power dynamics of warfare and the rise and decline of England's imperial influence. Jed Esty has made crucial observations in *A Shrinking Island: Modernism and National Culture in England* about how the dialectic of imperial expansion and contraction created different uses of "metropolitan perception" that swing a global cosmopolitan gaze inward "to Anglocentric representations of meaningful time and bounded space."[32] Giving this question a turn toward rural perception, Alexandra Harris's ground-breaking *Romantic Moderns: English Writers, Artists and the Imagination from Virginia Woolf to John Piper*, reminds us that beyond the first decade of High Modernism, modernists were looking to the countryside for inspiration and "drawn to the crowded, the detailed, old-fashioned and whimsical, gathering souvenirs from an old country that may not survive the fighting."[33] Modern artists' representations of country life inform a desire to reclaim a sensitivity to heritage and local place, which play their own significant role in motivating the modern aesthetic. This book adds to that critical conversation by showing how modernist literature revises environment-as-object to acknowledge environment-as-being. This conceptualization of self in world arises from the personal, local embodied experience of rural environment Harris identifies, yet prompts wider cultural reevaluations of what it means to be a member of an expanding community in ways that contradict the idea of man as island. That burgeoning environmental consciousness of nature's agency resists insularity; once internalized, it puts forth its own green shoots in an outward movement, influencing modernist assessments of the politics of aesthetics and the role of humans on a wider national, ecological, and sometimes even global stage. Both Esty and Harris highlight how Modernism registers a self-awareness of doubt about assumptions of superiority. In this work, that theme is amplified through the rebellious potential of nonhuman lives and human characters' palpable awareness of their surroundings, prompting efforts to imagine the thoughts and feelings of nonhuman characters.

Nature's dialogue in three modernist voices

Modernist works often depict the voice of the nonhuman as having its own source of agency and situated perspective. In the culminating sections of *A Passage to India*, quoted as an epigraph, Nature gets the last word. Forster's "not yet" posits Nature as an actor beyond political control, outside the purview of British, Indian, Anglo-Indian, Muslim, Hindu, or even Jainist humans. In terms of Raymond Williams' conception of the British colonial movement of retreat and return, this pattern of human expectation for escape and reflective insight is denied by Nature's own ability to turn the gesture of tourist "retreat" on its head by figuratively foisting the British out as an "other" within *its* dominion, incapable of truly understanding the wild diversity of India's larger environmental culture. Woolf's inclusion of the cows that save the pageant play in *Between the Acts* because they "annihilated the gap; bridged the distance; filled the emptiness and continued the emotion" similarly acknowledges the presence of nonhuman actors in a larger environmental historical drama.

Woolf's pageant scene recalls a performance of one of Forster's own pageant plays, published as *England's Pleasant Land*, which begins with an author's note describing a production of it performed in Surrey, 1938: "Naturally, it rained . . . and of course aeroplanes messed about overhead and anticipated the final desolation. But there was also a lovely flock of white pigeons, which descended on one occasion among the ghosts, and on the whole the unrehearsed blessings exceeded the unexpected evils."[34] Forster may have lamented the rain shower and the presence of modern technology, but, like the character of Miss La Trobe, seems grateful for the improvisational nonhuman actors. Yet Woolf's representations of Miss La Trobe's "unrehearsed blessings," unlike Forster's dialogue of the thoughts of horses, sky, and rocks in the concluding pages of *A Passage to India*, refuses to translate the moo of the cows into human language. The affect is to suggest the ways in which the nonlinguistic sound carries a meaning which – far from diminishing its significance to the human script – exceeds the "failing" moments of the human speech. Louise Westling illuminates the potential of sensory communication within Woolf's fiction: "Woolf suggests the radical sense in which language belongs not only to the animal community, but to the whole of the natural world,"[35] going beyond even the moo of the cows, to embrace the rain and the skin of the earth.

During the first half of the twentieth century, both literature and philosophy became deeply attentive to language, yet grappled with a new distance between the signifier and the signified that hinted at profundities language could not contain. Maurice Merleau-Ponty theorizes the presence of the "invisible" as a necessary and ever-present corollary to conscious thought. For Merleau-Ponty, the kind of knowledge we can intellectualize and put into words is the visible manifestation of all the other bodily impulses of flesh that are constantly in contact with a larger environmental context. In "Metaphysics and the Novel," Merleau-Ponty explains the similarities between philosophy and literature:

> The tasks of literature and philosophy can no longer be separated. When one is concerned with giving voice to the experience of the world, one can no longer credit oneself with attaining a perfect transparence of expression, if the world is such that it cannot be expressed except in "stories" and, as it were, pointed at.[36]

The embodied experience that mediates Woolf's nonhuman descriptions encompasses the kind of relationship Merleau-Ponty gestures toward in his philosophy of what is now termed ecophenomenology.

Auden's work runs the gambit of experimentations in nonhuman voice. His theatrical scripts and libretto lyrics also give voice to animals. With a wryly humorous tone, which has sometimes been mistaken as mere whimsy, Auden plays with nonhuman voice in multiple genres. The prologue of *Paul Bunyon*, another kind of history pageant, decenters the human narrative of conquest:

1st GOOSE: You are all going to leave here.
YOUNG TREE: What.
OLD TREE: It's a lie.
YOUNG TREE: Hurrah.
OLD TREE: Don't listen.
YOUNG TREE: How?
1st GOOSE: Far away from here, a mission is going to find a performer.
OLD TREE: What mission?
1st GOOSE: To bring you into another life.
YOUNG TREE: What kind of performer?
1st GOOSE: A man.
YOUNG TREE: What is a man?
1st GOOSE: A man is a form of life, that dreams in order to act, and acts in order to dream, and has a name of his own.

ALL TREES: What is that name?
1st GOOSE: Paul Bunyan.
OLD TREE: How silly.[37]

These lines of dialogue allow nonhuman characters a more readily translatable voice, but Auden's poetry – which will take center stage in this book – takes up similar themes of critique in a wider variety of experimentations with rhythm and meaning. In several genres, including theater, librettos, poetry, and essays, Auden suggests that actions which may seem valuable when measured by monetary and national accomplishment, become detrimental, or even downright "silly" when reimagined from a nonhuman or global consciousness. Moreover, his poetic experiments with the relationship between consciousness, emotion, and the subjectivity of "otherness" offer provocative insights into modern (and arguably postmodern) conceptions of animality. As in the quote from "First Things First" on the opening page of this introduction, Auden's poetry explicitly questions the layers of human syntax and personification at stake in any effort to depict how responses to the nonhuman environment are filtered through one's experiences. Thus, Auden simultaneously acknowledges the boundaries of language while experimenting with the existence of nonhuman sentience – questions central to the formation of ethics that inform animal studies. And, as Carrie Rohman has suggested, these questions are also pivotal to examining animality within modernism, as Kurtz's character so aptly demonstrates: "Language's ability to transcend the body is called into question because of Kurtz's participation in animality. . ... As the novel continues, Kurtz's voice is irreducibly linked to the materiality of the mouth."[38] In Conrad's text, a reader is thus left with a depiction of animality as reversion and diminishment of human morality. To be sure, not all modernists represent enigmatic environmental agency with the same connotations. For Conrad, Kurtz's own animality, the atmosphere of the gathering dusk, and the currents of the Thames are implicated in "the Horror" of Marlow's realization and what cannot be said. However, as Auden's work will show, fear is not the only modernist response to the realization that humans are merely one of many bodies making meaning within a larger, animate world "enjoying its storminess." And, as has often been epitomized through poetic connotation, sometimes what cannot be said is equally meaningful as what can be said.

Modern ecology and the view from above

Modern life science, like modern literature, was also conceptualizing a more complex network of organic relationships, as ecology gained recognition as a field of study. As Westling has noted, "during most of modernity, a continuous interplay between scientific and artistic exploration"[39] existed, though admittedly these writers were imaginatively engaged with the public discourses surrounding these sciences, rather than the primary scientific studies, in order to "expose ethical dilemmas" posed by those discoveries.[40] Indeed, there is evidence that scientists, as "swimmers in the same cultural sea,"[41] are likewise influenced by literary discourses. The interdisciplinarity of scientific metaphors and rhetorical language around the discourse of ecology is elucidated in Peder Anker's *Imperial Ecology*, including how the structure of the human mind and human society served as analogies for the systems devised to represent ecological habitats:

> [Arthur] Tansley, a [follower] of Sigmund Freud, wrote extensively on the nervous systems while developing his ecosystem theory; [Jan Christian] Smuts first laid out his theory of holism and evolution inspired by the poet Walt Whitman's thinking. These uses of psychology to develop ecological methodology help to explain why from the very beginning botanists thought it was possible to expand ecology to include human beings.[42]

Like many modernist authors and poets, ecologists were influenced by source material from psychology and literature. They too attempted to include human beings as participants in the wider organic webs they were classifying and struggled to find appropriate language to represent these new relationships. Yet, as we can now begin to assess through the work of Jacques Derrida and other poststructuralist philosophers, the rules and codes of human language are loose reins for securing any frame of knowledge that one might want to deem objective and factual: "The terminology that describes plants and vegetation resembles colonial language. Plants 'establish themselves on soil 'prepared' for them,' higher forms of plants 'kill out the lowly pioneers,' and establish new plant 'associations,' 'kingdoms,' 'societies,' 'clans,' and 'colonies,' and certain species 'dominate' these 'communities.'"[43] Thus, even in ecologists' attempts to present a modern method for rationalizing the nonhuman in terms of predictable, measurable patterns of practices and outcomes, the terminology of ecology evidences some of the same problematic assumptions – though not the same ameliorating attitudes of uncertainty – manifested in the larger literary environmental themes.

The ability of modern technology, such as the airplane, to shape social power looms large in modern environmental thought, even though it carried different signifying meanings. For the ecologists, aerial observation offered the ability to monitor and manage grand sweeps of terrain: "This aerial view on nature, society, and knowledge – *the master perspective from above* – was at the very core of British ecological reasoning."[44] Aviation provided new insights and new fears related to how humans both comprehend their environment and choose to act upon it, offering a glimpse of the ephemeral smallness of humanity at the same time it threatened to become a prime symbol for humanity's obsession with speed and the ability to master, or "fly" above, natural forces that had previously limited human greed. The potential and the dangers of these new opportunities to experience oneself in relation to an expanding mass of topography and stratosphere is poignantly exemplified in ecologist Jan Smuts' own theoretical over-reaching:

> While Smuts stressed that 'we do not want to recreate Nature in our own image,' from a historical perspective this is exactly what he did. He modeled nature according to his own social and political values. His ecophilosophy served him as a glorification of white supremacy, with a division of society into high and low personalities, while still defending unification of South Africa, the British Empire, and ultimately the world through the League of Nations.[45]

Artistic conceptions of human relationships with an increasing ecological awareness of interrelated human and nonhuman life wrestle with similar worries about the ethical problems of hierarchies and classifications. Yet, a number of writers were resisting the impulse to classify in favor of embracing the disorienting wonder and destabilizing potency of nonhuman life. This, of course, does not mean their language was totally free from the same prejudicial stereotypes that tainted Smuts' environmentalism. This is painfully evident in Forster's own conflicted self-awareness of his prejudice towards Arabs as "damnable and disgraceful and it's in me,"[46] or Woolf's much less self-aware description of Paul Robeson – a world-renowned American-born singer who graduated as a valedictorian from Rutgers University and earned a law degree from Columbia – as "all warmth & the hot vapors of the African forests" in her diary.[47] Such a description betrays how Conrad's troubling racial stereotypes conflating people and place haunt the modernist literary environmental consciousness as well as the scientific one. Further, the same aviation technology that figures predominately in the study of ecology is a repeated symbol for modern technology in modernist literature. As Harris reminds us, the airplane became the "ally of abstraction"[48] in Piper's modern art and yet "the ariel view was already the view of the bombing pilot"[49] too, demonstrating its potential as a symbol for both new creative perspectives and destructive political aims. It appears alternately as an instrument of society's rupturing noise in both Forster's *England's Pleasant Land* and Woolf's *Between the Acts*, or a more benign source of communal gaze and sky-writing in *Mrs. Dalloway*, as well as a subject of indiscriminate harm in several works within Auden's oeuvre warning against the scientific and technological might of aerial bomb attacks.

E.M. Forster, Virginia Woolf, and W.H. Auden

Although E.M. Forster and Virginia Woolf were both members of the oft celebrated and equally maligned Bloomsbury Group, the lives and writing of all three writers intersected at times. Forster and Woolf published reviews of each other's work that underscore a shared awareness of the significance of the environment in their literature, as when Woolf acknowledges that the land seemed to be the most important element of *A Passage to India* in "The Novels of E.M. Forster."[50] Likewise, Forster describes Woolf's work in terms of a plant that refuses the confines of its "well-prepared garden bed" and surprisingly "pushes suckers up . . . even through the flagstones of the kitchen yard."[51] Yet, in this same summation of Woolf's legacy, Forster did not feel Woolf was as strident about resisting modern progress, in hindsight, as she should have been:

> Decay she admitted: the delicate grey churches in the Strand would not stand for ever; but she supposed, as we all did, that decay would be gradual. The younger generation – the Auden-Isherwood generation as it is convenient to call it – saw more clearly here than could she, and she did not quite do justice to its vision, any more than she did justice to its experiments in technique – she who had been in her time such an experimenter. Still, to belong to one's period is a common failing, and she made the most of hers.[52]

In contrast, Forster felt Auden's more pointed elegies on the folly of uncertain notions of "progress" and the impact of global tools of destruction on a fragile planet – exemplified in poems such as "Ode to Terminus," "Ode to Gaea," and essays such as "The Bomb and Man's Consciousness" – more accurately foretold the alarming doom presented by the reach of human achievement. In a review of Auden's mountaineering drama, *The Ascent of F6*, Forster applauds the play's warning against measuring human advancement in terms of a contest with nature: "[The protagonist] suffers from the last infirmity of noble minds: thinking he pursues virtue and knowledge, he really pursues power. And at the crisis, in the nightmare-cloud on the summit, he sees that his motive has been impure, and, as evidence of this, the ghosts of the friends whom he has killed."[53] While some of Auden's work, including *The Ascent of F6*, does offer a didactic moral against uses of technology that ignore the consequences to earth and those who inhabit it, he also shares Woolf's complex sense of experimentation with subjectivity, otherness, and empathy when he plays with representing animal consciousness. Indeed, Woolf saw a bit of the animal in Auden, himself, when she was first introduced to him at an event sponsored by the National Joint Committee for Spanish relief to raise money for Basque refugee children on June 24, 1937 (the same evening she heard Paul Robeson). On the pages of her diary the next day, Woolf exclaims, "Oh, but I liked being introduced to Auden", whom she describes as, despite his considerable height, "a small, rough-haired terrier man: slits for eyes; a crude face; interesting, I expect, but wire haired, yellowish white."[54] Usually, Woolf's use of animal associations for friends and loved ones was something developed over time, but her use of this form of intimate connection seemed possible with Auden at the start. In the same entry she notes that, even though she "took several snubs and benedictions" at the occasion, she felt "Auden [to be] warm."[55] Woolf also poignantly recognized some of Auden's anthropocentric tendencies as emanating from a desire to expose something more rudimentary beneath the cloak of language. As Auden would indeed work through oscillating notions of the human ego, nonhuman egos, and what it means to inhabit an animal body, Woolf, after reading *Letters to Iceland*, acknowledges that Auden's writing prompts her to ponder these anthropocentric concerns and the limitations of human language: "Do I ever write, even here, for my own eye? If not, for whose eye? An interesting question, rather. I'm musing on the nature of Auden's egotism. Suspect it's something to do with uneasiness. He wants to write straight from the heart: to discard literature; egoism may be his way of orienting himself. What I mean I don't quite know. [P]erhaps that it seems to him that['s] being honest, simple, naked, taking off literary clothes."[56] Auden's later writings particularly acknowledge a desire to give feelings and experiences that are difficult to express a coherent shape. Two essays describing the craft of writing are titled "Squares and Oblongs," a reference to Woolf's use of this phrase in a passage of *The Waves* where Rhoda is trying to describe a symphony. In a 1948 essay he identifies the project of poetry as "bringing to consciousness, by naming them, of emotions and their hidden relationships,"[57] and in another, published in 1957, he metaphorically links the relationship between poetic art and environmental consciousness as well: "As a natural object, the verbal system of a poem belongs to the organic rather than the inorganic order, i.e., instead of the mathematically exact symmetry of the inorganic, it is rhythmical, its symmetries are perceptible but unmeasurable."[58] These homages to Woolf get at the literary task of trying to balance idea and articulation of thought into "squares and oblongs" that would suggest essential understanding within gestural shapes. A concern that ironically led Auden to spend pages of inquiry distinguishing nonhuman animal modes of communication – gestural, odiferous, and sonorous – from human speech in "Words and the Word," betraying that the question of what it means to be human and what it means to be animal were inherent to his dialectic consideration of Being. The way Auden sounds those chords within his work, whether it be "Talking to Mice" or an elegy for one of his own beloved feline family members, reveals the frustration of getting at how to both write within a human consciousness and yet point beyond familiar structures of meaning toward a shared human-and-nonhuman-animal consciousness. Issues that continue to prompt contemporary theorists and scientists to understand the yelp of prairie-dogs, the grief of elephants, and the ways our pets know more about us than we do ourselves.

This isn't to say that these three figures represent the whole of modernist responses to modern identity in terms of environmental questions; rather, they provide three noteworthy case-studies with fertile intersections from which to examine modernist perceptions of the natural world.

Chapter 1, "Passage from pastoral: E.M. Forster," uses pastoral ideology articulated by theorists such as William Empson, Raymond Williams, and Terry Gifford to show the centrality of pastoral symbolism in registering Forster's growing opposition to social prejudice and colonial politics. The first section of the chapter, "The lure of the pastoral in 'The Story of a Panic' and 'The Other Kingdom'," evaluates how the classic pastoral genre of Theocritus and Virgil influences Forster's early short stories. While Forster uses natural imagery in these stories to replicate classical ideas of stewardship and conservation, his pastoral tropes also repeat troubling stereotypes that use rural people to represent nature itself. In the second section, "Anti-pastoral and the fantasy of the green retreat in 'The Machine Stops,' *Howards End*, 'Arthur Snatchfold,' and *Maurice*," I illustrate how the promise of leisure and bounty associated with the rural countryside fails to provide satisfying happy endings because nature does not actually function as a haven or panacea for social ills, be they economic or sexual. In the last section, "Beyond the pastoral: *A Passage to India*," I argue that it isn't until Forster makes pervasive use of modernist techniques in *A Passage to India* – such as eschewing traditional plot devices in favor of repetition, indeterminacy, and a profusion of sensory stimuli – that a fundamentally different depiction of the environment as embodied and independent emerges. Forster's India exerts a palpable presence embodied by heat and terrain. It is endowed with the speech of its "hundred voices," particularly the central echo of the Marabar caves – "'Boum' is the sound *as far as the human alphabet can express it*, or 'bou-oum,' or 'ou-boum'"[59] – which acquires different valences of meaning as it radiates through the novel. The environment is crucial to the novel's surprising resolution where the nonhuman world intervenes to prevent easy reconciliation between British and Muslim characters, suggesting that greater understanding must encompass not only a respect between people, but also deference to nonhuman interests. Thus, a study of how Forster manipulates pastoral tradition and notions of the wild marks his changing relationship to the humanist tradition and empire.

Chapter 2, "The phenomenological whole: Virginia Woolf," employs Maurice Merleau-Ponty's ecophenomenolgy and recent work in material ecocriticism by Serenella Iovino, Serpil Oppermann, and others to argue that Woolf's work consistently relies on embodied realizations to articulate a loosely constructed "whole," both formally and thematically. Forster's India is protean, gliding between positive and negative outcomes; its meaning is frequently misunderstood by British, Muslim, and Hindu characters. In contrast, Woolf's nonhuman presences often provide a source of cohesion, either enriching understanding between human characters or offering thematic connections for the reader. Her use of the nonhuman environment allows her to conceive of a more-than-human community. This wider environmental awareness generates nonhuman perspectives on social injustice and imagines natural flux as a response to trauma. In the first section, "Woolf as a green reader," I show how Woolf's evaluation of other authors often hinges on how they depict the environment and nonhuman animals. In other words, Woolf privileges many of the same questions posed by current ecocritics, offering insights into the significance of the physical environment and nonhuman forms of intelligence to modernist concerns, as well as her own methods for constructing representations of the various settings and creatures that inhabit her own stories. The second section, "Humans and nonhumans in "Kew Gardens," *Flush*, and "Thunder at Wembley," shows how Woolf underscores the possibility that other animals share capacities for human-like emotion and thought while still granting other animals motives and opinions that differ from human attitudes. Nonhuman animals often appear as agents of social critique that correct human assumptions of superiority. The chapter culminates in "The meaning of a more-than-human life in *To the Lighthouse*", which demonstrates how characters' thoughts are informed by an awareness of the sensory environmental prompts and embodied knowledge. Nature in the "Time Passes" section of *To the Lighthouse* has generally been analyzed as an elegiac commentary on the apocalyptic crisis of the First World War. I complicate such accounts by contending that Woolf's vision of human experience within a larger natural world depends on a dialectic that has despair and loss as one pole, but unity and hope as the other. When Lily Briscoe is overwhelmed by the blankness of her canvas and her desire to express herself to those who are absent, the impulses of the surrounding sea and hedge direct her strokes, participating in the creation of art and meaning. Nature functions neither as a sympathetic mirror for humans, nor an antagonistic foil, but rather as a force intertwined with humans in a larger community of reflexive exchange.

Forster and Woolf both influenced the development of Auden's poetry, the focus of my final chapter. "Brute being and animal language: W.H. Auden" concentrates on Auden's later poetry, which has been largely neglected by both modernist and ecocritical scholars. I argue for the renewed importance of these poems, analyzing them through the lens of animal studies as it has been honed by scholars such as Donna Haraway, Cary Wolfe, and Carrie Rohman, demonstrating how dexterously Auden's poems weave themes of human and animal kinship with startling formal maneuvers. For Auden, poetic ruptures and metaphoric conflations promote an interrogation of boundaries and formal categories that ostensibly differentiate human and nonhuman. But the resulting slippages invite identification and empathy with other beings. In the first section, "Subversive natural science and the human subject," I explore how poems such as "After Reading a Child's Guide to Modern Physics," "Bestiaries Are Out," and "Ode to Terminus" create a lexicon of common cultural assumptions about human identity in a firmly ordered relation with the world, but combat their own hermeneutics by hurtling toward the opposite binary in any dialectic the poem presents, whether it be scientific order versus organic chaos, nature versus culture, or human observer versus nonhuman subject. By pointing out that humans strive to construct and control the environment, Auden accentuates the reader's awareness of how society divests nature of its own independent beauty or authority. In the section titled "Talking animal" I establish how Auden's poetic strategies pluck at the linguistic barrier between humans and other nonhuman forms of communication. Auden manifests simultaneous resistance to and curiosity about breaking down the assumption that human language provides irrefutable proof of human superiority over the rest of the animal kingdom, particularly in poems such as "Talking to Mice" and "Talking to Dogs." Combining animal studies and ecophenomenology, the last section, "Words in the flesh of the world," offers close-readings of "Natural Linguistics" and "First Things First," which insinuates that the nonhuman world might contain other languages of its own, arising from the Logos of the natural world.

Despite these differences in approach and technique, all three authors sustain a tension between representing nature as a chaotic force scrambling access to meaning and depicting nature as a source of harmony where truth and meaning ultimately coalesce. While each may have a different place along the spectrum of those extremes, nature remains a complex entity within their work. *Ecocriticism in the Modernist Imagination* echoes John Parham's claim for the significance of ecocritical literary study: "Literature is one of the key places where we mediate ideas about nature, self and society."[60] Writers who are attuned to representing the material world make some of the culturally hidden bonds between humans and nonhumans immanent as they read and represent what Oppermann and Iovino term "the storied world" beyond ourselves, intermingling agencies and subjectivities in ways that "are means of understanding the creative experience that characterizes both humans and non-human natures."[61] Burgeoning international attention to environmental literary and cultural criticism prods us to reconsider constructions of knowledge that have influenced not only art and literature, but also ethics, politics, and science. As the early twentieth century had its horrors, the early twenty-first century has also been defined by crises, including global warming, depletion of natural resources, terrorism, corporate greed, and wars created by assumptions of dominance. By demonstrating how some modernist writing engages in forming an environmental consciousness, I also suggest that the environmental modernisms of Forster, Woolf, and Auden have implications for our discussion of questions related to the interconnectedness of humans and the larger environment we all share. As the epigraph above from Woolf's *Between the Acts* suggests, when our cultural and linguistic "illusions have failed," initiating a faltering pause, the presences within those silences – cows, rain, or even the verdant darkness – may have something to insert to "annihilate the gap; bridge the distance; fill the emptiness and continue the emotion." Moments of crisis and fragmentation may present the best opportunity to become aware of new forms and alternative solutions.

CHAPTER I

Passage from pastoral
E.M. Forster

Traditionally, Forster has been considered a liberal humanist; yet, this perspective doesn't account for the centrality of the environment to Forster's canon.[1] Although Forster's work undoubtedly reflects what might now be deemed a naive belief that all humans are bound in a communal sympathy, the ecocentric foundations of his ideals productively complicate the very definition of what it means to be human. In this sense, Forster's work could be linked to Timothy Clark's definition of a "romantic humanism" which "celebrat[es] engagement with the wild, either immediately or in literature, as the recuperation of some supposed natural part of a human identity seen as suppressed by the effects of abstraction, instrumentalist rationality, urban culture, and so forth,"[2] but inevitably still seeks to use these forces to better shape and refine some definition of humanity. Indeed, frequently in Forster's work, what it means to be human is only realized by confronting what it means to be a creature in a larger environmental habitat that informs so-called essential human qualities. Yet, this doesn't necessarily mean the work should be relegated to a pejorative category; its twists and inversions complicate the definition of humanism in ways that leave it more productively tensile, even though admittedly not constituting a representation that is fully posthumanist. In particular, the dialectic of the pastoral is foundational to Forster's vision of a modernist humanism – one that is fraught with the tension of looking back to a nostalgic past as it negotiates a diversified present, as well as one in which individual morality is often achieved only through pilgrimage to a rural touchstone that prompts the protagonist to experience an epiphany about social morality. This pastoral movement of retreat and return thus provides a renewed connection with a sense of place endowing the human animal with an ironically "civilizing" humility and a wider sense of responsibility for both human and nonhuman life. Paul Sheehan describes the modern age as "'anthropometric'... taking the measure of the 'human': as transcendental category, empirical reality, or malleable, indeterminate becoming."[3] But modernism is also part of the Anthropocene era, what John Bellamy Foster defines as "a new geological epoch in which humanity has become the main driver of rapid changes in the earth system." [4] Forster's liberal humanism evidences Sheehan's anthropocentric shift while still retaining a critique of the effects of human industry that mark the Anthropocene. Thus, Forster's use of the pastoral as a means to explore how environmental consciousness develops human ethics is as fluctuating, problematic, and shape-shifting as the genre itself. Terry Gifford explains:"It is this very versatility of the pastoral to both contain and appear to evade tensions and contradictions – between country and city, art and nature, the human and the nonhuman, our social and our inner selves, our masculine and our feminine selves – that made the form so durable and so fascinating."[3] Likewise, as Forster's texts progress from what we would now recognize as classic, Virgilian pastoral stories contrasting urban ills with rural virtues, to anti-pastorals such as *Howards End* and *Maurice*, and finally, with *A Passage to India*, postpastoral modes, Forster's idealism is just as often undercut by latent prejudice and preservationist conservatism, tempering any facile promise of the Arcadian idyll. Gifford claims that "at its best," what the pastoral delivers is "an implicit realism";[4] similarly, in Forster's work, characters' bucolic fantasies are either denied or dissatisfying, and the environment, if it is to endure at all, must often become an antagonist in its own right – the Indian caves strike out in violent, self-preservation while the passive English countryside risks being devoured by the "rust" of urban industry as Helen and Margaret look on. Thus, rather than provide a romantic escape of Edwardian pleasure, Forster's pastoral often attempts to highlight the limitations of the humanist ideal and the improbability of environmental harmony in a modern age.

Examining Forster's environmental representations affirms his position in the modernist canon and offers new critical insight into the meanings of particular scenes in his novels. Admittedly, most of Forster's prose, apart from the language used in *A Passage to India*, does not exhibit much formal modernist innovation. However, this does not necessarily justify one critic's claim that: "Discussion of E.M. Forster and modernism might well be brief. Forster was scarcely a modernist."[5] Most critics do concede that *A Passage to India* exemplifies the fragmentation of language, at the level of the word, which is the hallmark of a modernist text. It is not my aim to show that *all* of Forster's work is modernist. His early fiction is clearly rooted in an Edwardian tradition, both in form and theme. Yet Forster's eventual rejection of the traditional pastoral motifs for more complex and innovative styles that would now be described as anti-pastoral and post-pastoral, typify modernist revisions of older literary forms. Paul Peppis aligns Forster's Maurice Hall and Alec Scudder with other modern characters who are famously "contemptuous of the timorous and soulless millions in their stuffy little boxes" and rebel by defying the tide of mainstream society: "Maurice and Alec join Paul Morel and Stephen Dedalus as modernist (anti)heroes, defiantly committed to 'live outside' the constraints, the nets as Dedalus would say, of respectable society and the classic bildungsroman."[6] A letter from Edward Upward to Christopher Isherwood in 1926 indicates that Forster's contemporaries did in fact regard him as a modernist, even in his less radical heterosexual fiction, specifically for his attention to "background" issues: "Forster's the only one who understands what the modern novel ought to be ... there's actually less emphasis laid on the big scenes than on the unimportant ones: that's what's so utterly terrific. It's the completely new kind of accentuation."[7] In an unpublished review, Auden would call Forster his "favorite living novelist" for a similar reason: "the peculiar qualities of his books lies in the contrast between the triviality of their objective incidents – things that would earn at most a few lines in the social columns of a local paper – and their immense subjective significance to the actors involved."[8] As with Woolf, this focus on the peripheral and the daily often results in a more rapt attention to the nonhuman environment. Thematically, Forster's novels grapple with how to sustain some kind of unity in an increasingly fractured world, a fundamental dilemma in the early twentieth century. Daniel Shwarz aggressively defends Forster's position within the modern canon, citing his depiction of "psychological nuance[d]" human characters and "his expectation that the reader will discover relationships and significance"[9] as aspects of his modernist style.[10]

Although Forster's homosexual literature was not published during his lifetime, queer ecocritical theory illuminates environmental and modernist aspects of these works too. By queering normative understandings of human society and discourses about "the natural," Forster betrays a consciousness of the cultural construction of codification of all beings while acknowledging a wider multiplicity of cross-currents within twentieth-century understandings of sex, evolution, and empathy. In this way the pastoral serves multiple functions within Forster's work, exemplifying Catriona Mortimer-Sandilands and Bruce Erickson's reminder that "ancient bucolic poetry contained a range of sexual acts, desires, and preferences, and subsequent romantic reinventions of the pastoral conventions have, despite homophobic attempts to the contrary, continued to include male homoeroticism as a central facet of the pastoral depiction of nature as a site for innocent, corporeal plentitude."[11] Whether it be the rebuke to what constitutes a "masculine" hero in *Howard's End* or "The Machine Stops" – associating the necessary ingredient of "nature" as one related to tender care rather than any violent conquest – or the use of park spaces and green retreat as a queer space, timorously claimed and only partially concealing homosexual trysts in "Arthur Snatchfold" and *Maurice*, queer ecology suggests how Forster's environments twine around and weaken structures of early twentieth-century heterosexual concepts of both masculinity and nature.

But perhaps the most striking aspect of Forster's modernist experimentation goes beyond his work with human characters, suggested by a growing awareness of the more-than-human world as having potential as a character in its own right – a technique that reaches its fullest manifestation in *A Passage to India*. For Forster does not solely use nature as a pastoral catalyst for a humanist bildungsroman; rather, as his career progresses, he also articulates his most poignant disillusionment with humanity by championing the environment over people, in statements that, despite his many calls to universal brotherhood, are nonetheless tinged with misanthropy. Complaining of T.S. Eliot's preoccupation with the pain of each individual's life, Forster rejoins, "Even if Man is wiped out other forms of life may get comfortable."[12] Reflecting back on *Howards End* in 1952, he prioritized the attachment to the place over the people he created: "[There is] not a single character in it for whom I care . . . Perhaps the house in *H.E.*, for which I once did care, took the place of people."[13] And in 1955, he writes that "Man will suppose himself the only form of life, that armed and capsuled imbeciles will penetrate the new regions accessible above and beneath us to murder whatever is stirring . . . There was a time when we – i.e. what we came from – communicated. . . . The man-modified earth [is] on the way to being man-destroyed."[14] Forster explicitly acknowledges that "we" are "what we came from" and that other forms of communication exist beyond human language. Thus, the liberal desire to "only connect,"[15] Forster's epigraph for *Howards End*, extends to nature as well as other humans.

This chapter will map the development of this ecocentric perspective within Forster's work. Tracing how his earlier short stories are patterned after the classic pastoral of Theocritus and Virgil underscores Forster's early concern for natural conservation and stewardship. These tales are also conspicuously tangled in pastoral class distinctions that take a patronizing view of romanticized rural characters. Thus, in these stories, the nonhuman environment often manifests itself through a transformed or metamorphosed lower-class individual, rather than operating as an independent being. Yet, at times, evidence of Forster's own self-critical awareness of these prejudices and the highly ironic deployment of a narrating consciousness unsettle the seemingly simplistic morality of the narrative voice and point toward the development of a more nuanced treatment of people and nature. As Gifford reminds ecocritics, "It is important to realize that a single writer, or indeed a single text, might shift between all three modes of pastoral, anti-pastoral and post-pastoral"[16]; Forster's use of the pastoral is just this kind of plastic art. "The Machine Stops," *Howards End*, and *Maurice* are thematically counter-pastoral, overtly politicizing the relationships classic pastoral conventions obscure and heightening the tension between romantic expectation and disturbing social critique. A finely tuned awareness of embodied knowledge, including the experience of a queer embodiment, begins to suggest ways in which all humans are capable of connecting – with each other across class-barriers and with the natural world. Not yet fully "modernist" in form, these texts begin to experiment with the play between genres of realism and fantasy, the use of mythic paradigms, and inverting devices such as personification and zooification, all of which work to formally disorient the reader's expectations. Fidelity to the natural world and physical experience serve as crucial barometers for Forster's critique of English society. Ultimately, however, *A Passage to India* represents the radical culmination of Forster's abandonment of the pastoral plot in favor of a postpastoral narrative with an animate environment that speaks in its own voice and dictates the comings-and-goings of human journeys.

The lure of the pastoral in "The Story of a Panic" and "The Other Kingdom"

Forster's early short stories incorporate a classic pastoral schema learned from Theocritus's *Idylls* and Virgil's *Eclogues*. As Raymond Williams notes, late nineteenth-century and early twentieth-century attitudes toward the country were influenced by men who were educated in elite universities endorsing a particular academic view of rural landscapes: "that set of ideas about the 'rural' and the 'pastoral', filtered through a version of classical rural literature, but which in the first decades of the century . . . was a deep if conventional intellectual conviction: an eyeglass that was lifted, deliberately and proudly, to the honestly observing eye. Fauns, Pan, centaurs, the Golden Age, shepherds, Lycidas, swain, tryst, staunch peasants, churches, immemorial history, demigods, presences, the timeless rhythm of the seasons."[17] While a nostalgia for an idealized greenwood as homoerotic retreat, a naïve attitude toward country people, and allusions to chimerical woodland spirits are present in Forster's short stories, his tales also reflect something often omitted from the classical pastoral – a prominent accent on land use politics. Although dilemmas related to property rights and agricultural livelihood are treated in Virgil and Theocritus, contemporary explanations of the pastoral genre dilute this emphasis. J.H. Stape's chronology dates Forster's reading of Virgil's *Eclogues* within his Lent term at King's College in 1899.[18] Like the original classic texts, it would be a mistake to regard Forster's early short stories merely as simple-minded romps through a romantic, magical-creature fantasy-land. Characters who experience moments of enchanted realization are often confronted with distressing choices between their own fate and fidelity to nature.

Accordingly, Forster's early fiction undoubtedly participates in the pastoral tradition Williams describes, but it has a focus on environmental ethics that is often disregarded because contemporary critiques of the pastoral in Forster's work don't explicitly acknowledge this aspect of Theocritus and Virgil's original texts.[19] In Virgil, nature's bounty was threatened not only by the winter season, but also by the problem of property rights when soldiers returned from war: "Have we done all this work / Upon our planted and fallow fields so that / Some godless barbarous soldier will enjoy it? / This is what civil war has brought down upon us."[20] Similarly, in Eclogue IX, Moeris laments to Lycidas, "O Lycidas, we never thought that what / Has happened to us was ever going to happen, / And now we've lived to see it. A stranger came / To take possession of our farm, and said: 'I own this place; you have to leave this place.'"[21] Political decrees and commercial transactions menaced the shepherds' traditions. Violence wrought by desires for money and ownership similarly shadows the lightness of Forster's short stories, evidencing his belief that monetary interests shouldn't dictate land use. Many of Forster's narratives recognize the intersections of material wealth, class, the blinkered limitations of assumed cultural power dynamics, and unfettered capitalistic accumulation of wealth and goods as part of the environmental story. In this way, he not only reaches back to the earlier pastoral emphasis on land use but also represents the trajectory now manifested in Marxist ecology, including Bellamy Foster's *The Ecological Rift*: "Ecologically, the system draws ever more destructively on the limited resources and absorptive capacity of nature, as the economy continually grows in scale in relation to the planetary system. . . . The essential nature of the problem resides in the fact that there is no way out of this dilemma within the laws of motion of a capitalist system, in which capital accumulation is the primary goal of society."[22] Whether it be the rudimentary metamorphosis of land, trees, and people as commodified objects in his early short stories, the dizzying spiral of property and objects that combine metaphorically to crush the laboring body of Leonard Bast, or the way valuing certain kinds of places and experiences in a monetary system leads to destruction, Forster, perhaps through fellow-Bloomsbury figure Maynard Keynes, expresses an awareness of the dangers of capitalist systems that rely on dubious notions of expansion.

In "The Story of a Panic," a party of English tourists having a picnic are discussing how the woods no longer give shelter to Pan due to the allure of commercial profit for timber cutting: "All the poetry is going from Nature," the self-important artist in the group laments, "her lakes and marshes are drained, her seas banked up, her forests cut down. Everywhere we see the vulgarity of desolation spreading ... the mere thought that a tree is convertible into cash is disgusting."[23] While they are having their conversation, Eustace, a young boy whom the staunch English narrator views as peevish, unhealthy, and spoiled, is whittling a whistle. It is reminiscent of Pan's pipes but also suggestive of cutting timber, highlighting the pipes' uncertain status as a positive symbol of ancient homage or as a harbinger of a destructive force. The group is unexplainably startled by a wind that kicks up in them "brutal, overmastering, physical fear, stopping up the ears, and dropping clouds before the eyes, and filling the mouth with foul tastes."[24] The English narrator admits, "I had been afraid, not as a man, but as a beast."[25] The storm assumes the status of an ancient pagan god reaching out to punish those who have abused the forest and the reactions of the characters betray their fear of being unmoored from usual assumptions of social control that make them confront their vulnerability as human animals. The young boy becomes the figure – either brave or abandoned – who is left to experience the encounter.

What occurs to Eustace is covertly linked to a homosexual experience, suggesting that in nature, sexuality is more invitingly diverse than in the strict confines of society and revealing that the common cultural reaction to both homosexuality and unfettered natural power is fear. After they flee the scene, the other characters realize that Eustace is missing and return to the spot to find him lying on the ground with his hands "convulsively entwined in the long grass,"[26] a "peculiar smile" on his face,[27] and "some goat's footmarks in the moist earth beneath the trees."[28] Whether this is a loving satyr who brings a beneficent epiphany of nature's transforming power or a figure of Satan is left ambiguous. The paradoxical possibilities play up the distance between the narrator's homophobia and the conclusions the reader is ultimately meant to draw from the tale, which point up the narrowness of the narrator's mindset. The narrator breaks his reminiscence of the telling of the event to comment "I have often seen that peculiar smile since, both on the possessor's face and on the photographs of him that are beginning to get into the illustrated papers."[29] The reference to Eustace's smile in the papers may also allude to a Wildean sense of naughty bemusement. An ex-curate in the party ventures to proclaim that, "The Evil One has been very near us in bodily form."[30] Thus, Pan takes on dual possibilities as a bearer of an innate knowledge of the earth's beauty that leaves the boy deeply happy, or the perpetrator of some unspeakable "evil," which is suggestively homosexual in its secrecy and the boy's reclined state of bliss. The pagan gods are equally poised to lurch toward good or evil, expressing the fear and longing associated with a particular kind of Eros: homosexual love in a heterosexual English society. One of the forms homosexual condemnation took was the idea that any queer identity was at odd with nature and a threat to natural evolution. As Mortimer-Sandilands and Erickson carefully document, biologists often discounted or refrained from recording instances of homosexual activity in their studies, instead participating in cementing an understanding of heterosexuality as "natural" and queer identities as deviant or even harmful to a functioning society or ecological system: "It is clearly not the case that all sex leads to reproduction, for humans and other animals alike, yet the presence of nonreproductive sexual activities is frequently read as a sign of ecological decline: another twist on degeneracy theory."[31] Contrastingly, in Virgil's Eclogue II homosexual desire is not scorned, but rather garlanded with all of the romantic conventions typical of celebrated love: "Corydon fell in love with a beautiful boy / Whose name was Alexis, the darling of his master,"[32] and Corydon sings his lovesick songs, "O come and live with me in the countryside, / Among humble farms. . . . Together singing we will mimic Pan, / Who was the first who taught how reeds could be / Bound together with wax to make a pipe,"[33] echoed in the references to Pan and pipes in "The Story of a Panic." Eros presented a particularly painful dilemma for the early twentieth-century homosexual, who was constantly forced to choose between a chaste and conventional civic existence and the desire to live in a loving homosexual relationship. Within this conflict of sexualities, organic nature often seems to be associated with homosexual desire in Forster's work (a theme that Forster will develop more fully in *Maurice*), yet, rather than use nature and the "natural" as a measuring-stick to prudishly upbraid homosexuality, the larger organic world inspires, shelters, and encompasses queer identities, correcting misappropriations of evolutionary theorists and Forster's own peevishly short-sighted heterosexual narrating personas.

Eustace is anxious to share his epiphany on the hill with another boy, Gennaro, an Italian working at the hotel. Eustace senses that the Italian youth will understand and sympathize with the revelation he experienced, in a way that the upper-class English presumably do not. Eustace leaps into his arms and Gennaro speaks to him using the intimate form of the personal pronoun, to which the classist adult narrator immediately takes affront. As night falls, Eustace runs out into the dark in his bedclothes, dancing and singing what the thick-headed narrator can only interpret as "ludicrous" songs "blessing the great forces and manifestations of Nature."[34] In order to put a stop to it, the narrator bribes Gennaro into tricking Eustace by promising him a profit of ten lire. The boy reluctantly agrees. Although Gennaro leads Eustace to the men who proceed to confine him to his room, which Gennaro has foretold will only conclude in the boy's death, Gennaro ultimately frees Eustace and they both jump from the younger boy's window. Eustace successfully bounds over the parapet of the garden wall and slides to the earth, running off until all that is heard of him are shouts and laughter. When the narrator demands his money back, Gennaro clutches his "ill-gotten" gains, precipitously toppling and dying on the spot like a felled tree, "sway[ing] forward and fall[ing] upon his face in the path."[35] Gennaro, like the wood discussed at the outset of the story, is a rustic who hasn't escaped the fate of "selling out" nature's spirit for money. While Eustace is permitted to escape, the Italian peasant boy and the woods of his native country are similarly cut down in the end, problematically conflating human and nature. The rural natives are implicated in selling natural resources for profit but also share the land's fate, ultimately becoming pawns of British capital.

As "The Story of a Panic" exemplifies, Forster's early short stories share the traditional pastoral's concern for land ethics, but they also replicate prejudices inherent in the archetypal motifs of leisurely retreat. Escapism and fantasy are often associated with travel to foreign countries. "The Story of a Panic" was written in 1902, when Forster was abruptly inspired by the landscape of Ravello, Italy, as a young man of 23 years of age: "I sat down in a valley, a few miles above the town, and suddenly the first chapter of the story rushed into my mind as if it had waited for me there."[36] Forster, like some of his characters, seems to relate a moment of his own exhilarating brush with a mythic natural muse. In this story and other works that are set in the Mediterranean, such as "Albergo Empedocle" (1904),

"The Story of the Siren" (written 1904, but not published until 1920), "The Eternal Moment" (1905), *Where Angels Fear to Tread* (1905), and *A Room With A View* (1908), the pastoral is evoked for the English traveling abroad – both Forster's characters as well as the author himself – when they find themselves in exotic locations for recreational pursuits. Williams' description of a colonial pastoral in this era of literature recognizes the myopic nationalism inherent in this model of environmental representation: "The lands of the Empire were an idyllic retreat, an escape from debt or shame, or an opportunity for making a fortune."[37] In this regard, Forster seems to uncritically cast the foreign landscape as a liminal or "othered" space – a land of rustic simplicity standing in stark contrast to the "culture" and "civilization" of England. A concern that will be reprised with different inflections in *A Passage to India*. Yet the classical pastoral mode, as seen with the character of Gennaro in "The Story of a Panic," frequently participates in the more unequivocal prejudicial stereotyping or dehumanizing of nonEnglish characters, erasing their individual dimensions as humans in favor of constructing them as symbols for the natural world.

In "The Other Kingdom," written in 1905 and published in 1909, Forster rewrites the story of Daphne and Apollo into a pastoral tale that is rife with the problematic elements Williams identifies. "The Other Kingdom" tells of a tragic demise of woodland caused by the incursion of private development in a natural greenwood; it also equates nature with a low-class foreigner. The story begins with a lesson on Virgil's *Eclogues*, showing that Virgil's pastorals were standard reading and explicitly evoking the pastoral genre. The tutor, also the tale's narrator, is instructing Mr. Harcort Worters' young ward, Jack Ford, and Mr. Worters' fiancée, Miss Beaumont. Miss Beaumont was "picked out of Ireland"[38] by Mr. Worter as one might pluck plants out of their native ground for a bouquet to decorate one's table. Miss Beaumont's status as a low-class Irish immigrant makes her another version of the peasant-figure. Indeed, the figure of the Irish man or woman in British literature is often mythologized on the one hand as not human at all, but rather a pagan spirit of ancient lore, or on the other hand, as an anachronistically primitive being who doesn't belong to the civilized world, thus becoming an object of scorn or pity.

Miss Beaumont, belonging to the former category of Irish peasant stereotypes, is repeatedly associated with the woods bordering the estate. Miss Beaumont is overcome with emotion when Mr. Worters announces that he has bought her the rights to a wooded property adjoining his manor. Disappointment disturbs her happiness when she learns that the lease is only for ninety-nine years, a problem of perpetuity that Mr. Worters later remedies for her. However, conflicts between the two become apparent when Mr. Worter announces his plans to "improve" the copse with a bridge, a paved walkway that "tether[s]"[39] the woods to the house, and a fenced boundary with a gate that locks, verbs that create associations with imprisonment and domestication of wild animals. Miss Beaumont unsuccessfully resists these schemes, making clear her desire to de-emphasize man-made structures when she plans a picnic "without servants" where she demands the attendees show respectful reverence for the place. She orders Jack Ford to stand with his tea so that he will block her view of the manor house, a request that Jack happily accommodates to the annoyance of Mr. Worters, who designed the house. Like Genarro and Eustace, Miss Beaumont and the youthful Jack have a close, sympathetic relationship with the natural environment that the adult, upper-class English characters don't have a capacity to share.

Similar to Genarro's narrative, Miss Beaumont, and particularly her physical body, become representative of the land itself. The most poignant disagreement over land use comes when Miss Beaumont begs her betrothed to leave the copse open for the rural folk to come carve their initials in the trees as they have done for centuries. Her knowledge of this local custom is surprising as is her switch to the first person as she goes on to plead: "Oh, fence me out, if you like! Fence me out as much as you like! But never in. . . . I must be on the outside, I must be where anyone can reach me. Year by year – while the initials deepen – the only thing worth feeling – and at last they close up – but one has felt them."[40] The personal pronouns in this section draw attention to the tradition of women being considered property, in Miss Beaumont's case a colonial property from Ireland, but the passage also critiques the sexual anxiety of male ownership over females and nature more generally. Mr. Worters' plans for a gate and lock are reminiscent of a kind of chastity belt, which ensures that the only couple that can express their love through carving initials are the two of them. His refusal of Miss Beaumont's appeal to allow others to roam the wood and carve their initials in the bark aligns the anxiety of property ownership with the desire for complete possession of the female. Worters takes out his phallic knife and "dr[aws] her away" to find a tree exclaiming: "Mine! Mine! My haven from the world! My temple of purity. . . . Year after year alone together, all in all to each other – year after year, soul to soul, E. B. Everlasting Bliss!"[41] His speech takes the values she attributes to the place she had deemed to be a natural refuge and relocates those values onto her own body – for him it is not the wooded copse that serves as a place of natural peace and retreat to remain unsullied, but rather her literal female form that becomes "the temple of purity" where he finds his "bliss." From one point of view, this story reveals Forster's criticism of prejudicial gender stereotypes, which would indicate a more complex social critique is embedded in this pastoral narrative; this seems to be a fair assessment of Forster's sensitivity to gendered stereotypes. However, the fact that Mr. Worter's prescient alignment of female and woods is blatantly affirmed when Miss Beaumont metamorphoses into a tree fails to recognize or distill the classist, racist, and anthropocentric prejudices inherent in the equation of "rustic" people with nonhuman nature.

The potentially dehumanizing racist treatment of characters such as the Italian Gennaro and the Irish Miss Beaumont reveals the pervasive prejudices that are likely to provide snags to any reader hoping to find only "good" progressive ideals within environmental literature. Yet, a more productive approach to ecocriticism, and environmental literature generally, is to recognize and consider the ways in which cultural biases are registered and what they might tell us about our own history of narrating people and place. More often than not, it is only through the patient perusal of these textual knots that a fuller comprehension of the complexity of dialectic oscillations within human depictions of the nonhuman world reveal themselves; seen as such they are rarely simply a pangaeic impulse of harmonic hegemony or a nest of latent prejudices and egotistic assumptions, but some layered mixture of both, grown from years of symbolic and metaphoric uses of nature within a shared literary canon. Forster is not unique in problematically reflecting harmful stereotypes of his era even while, in other instances, his fiction displays a conscious effort to create narratives that bucked against them. As Catriona Mortimer-Sandilands and Bruce Erickson explain, the pervasiveness of racial prejudice is interwoven into thinking about biology as was condemnation of homosexuality:

> These experimental forms of physical/environmental measurement were part of a larger emergence of scientific racism, in which different 'races' were characterized by distinct physical characteristics as part of a colonial project of intellectual as well as economic dominance (sexual narratives intersected with and supported many of these racist stories, and both Darwin and Ellis use examples from 'primitive' peoples to substantiate their evolutionary views.) As with homosexuality, the application of evolutionary narratives to the explanation of race was fraught with difficulty: in

particular, the ongoing tendency to equate reproductive fitness with the possession of those characteristics that happened to be (in their own minds, at least) associated with white, upper-class, western heterosexual men was certainly at play in many of the evolutionary and sexological accounts of the time.[42]

Thus, while some aspects of Forster's pastoral stories clearly critique the perspective of his white, upper-class, male narrators, the tendency of these narratives to change lower-class characters of nonEnglish race into objects – even if those objects are idealized organic trees, a possible symbol of transcending oppression to become "one with nature" – replicates troubling treatments of nonwhite "peasant-folk" as somehow less than civilized or human.

As many heroines threatened by rape do in other classical tales, especially Ovid's *Metamorphosis*, the story implies that Miss Beaumont is transformed into an organic, nonhuman shape. This conclusion is foreshadowed by her use of the personal pronoun discussed above, as well as by her literal acting out of the role of a birch tree when determining which species of trees populated the copse: "She flung her arms up above her head, close together, so that she looked like a slender column. Then her body swayed and her delicate green dress quivered over it with the suggestion of countless leaves."[43] Thus the reader is prepared to assume she has become a part of the wood when she runs through the foliage and disappears from Mr. Worters, who fears she has been dallying with his ward, Jack Ford. In parting she cries, "Oh Ford, my lover while I was a woman, I will never forget you, never, as long as I have branches to shade you from the sun."[44] This declaration could have been misinterpreted by Worters, if one considers that Miss Beaumont is not speaking of herself as a human woman intending to cuckold him, but rather as a personified Nature more generally. The name "Ford" has provocative connotations suggesting his own alignment with nature, referring to the shallow stream surrounding the copse, a fluid that mingles with and nourishes the trees' roots. The fact that Ford as a character is a lover of the classic pastoral and a better scholar than the tutor suggests that he would have guessed Miss Beaumont's metamorphosed fate. When Mr. Worters confronts Jack Ford, Ford admits that he knows what happened to the missing fiancée but refuses to explain. Those who share an emotional connection to the land – rural peasants and the young – can "ford" the gap in understanding that someone who is too bound to the conventions of society cannot. As a result, the story enacts the stereotyping and prejudice that Raymond Williams associates with the colonial pastoral, but it also uses these devises in order to blatantly critique a narrow-minded English model of economic use-value as justification for denuding the landscape.

Although Forster's treatment of human characters, particularly women, becomes arguably more complicated in this story, the environment remains a relatively inert entity. While conserving nature for public enjoyment may be a more laudable purpose than corporate consumption or private development, it still involves acquisition for the pleasure of people. It is not only Mr. Worters who represents the salacious desire for ownership in this story. Miss Beaumont requires a full lease in perpetuity and performs a count of the number of beech trees she owns.[45] At the time of the gift, the narrator notes, "The joy of possession had turned her head."[46] Her motives are directed by stewardship rather than exclusive ownership, but she ultimately wants to control the way the grounds are used. In other words, Miss Beaumont's valuation of the land suggests an aesthetic model that still prioritizes human notions of beauty. Thus, the goals the story privileges are still largely anthropocentric and do not represent the environment as having purposes distinct from human interests.

In 1926, Forster had an experience with land ownership that attests to his later, more biocentric approach to nature. When Forster learned that a four-acre wood, called Piney Copse, was threatened by the possibility that its owner might choose to develop it, he purchased it himself.[47] Just as Miss Beaumont wishes her copse to be open for the amusement of other country people, Forster, "would throw the wood open for an annual school treat, going about it on the previous evening hanging the trees with toys, bags of sweets, and swatches of bananas."[48] Yet Forster also recognizes his own penchant toward a zeal for possession, once going so far as to note:

> I saw it was not a man who had trodden on the twig and snapped it, but a bird, and felt pleased. My bird. The bird was not equally pleased. Ignoring the relation between us, it took fright ... and flew straight over the boundary hedge into a field, the property of Mrs. Henessy, where it sat down with a loud squawk. It had become Mrs. Henessy's bird. Something seemed grossly amiss here, something that would not have occurred had the wood been larger ... Mrs. Henessy's bird took alarm for the second time and flew clean away from us all, under the belief that it belonged to itself.[49]

Forster's sense of satiric self-deprecation hints at the theme of the "My Wood" essay, which is *not* a manual on the virtues of ownership and preservation but rather a warning that possession can have a detrimental effect on human character. His essay encourages the reader to adopt the bird's belief that "it belonged to itself." He decides, "(in the words of

Dante) 'Possession is one with loss.'"[50] Later, due to a hitch in the lease, Forster was forced to sell his woods, and he determined to sell them to the National Trust rather than another individual.[51] These biographical insights show Forster's shift in understanding nature and the nonhuman as part of one's "property" – an entity that should be controlled by humans and might even be used to equate owners with the land of their country homes, as we saw with the conflation of people and nature in "The Story of a Panic" and "The Other Kingdom." In Forster's later years, he advances the idea that nature and the nonhuman animals that inhabit it may have emotions and desires of their own, an attitude that will also become evident in his later fiction.

These early stories represent a classic pastoral vision of nature that Forster later rejected in favor of more diverse environmental representations, such as those seen in *A Passage to India*. But even these early tales of metaphysical transformation and folkloric mystery are charged with themes that will continue to shape Forster's environmental ethic. Miss Beaumont's metamorphosis into a tree as protest against private development prefigures the problem of industrial, urban encroachment on rural landscapes that Forster will take up more explicitly in *Howards End*, and even hints at the somewhat supernatural presence of Ruth Wilcox shaping the fate of her property even after her death. Similarly, the uneasy conflation of people from other national or ethnic origins, children, or lower-class people with nature, while not entirely eradicated from later novels, functions more explicitly as a social critique in *Howards End* and *Maurice*. Forster's intermediary fiction becomes counter-pastoral, using conventional pastoral motifs as a sophisticated instrument for pulling back the softer, more playful layers of rustic pipes and flirtatious chases to reveal very real, pressing social concerns. In this process, nature is associated with the health of the human body generally, rather than the body of a particular class of persons.

Anti-pastoral and the fantasy of the green retreat in "The Machine Stops," *Howards End*, "Arthur Snatchfold," and *Maurice*

Raymond Williams explains that Victorian literature of urbanity was predominately "an imagery of the inhuman and the monstrous"[52] that "identified the crowding of cities as a source of social danger" and included "the loss of customary human feelings."[53] The encroachment Williams describes resembles an English version of Leo Marx's "Machine in the Garden." The startling incongruency of the speed and noise of industrialism ripping its way through a reflective and sedate pastoral setting creates what Marx terms a "complex pastoral." The countryside pastoral conceived by Virgil is changed by a power "that does not remain confined to the traditional boundaries of the city"[54]; instead, "tension replaces repose: the noise arouses a sense of dislocation, conflict, and anxiety."[55] As the use of the term "pastoral" has expanded, it has been used "as an oblique way to criticize the values and hierarchical class structure of the society of its time."[56] In order to clarify the distinction between Forster's use of classic pastoral tropes in the early short stories and a more conscious use of the pastoral as a critique of his own social moment in the three narratives featured in this section, I refer to Terry Gifford's term, anti-pastoral, or counter-pastoral. According to Gifford, anti-pastoral literature "expos[es] the distance between reality and the pastoral convention when that distance is so conspicuous as to undermine the ability of the convention to be escaped as such."[57] This theory of the pastoral grafts social realism to the classic pastoral, creating a more disturbing pastoral myth designed to agitate society's awareness of themes related to both class and conservation. Dissonances between upper and lower classes highlight the problem of erasing the presence of labor in the landscape or associating peasants with spirits of nature. Forster's anti-pastoral stories also associate the organic world with the health of the human body. These themes are evident in "The Machine Stops" (1909), *Howards End* (1910), and *Maurice* (written in 1914, although not published until 1971). Further, in *Maurice* and "Arthur Snatchfold" (written in 1928) Forster folds the pastoral tradition of homoeroticism into his social critique of the "natural" and the "good," using the association of male love with nature and innocence in the classic pastoral to amplify his twentieth-century critique of homophobia and socially learned repression of the queer desiring body.

"The Machine Stops" presents an apocalyptic drama of the combustion of the mechanized city, while *Howards End*, published only a year later, treats the threat of the machine's incursion into the English countryside. Forster locates England's social decline in its detachment from nature, precipitated by the hurried pace and increased mechanization of city centers. "The Machine Stops" literalizes the atrophy that occurs in both the body and man-made civilization during prolonged separation from immediate sensory experience and the natural world. In "The Machine Stops" human life has moved underground after devastating the earth's surface, and people live in separate cubicles tended by a vast machine, not unlike Forster's later description of London's Adelaide building:

It [the Adelaide] towers into the sky, it plunges into the depths; in its vast cube are accommodated hundreds of business men with their clerks, typewriters, and anxieties all complete, all making money as hard as they can for the sake of the Empire, and upon its roof, which is flat, are a garden, an orchard, and a putting green, where the anxieties of the business men can take another form.[58]

Society is reduced to geometric cubicles of mechanical production with nothing but an artificial pastoral icing smeared on top. This hierarchical representation of the pastoral desire to obscure the lower-class labor it depends on resembles a bottom-dweller and top-feeder image that recurs in other depictions of urban dystopias, such as Fritz Lang's 1927 film, *Metropolis*, which opens with scenes where the wealthy Freder is seen sporting and cavorting in the sun-filled gardens on top of a city structure, while uniformed laborers repetitively toil unseen and underground. The leisure and camaraderie the pastoral are meant to engender are compacted into a man-made spectacle designed for furthering competitive sport, what Forster calls "another form" of business anxiety, rather than genuine recreation. Human frailty is not represented by a failure to conquer the environment; instead, the degradation of the human species is marked by a failure to live in symbiosis with the natural environment.

In "The Machine Stops" the increasing industrial negation of tactile experience and the erosion of rural environments degrade social structures and healthy independent thinking. Initially, the future society appears to be an industrial utopia of shared intellectualism. It features individual rooms, each "hexagonal in shape like the cell of a bee. It is lighted neither by window nor by lamp, yet it is filled with a soft radiance. An arm-chair is in the center, by its side a reading-desk – that is all the furniture. And in the arm-chair there sits a swaddled lump of flesh."[59] Like babies, every human's need is effortlessly met so that the life of the mind can be the sole concern. It is worth noting here that, although Forster draws a comparison to bees, it is in reference to social metaphors that suggest mindless drones who don't participate in finding flowers and pollinating them, rather than any real knowledge of the habits of the labor of different sets of honeybees within a hive. Rather, the emphasis here is on a stultifying ease. Two-dimensional "plates" on the wall, not unlike flat-panel television screens today, convey "blurred" images of anyone with whom a person wishes to communicate. With the mere flip of a switch, the room is filled with the messages of correspondence: "All the accumulations of the last three minutes burst upon her. The room was filled with the noise of bells, and speaking tubes. What was the new food like? Could she recommend it?

Had she any ideas lately? Might one tell her one's own ideas?"[60] The infantilized figure, Vashti, is, ironically, a mother and an academic. Vashti can communicate with a wide range of people anywhere, listen to music, and even give lectures in the modernized society of "the machine." Yet, as the story progresses, a heightened sense of isolation siphons emotion and insight.

When Vashti's son, Kuno, has something he would prefer not to tell his mother over the Machine, the reader gets an initial clue that there might be something pernicious about the machine's paternalism. Vashti treats the machine like a god.[61] The analogy to an empire that quells sedition and encourages a nearly religious fanaticism for progress is readily apparent. Vashti's son finally convinces her to venture from her cubicle and she is exposed to "the horror of direct experience."[62] Vashti is driven by the pursuit of ideas, but when her son forces her to unaccustomed bodily travel via a flying device, "a relic from the former age,"[63] she scrupulously shuts out any possibility of natural inspiration: "'Cover the window, please. These mountains give me no ideas.'"[64] The forces that stirred Keats and Shelley to sublime inspiration have no ability to reach the urban mind: "All the old literature, with its praise of Nature and its fear of Nature, rang false as the prattle of a child."[65] Vashti's attitude mirrors modernist concerns with exculpating romantic sentimentality in favor of realism. Nature has been driven out of the human imagination; yet, ultimately, the human characters must rely on the daunting and unknown wilds of their planet's exterior to survive.

When they meet face-to-face, Kuno tells his mother that he has risked exile to climb out of the machine to the forbidden natural world. There, he begins to grasp the extent of what has been lost to the "poisoned darkness" of the machine and comes to believe salvation exists with the few "homeless" people who still live in the outer environment: "'I have seen them, spoken to them, loved them. They are hiding in the mists and ferns until our civilization stops.... Humanity has learnt its lesson.'"[66] Further, Kuno's knowledge of those living in the natural world is not described with abstract, second-hand information, but rather in terms of direct physical interaction – Kuno has "seen," "spoken" and "loved" them. But Kuno's adventure is abruptly halted as he is dragged back by the machine's worm-like tentacles. It is not that Forster celebrates the condition of homelessness, which he personally abhorred in his own experience of renting and leasing property throughout his life, but rather that homelessness is the ultimate sacrifice for any Forster character. The decision to permanently uproot oneself from one's local place and protective architectural shell, without the promise of a reflective pastoral return, denotes a detachment and devaluation of locality and home that thwarts growth of character and body. It is the outward momentum of discovery paired with the impetus to return and educate that creates the pastoral balm.

The epiphanies Forster values most are those that directly engage the senses and stimulate feeling as well as intellectual development. The machine retaliates against Kuno's insurrection by warning humans from first-hand ideas that "do not really exist. They are but the physical impressions produced by love and fear, and on this gross foundation who could erect a philosophy?"[67] The machine begins to pause and flicker with malfunction, "disfigure[ing] the symphonies"[68] and causing interruptions in medication. The people living in the machine, however, readily adapt to these erratic failings and they are uncritically subsumed into daily existence. Here, one can sense Forster's critique of society's apathy even though he risks oozing into vague notions of love and fear that remain unexamined. The citizens are so accustomed to having their needs met by others that they have grown into dependent sycophants incapable of revolution, or they are so caught up in being polite and well-bred that all the critical inquiry of true advancement is euthanized, creating an unfeeling and inhumane society.[69]

Before Kuno can persuade his mother to climb out with him on a second attempt at escape, they both perish when the machine explodes. The final image, eerily prescient of recent American imperial history, is of an airplane crashing through the machine "exploding as it went, rending gallery after gallery with its wings of steel."[70] The attainment of a fully intellectual, mechanized existence is a dystopia rather than a utopia. Further, the upper earth, where the "sun grew very feeble" against the "low colourless hills" is not rendered as a jubilant Eden either. The looming threat of danger and extinction in the nebulous "mist" is a rather bleak new world. The only hope for the future life is left to the "outcasts" who roam the grassy hills, not in a Virgilian idealism, but as exiles who know that to start over is still preferable to the solipsistic steel trap of urban intellectualism. Kuno and Vashti face their doom mourning for "the sin against the body ... the centuries of wrong against the muscles and the nerves, and those five portals by which we can alone apprehend,"[71] recognizing that the very means of intellectual understanding is the body's ability to feel and "apprehend" the surrounding world.

Although the characters in both "The Machine Stops" and *Howards End* seem to find a remedy in pastoral escape, neither is satisfactory; as a result, Forster's natural spaces begin to resemble the anti-pastoral tradition. The promise of a redemptive green world is no longer realistic. In these works, the hope for a green retreat, described by Forster in his *Common-place* book as a place where humans can "revert with a tired sigh to the woods"[72] seems to be a bathetic solution at best or, for more tragic figures such as Kuno and Leonard Bast, a bitterly satirical fantasy. As in the earlier short stories, industrialized urbanity is shown to be a dystopia, but now the country is no utopia either. The homeless outcasts from the machine are furtive exiles, struggling to exist in the indeterminate mist of the outer green world; and while the protagonists of *Howards End* may seem to secure an idyllic pastoral home, Forster's conclusion promotes an anti-pastoral real-ization, subtly undermining the expected conventions of the pastoral genre, and challenging his readers to critique the pastoral fantasy rather than "buy" into a false sense of ease. In other words, the city is rejected, but the wished-for panacea of beginning again in an unspoiled countryside is also subtly questioned; in these works, a pastoral ending does not successfully erase the problems of class or the hardship entailed by a green retreat.

The tension between the degradation of urban spaces and the renewal of natural spaces has long been recognized as a prominent theme in *Howards End*, but the health of the flesh is also a central environmental issue in the novel, particularly as it applies to Leonard Bast. Leonard Bast – a kind of anti-pastoral shepherd-figure – is a struggling London clerk, a "grandson to the shepherd or ploughboy whom civilization had sucked into the town."[73] The Schlegel sisters, most notably Helen, disastrously employ their roman-ticized ideals in an attempt to rescue him from the abyss of poverty, and before they unconsciously bring about circumstances that will cause his death, Bast sires the child who symbolizes the novel's tenuous hope for future generations. Yet despite his importance as a progenitor for a better future, Bast's own body is afflicted by urban poverty. Although Forster does undoubtedly reify agricultural laborers, it is important to note that he does not locate modern decline in a eugenic argument, but rather in a pointed condemnation of upper-class mobility that negligently treads on those, who but for the fetters of modernization, could have been the kind of rural farmer or shepherd-figure whom Forster identifies as the backbone of English moral character:

> A young man, colourless, toneless, who had already the mournful eyes above a drooping mustache that are so common in London, and that haunt some streets of the city like accusing presences. One guessed him as the third generation, grandson to the shepherd or ploughboy whom civilization had sucked into the town.... Margaret, noting the spine that might have been straight, and the chest that might have broadened, wondered whether it paid to give up the glory of the animal for a tail coat and a couple of ideas.[74]

Ideas will not fortify the body. The fact that humans are also animals is not only acknowledged in Forster's fiction, but also praised rather than being shunned as bestial. Indeed, "the glory of the animal" must be recognized as a necessary aspect of the best kind of human. Forster's mocking reference to the "tail" biological evolution has divested from the human body is cunningly refigured as a fashionable social appendage marking the abject decline of our "urban" species. The proverbial "monkey suit" is more appalling than any real component of our animal kinship with other species.

The novel's satirical stance toward "progress" is also evidenced by city dwellings that deaden any aesthetic infusion of health or inspiration. The impoverishment of Leonard Bast is typified by squalid urban living conditions. Leonard attempts to elevate his mind by reading the aesthetic principles of John Ruskin: "Let us consider a little each of these characters in succession, and first (for of the shafts enough has been said already), what is very peculiar to this church – its luminousness."[75] But the beauty of Ruskin's words and ideas can't paper-over the reality of Leonard's flat: "First (for the absence of ventilation enough has been said already), what is very peculiar to this flat – its obscurity. . . .. 'My flat is dark as well as stuffy.' Those were the words for him."[76] Imagining what he would write about his own surroundings, Leonard can copy the style of Ruskin's prose, but he can't replicate the sense of sanctuary – his own space won't allow him the words. Forster implies there is no possibility for creative fulfillment or uplifting sentiment in urban architecture designed for the lower classes.

Like Leonard – the shepherd denied his proper pastoral role – even food, itself, is deprived of its expected beauty and sustenance when it is too far removed from its organic origins:

> They began with a soup square, which Leonard had just dissolved in some hot water. It was followed by the tongue – a freckled cylinder of meat, with a little jelly at the top, and a great deal of yellow fat at the bottom – ending with another square dissolved in water (jelly: pineapple), which Leonard had prepared earlier in the day.[77]

The geometric shapes of the gelatinous molds suggest mechanical reproduction. The compact "square" and "cylinder" no longer resemble any organic matter, but are rather artificially flavored with exotic "pineapple" to lure one's imagination to some tropical fantasy rather than the reality of the dismal food itself. The sensual activities of food preparation and the pleasure of eating have been replaced by artificial flavoring. The language is also devoid of sensory modifiers, taking on the shape of the jello's cube in a condensed block: "(jelly: pineapple)." The quality of the food is part of the atmosphere of Leonard's flat, which resists beauty, both rhetorically and physically. Instead the description hints at the urban consumerism that causes such a dismal product. There are whiffs of human labor, the bodies that industry consumes or the people who have been "sucked into the town" in words like "tongue" (a human part as well as an animal part) and "freckled," suggesting the skin of country children exposed to the sun. As Stacey Alaimo reminds us in *Bodily Natures*, "Workers' bodies are not only the sites of direct application of power, but permeable sites that are forever transformed by the substances and forces – asbestos, coal, dust, radiation – that permeate them."[78] Society's failure to adequately address the slimy underbelly of industry and the impoverished health of disempowered citizens is the "yellow fat at the bottom," the unhealthy greed and coward-ice that no preprepared promise of riches and leisure can eviscerate.

The bottom dregs of the lower class – those who don't have a job or tenement rooms – don't even appear as characters: "We are not concerned with the very poor. They are unthinkable, and only to be approached by the statistician or the poet. This story deals with gentlefolk, or with those who are obliged to pretend they are gentlefolk."[79] That Forster's narrator explicitly points out this absence not only participates in a middle-class myopia, but also acknowledges it in a way that invites censure. Within the upper-wedge of the lower class that the narrator does deign to observe, it is clear that hand-to-mouth urban wage-earners are impoverished not just monetarily, but also bodily, emotionally, and intellectually by their com-plete separation from nature.

By using Leonard as a thwarted peasant-figure of the pastoral tradition, Forster's relationship with the pastoral tradition becomes more complex. While Forster seems to be sustaining the traditional ideal that those who work the land are blithely happy figures, as Leonard might have been if the availability of jobs had not encouraged migration to urban centers, Forster is also explicitly drawing the reader's attention to the politics of class and mobility to reveal the precarious position of the lower class. In this manner *Howards End* borrows from the pastoral, but it also exposes what the pastoral is traditionally meant to evade. William Empson explains the primary function of the pastoral convention: "The essential trick of the old pastoral, which was felt to imply a beautiful relation between rich and poor, was to make simple people express strong feelings (felt as the most universal subject, something fundamentally true about everybody) in learned and fashionable language (so that you wrote about the best subject in the best way)."[80] Leonard's pointed inability to make Ruskin's language fit his circumstances is the exact opposite of allowing lower class characters to speak in "learned and fashionable language." Moreover, the relation Forster depicts is anything but "beautiful." It encourages repugnance.

This reaction isn't limited to the aforementioned body, home, or food either. The Schlegel sisters' initial efforts to encourage Leonard Bast – which seemingly create a "beautiful relation between rich and poor" through intellectual conversations about midnight walks – all go dreadfully awry. Helen's desire to help becomes an inappropriate and regretted sexual tryst with the married Mr. Bast, after which she attempts to assuage her guilt with payment. Her behavior is not unlike Henry Wilcox's treatment of Mrs. Bast, a former prostitute he frequented when he was married to his first wife. Even the well-intentioned Margaret engages in reproachable behavior. After her marriage to Henry Wilcox, she becomes embarrassed at how Helen and the Basts crash her step-daughter's upper-class engagement party, and does everything in her power to shuffle them off after Mrs. Bast's undecorous displays of sloppy drunkenness. There is nothing "pretty" about these class relations. The crucial aspect of the text that many critics overlook is the way the text shows up the errors of the Schlegel sisters' idealist middle-class morality. David Bradshaw's analysis is helpful on this point. Commenting on Margaret's relief that she and her sister will live contentedly at Howards End, Bradshaw explains:

> Margaret ... seems oblivious to the fact that Jacky, at that very moment, must either be teetering on the edge of a far from figurative abyss or, more likely, already well on her way to the bottom of it. This further evidence of the Schlegels' blindness, crassness, hypocrisy and bigotry might be parceled together in support of the view that Forster never intended us to be as favourably disposed towards them as the first few chapters of the novel seem to encourage us to be. Forster's aim may have been to discredit the Schlegels by exposing them as merely skin-deep progressives.[81]

The text's deliberate smashing of the sisters' original social aims further explains Margaret's marriage into and the narrator's subsequent justification of capitalism. Even the rebellious Helen is glad to be relieved of Leonard and is warming up to Henry Wilcox by the end. The novel couldn't be more emphatic about how the sisters have destroyed Leonard, their prodigal liberal project: Margaret's wealthy step-son, Charles Wilcox, who stands to inherit his father's corporate fortune confronts Bast with a drawn sword, and Leonard, thrown off-balance, is killed when he collapses underneath the weight of a toppling bookshelf, representing the ideas and privilege his circumstances have made inaccessible. Emblems of power, money, and education coalesce to produce Bast's death. Again, this maneuver inverts the usual pastoral plotlines of upper and lower-class characters described by Empson: "Their fundamental use was to show the labour of the king or saint in the serious part and in the comic part the people, as 'popular' as possible, for whom he laboured ... Usually it provides a sort of parody or parallel in low life to the serious part."[82] In *Howards End*, the lower class plot is decidedly tragic and the trajectories of the silly and foolish lower and middle/upper-class characters are starkly contrasted rather than paralleled.

Even Ruth Wilcox, a member of the landed gentry who is endowed with the classic pastoral qualities of nature goddesses, can't survive the poisonous airs of the city. At times, Ruth Wilcox resembles a personification of a mythological Demeter, recalling Forster's fascination with pastoral mythology in other short stories such as "Other Kingdom" and "The Story of a Panic." However, in this narrative, an upper-class matriarch, rather than a foreign peasant, is associated with nature, suggesting that all classes of humans are capable of being tied to the land. Mrs. Wilcox carries the symbol of summer harvest as she takes her evening walk: "Trail, trail, went her long dress over the sopping grass, and she came back with her hands full of the hay that was cut yesterday."[83] Although Mrs. Wilcox married into the nouveau-riche commercial class to save her rural home, and voices socially conservative views on female domesticity, she remains firmly rooted in a generosity that seems to emanate from her connection to the rural landscape. She takes no heed of her trailing gown getting ruined by the dew. And although she disagrees with the progressive notions of the Schlegel sisters, she not only invites them into her home, but also chooses Margaret as a spiritual heir who will value the natural state of her home, rather than a familial heir who might have the whole place razed for a profit. Margaret proves her ability to appreciate Ruth Wilcox's identification with her home when she rushes to join her for an impractical, and eventually thwarted, journey from London to Howards End. Margaret is willing to prioritize place-based values that the rest of the Wilcox family scoffs at. Ruth Wilcox's wish to pass on her home to Margaret reveals that sustaining the rural landscape matters more to her than upholding social convention. In other words, Mrs. Wilcox rejects expectations of primogeniture in favor of privileging alternative connections based on environmental values. Her presence permeates her country home, and even those who inhabit it, after her death. Margaret reflects: "I feel that you and I and Henry are only fragments of that woman's mind. She knows everything. She is everything. She is the house and the tree that leans over it."[84] In this quote, Forster's idea of flesh seems to expand. Unlike Miss Beaumont's metamorphosis, Ruth Wilcox doesn't exactly become the tree, rather she is a presence embedded in the place. Therefore, while the environment itself is not represented as an alive, independent being in this text, the relationship between humans and environment does become more complex as Forster begins to experiment with mixing genres of realism and pastoral fantasy.

The architecture of the home becomes yet another kind of animate body. For Forster, the rural landscape and the robust body are corollaries of England's best virtues, and both are threatened by urban encroachment. As Jon Hegglund succinctly remarks: "The health of the individual bodies and the collective health of the nation are intimately connected in the quasi-organic space of the house."[85] The Schlegel family home is personified in its final demise – "a house which had always been human, and had not mistaken culture as an end."[86] Similarly, Howards End is given a prescient consciousness and haunting sense of being a fleshly organism: "It was the heart of the house beating, faintly at first, then loudly, martially."[87] Yet Forster also reverses the expected literary device of personification by imbuing human bodies with the attributes of architecture. When Leonard Bast reflects, "'My flat is dark as well as stuffy.' Those were the words for him,"[88] the phrase "the words for him" implies that he is describing the condition of his own body as well as his flat. Moreover, Leonard's body takes on the qualities of a home when he approaches Howards End. The house that had been personified by a beating heart now is used to describe the portals of Leonard's palpitating aorta: "He felt in curious health: doors seemed to be opening and shutting inside his body."[89] The valves of his heart become doors to the cramped rooms of his chest. Place is fused with body as Forster suggests that both a proper home embedded in the living land and a strong body invigorated by outdoor activity are what England needs. In this way, Rob Nixon's critique of Forster's postcolonial blind-spots in this novel are keen: "Although imperial spaces trouble the edges of *Howard's* [sic] *End*, Forster anxiously seeks to screen out their implications by advancing a pastorally contained vision of English regeneration."[90] Forster's vision of place and the "slow violence" done to laboring bodies certainly does seem myopically limited to the boundaries of England's isle and the English working class. Yet, where I part ways with Nixon is that I do not think it necessarily follows that the novel as a whole "deploys geographical synecdoche and panoramic pastoral to foreclose from the idea of England, people, places, and histories that unsettle the books project of selective national regeneration and redefinition." Rather, Forster's attentiveness to the far-reaching and

exploitive effects of an overly ambitious capitalism does have something
to contribute to an awareness of "slow violence."[91] Not in terms of
postcolonial exploitation, but in terms of histories that expose the limitations of material, consumptive matrixes that are often assumed to be
foundational to national regeneration.

Margaret's eventual acquisition of Howards End seems to signal
a hopeful promise that society may learn to value the nonhuman environment – a maneuver that initially resembles a more conventional pastoral –
but the movement from the London flat to Howards End is fraught with
the kind of compromises that promote an anti-pastoral theme. The
circulation of commodities and their entanglement in the personal relationships of the Schlegels and the Wilcoxes is the pivotal conflict of the
novel. As Henry Turner has noted, the degradation of English character
seems to be prompted by "a *super*-abundance of objects, people, property,
and spaces."[92] The material environment becomes transformed from substance to monetary value. The dizzying array of property owned by the
Wilcox family illustrates this phenomenon of industrial commercialism
and capitalism, which Marxist ecocritic John Bellamy Foster theorizes is
the "catalyst for the unprecedented acceleration of changes in the atmosphere, the climate, the ocean, and the earth's ecosystems."[93] In the conclusion of *Howards End*, Forster seems to suggest that the solution to urban
consumption is seeded in the same alternate natural environment he
gestured to at the end of "The Machine Stops." As Alexandra Harris also
notes about this novel and its glut of homes and objects, "The possessions,
as Forster had suggested, were a symptom not a cause, a symptom of
having no fuller sense of belonging,"[94] a belonging that seems particularly
tied to rejecting a market-based economy of value or culturally imposed
monikers of class and colonial market power in favor of a value-system that
is based on a respect for all human life and the dynamic community of a
more-than-human world. Margaret Schlegel observes: "This craze for
motion has only set in during the last hundred years. It may be followed
by a civilization that won't be movement, because it will rest on the
earth."[95] One's awareness of an identity that is anchored in a specific
genius loci and nurtured by valuing land and organic life over human-
centered industrial progress is posited as the salve to modernity's ills.
Indeed, the most celebratory of Virgil's eclogues involves a group of friends
who have "left the city" to go to a country house: "A harvest home was
being held for Demeter."[96] The friends enjoy their satiated stupor while
around them, "the scorched cicadas carried their chirping labour on, and
the tree frog croaked far off in the dense thorn break ... bees zoomed
around and about the fountains. All things smelt of a rich harvest and

fruiting–abundance of pears by our feet and apples rolled at our side and branches burdened with damsons earthward drooped"[97] The analogy of Howards End to the "country house" that the urban dwellers, like the Schlegels, are journeying toward, and the feast in honor of "Demeter," or Mrs. Wilcox, tempts readers to expect a surfeit of bountiful goodness.

Yet Forster's conclusion is anti-pastoral in its darkly shaded subversion of a classic Virgilian ending. Margaret acknowledges: "'London's creeping.' She pointed over the meadow – over eight or nine meadows, but at the end of them was a red rust."[98] As Daniel Born points out: "The concluding hymn to pastoral calm does not drown out the more disturbing urban sights and sounds."[99] The looming threat of urban expansion is a reminder that England's future is by no means secure; Forster's agrarian resolution is neither tidy nor pat. Even Helen's final exclamation of a flush summer harvest invokes ominous echoes of the dead Mrs. Wilcox and Leonard Bast, who was also "cut" down by a "reaper" of sorts when Charles wielded a scythe-like sword. Helen's proclamation that "We've seen to the very end, and it'll be such a crop of hay as never!"[100] contains troubling ambiguities. Helen's optimism directly contrasts with her more practical sister's view beyond the "very end" of their meadow. Additionally, the term "never" has dual connotations – it can mean that this is the best crop yet, or that this is the final crop of such a yield and its equal will never be seen again. As Gifford notes of William Blake's anti-pastoral poetry, "he exposes pastorally-comforting images, images of Heaven as self-deceiving constructs."[101] Forster's reliance on a "happy" harvest ending strains the limits of believable optimism and actually creates an anti-pastoral effect. The effect of a conclusion where nationalities intermarry, middle and upper classes mingle wealth, and the atavist progeny of society is the offspring of an unwed mother and a father who poetically walked the fields at night in an Emersonian quest for enlightenment is meant to be unsatisfyingly unrealistic. The disruption of verisimilitude suggests that part of Forster's strategy is to show his readers that such a resolution can only exist in the realm of fantasy and could never be realized in current English society. As a result, the novel protests against the feeling of satisfactory ease the stereotypical pastoral is expected to evoke.

However, on an individual level, valuing nature and one's own connections to the earth more convincingly improves several of Forster's fictional protagonists. Although the fate of humankind is doomed in "The Machine Stops" and Vashti cannot be convinced to reexamine her revulsion toward "the terrors of direct experience,"[102] her son Kuno does achieve greater awareness through discovering the power of sensory perception. The machine routinely executes athletes because it is "a demerit to be muscular"[103] in the "advanced" society of abstract ideas, yet Kuno comes back from his struggle to make contact with the outside environment enlivened by a new perspective: "Man's feet are the measure for distance, his hands are the measure for ownership, his body is the measure for all that is loveable and desirable and strong."[104] Therefore, Kuno learns that one's connection to the land is also dependent upon a familiarity with the terrain of one's own body. Both Kuno and Leonard are characters who test the limits of bodies and minds that have been enervated by urban culture. They aspire to a full, virtuous life emanating from an appreciation of sensory, physical experience in natural settings. Yet these pastoral transformations are incomplete. Society does not benefit from what Kuno and Leonard have learned because both characters are denied the necessary "return." Kuno dies before he can share his discoveries with anyone but his mother, and Leonard is actually killed in the pastoral retreat of Howards End, unable to achieve resolution with Helen or teach his son the dangers of the city. Instead, it is the reader who must learn the lesson and complete the social change. The reader is challenged to question why the "happy endings" of Forster's pastoral novels seem fanciful and unsatisfying. Forster's anti-pastoral disquiet points toward values that must be adopted by an entire culture if any actual resolutions of tolerance and understanding are to be achieved for individuals in Forster's real, contemporary society.

Learning that truth and value are inherent in physical experiences and not just confined to abstract intellectualism is the defining lesson of Forster's novel concerning homosexuality, *Maurice*. Forster publicly denounced the elevation of intellect over the primacy of the body during his lifetime in essays such as "The Challenge of Our Time," saying, "But the difficulty is this: where does the body stop and the spirit start?"[105] His most profound expression of this belief is conveyed in *Maurice*, which was published posthumously. Living through the Oscar Wilde trials may have stimulated an interest in Wilde's mores and the "wild" impulses of the body.[106] Indeed, a homosexual writer who values the environment may have an innate investment in defining what is "natural." While serving as Secretary to a Maharaja in India, Forster and the Maharaja had to discuss advances Forster had made to another man; the conversation was reportedly framed in terms of what is "natural":

> "Why a man and not a woman? Is not a woman more natural?"
> "Not in my case. I have no feeling for women."
> "Oh but that alters everything. You are not to blame."
> "I don't know what 'natural' is."

"You are quite right, Morgan – I ought never to have used the word. No, don't worry – don't worry. I am only distressed you did not tell me everything before – I might have saved you so much pain."[107]

The Maharaja was quite accepting of Forster's sexuality and insinuates by his apology that the word "natural" connotes one's own instinctive sexual impulses, including a desire for a person of the same sex. Yet British society was not so open-minded. Catriona Mortimer-Sandilands and Bruce Erickson document the shared history of Darwin's evolutionary biology and cultural presumptions about sexuality that result in "notions of natural sexuality from which nonreproductive sexualities are understood as deviant,"[108] even leading many scientists to ignore or pathologize the wider variety of sexual activity observed in nonhuman animals: "It is clearly not the case that all sex leads to reproduction, for humans and other animals alike, yet the presence of nonreproductive sexual activities is frequently read as a sign of ecological decline: another twist on degeneracy theory."[109] This degeneracy was linked with the urban homosexual, "the idea that the work men did in cities no longer brought them into close and honorable contact with nature,"[110] an idea that Forster seems to have some agreement with, but only as it concerns the fate of all human bodies. Yet, Forster completely inverts these assumptions as they relate to queer sexuality. Although works like "The Machine Stops" and *Howards End* clearly indict the increasing encasement of human activity in urban environments as a source of problematic development in the human species, the homosexual does not represent the product of that degeneracy. Rather, the homosexual impulse is the natural impulse – wild, free, and organic. Forster's fiction repeatedly and emphatically associates queer sexual identity with the "natural" state of prolific diversity and profuse flowering of color and organic beauty. Indeed, the homosexual element often corrects what was "missing" from the natural scene, and is the component of its harmonizing completion. Redefining what is "natural" in terms of biodiversity – being able to show how what might initially be considered gross or marred is actually necessary to a well-functioning ecosystem – begins to offer possibilities for redefining what is natural sexually as well. Forster hints at this in an enigmatic statement made in April 1904: "He asked himself, in a dreamy way, why people were so sure that plants were not conscious of procreation, for it might be 'the side by which we might understand them.'"[111] Society's assumptions that it knows nature's secrets and can master environmental forces represent the same kinds of fearful and repressive control it attempts to exercise over sexuality. Forster explores the nexus between nature and sex more fully in *Maurice*. Indeed, Mortimer-Sandilands and Erickson have suggested that Edward Carpenter's role in Forster's writing the novel would indicate that he was motivated not only by a desire to tell a homosexual love story, but also to advance a preservationist agenda through that narrative: "English gay activist and utopian socialist Edward Carpenter was strongly committed to a rural socialist project of vegetarianism, voluntary simplicity, and manual agricultural labor; he also considered rural natures suitable places for what he called the 'Uranian' temperament (indeed, it was a visit to Carpenter that inspired Forster to write *Maurice*)."[112] The bildungsroman of *Maurice* positions the naturalness, or acceptableness, of homosexuality as the enlightened goal of Maurice Hall's education. For Forster, embodied knowledge, which one learns from the queer pastoral retreat, challenges cultural assumptions. Forster's work consistently insinuates that intellect detached from embodied knowledge, including a consciousness of the queer body, is often turbid, repressed, and ineffective.

Thus, the pastoral impulse is one involving a rural lesson of bodily, animal awareness, which, in return, promotes a more healthy and balanced antidote to social repression. *Maurice* encourages a respect for knowledge defined by an embodied interaction with the world and a verification of one's own instinctive drives: "The 'vast curve' of Maurice's life includes progress to a relationship in which the flesh educates the spirit and develops 'the sluggish heart and the slack mind against their will.'"[113] Maurice's first lover, Clive Durham, attempts to confine homosexual love to a platonic, artistic philosophy: "Landscape is the only safe subject – or perhaps something geometric, rhythmical, inhuman absolutely."[114] Clive has to abandon organic subject matter for something entirely mathematical and synchronized. This allows the wild to be framed in neat shapes and governed by known formulas. The application of Clive's philosophy to their relationship is apparent when Clive declines Maurice's request for a kiss, a desire inspired in part by a response to the natural surroundings – the waking sparrows and the sound of the ringdoves beginning to coo in the woods.[115] When Maurice finally begins to realize that Clive's meta-physical love will not satisfy his own ideal of passion and romance, he asks himself, "Did [Clive] suppose he was made of paper?"[116] emphasizing the distinction between the abstract life of purely intellectual pursuits and a fuller life acknowledging the pleasures of the body. When Maurice finally does find a partner who shares his ideal of a more physical love, in the gamekeeper Alec Scudder, the novel's discourse also becomes more embodied. In contrast to the abstract level of communicative language used to define Maurice and Clive's relationship, Maurice tries to explain his feelings to Alec by "trying to get underneath the words. He continued, feeling his way to a grip."[117] The prose is charged with sexual innuendo, but also suggests that language merely clothes the truth Maurice and Alec seek to articulate through direct and tangible action, rather than intellectual justification.

Forster inverts the values normally associated with homosexuality through making what might be considered "deformities" in nature into something positive. Maurice initially perceives nature with an unappreciative eye, wanting to see what is supposed to be aesthetically pleasing. Yet when Maurice ponders the imperfections of nature, hoping to find one example of nature's beauty fulfilled, he finds himself confronting Alec and homosexual desire: "On one spray every flower was lopsided, the next swarmed with caterpillars or bulged with galls. The indifference of nature! And her incompetence! He leant out of the window to see whether she couldn't bring it off once, and stared straight into the bright brown eyes of a young man."[118] Maurice must reconfigure what he considers "natural" not only in how he defines "errors" in nature's flowering plants, but also in the bloom of sexual love that Alec stirs within him. Maurice's desire doesn't erase the boundaries these distinctions evoke as much as it challenges the standard dialectic. Moreover, the natural imagery is less symbolic of the traditional pastoral and tuned to a finer understanding of ecological operations that slyly suggest what initially appears repulsive to social aesthetics, may actually be quite natural. Lopsided flowers weighted with insects in symbiotic relation to the floral environment are part of a thriving ecosystem. It is not coincidental that when Maurice poses his apostrophe to nature, requesting a perfect specimen, nature responds with Alec. Likewise, the reader is invited to reconsider whether natural "imperfections," be they caterpillars or supposedly deviant sexual desires, don't all have a proper place in the overall health of the naturally abundant world. Now that he has met Alec, Maurice's impulses to express love as an embodied act are aligned with a flight into nature's own fecundity: "How the tangle of flowers and fruit wreathed his brain!"[119] Forster remakes homosexual desire into something overflowing with organicity. The short story "Arthur Snatchfold," (written 1928) which takes on a more capitalist critique, similarly begins with Richard Conway – a queer widower who is "not a sentimentalist"[120] but who has become rich from the aluminum industry – leaning out of the window of a country house in the morning, critiquing the "too green" monotony of the garden, noting that "of course what was wanted was colour,"[121] when the promise of homosexual romance in the form of a young milkman changes the landscape and provides the desired "blaze": "He looked at the dull costly garden. It improved. A man had come into it from the back of the yew hedge. He had on a canary-coloured shirt, and the effect was exactly right."[122] In *Maurice*, the critique involves the correction of perceiving nature's beauty, and homosexuality, as something one might not initially understand as vital to its thriving ecology in order to attain a more fulfilling love. This contrasts with the plot of "Arthur Snatchfold," where the closeted, business-minded main character will ultimately be the impetus of the younger man's doom as nature's "color" is only superficially "fulfilled" in both the purely aesthetic gaze of Sir Conway and the monetary transaction that spoils what would otherwise have been a mutually appealing forest tryst. Even though Snatchfold is a wealthy financier, the milkman initially protested corrupting the mutual nonmonetary value of the exchange with payment: "'Naow, we was each as bad as the other . . . Naow . . . keep yer money.'"[123] In the end, even after being caught and tried for indecency, the young man refuses to identify the older business-man, revealing the superiority of his country ethics to that of Sir Conway, who silently wallows in his shame and hypocrisy thinking he was "safe, safe, he could go on with his career as planned" as he learns of the young man's fate over drinks at his club. Thus, "Arthur Snatchfold" uses the laboring country lover not only to create a critique of upper-middle-class heterosexual prejudice, but also, akin to Leonard Bast, as a reminder of the frequent victimization of the lower class.

An ability on the part of the rustic to point out flaws in the mainstream society is a feature of the anti-pastoral or, as Empson calls it, the "mock-pastoral": "So far as the person described is outside society because too poor for its benefits he is independent, as the artist claims to be, and can be a critic of society; so far as he is forced by this into crime he is the judge of the society that judges him."[124] Similarly, Alec, and to a much lesser extent, Arthur, becomes an authoritative rural critic of an effete and ineffective upper class society. Alec is still prominently used as a rustic peasant who is closer to nature, but unlike the earlier stories or "Arthur Snatchfold," the upper-class character, Maurice, explicitly acknowledges the superiority of Alec's knowledge. Maurice ruminates, "How did a country lad like that know so much about me?"[125] Maurice learns from and defers to Alec's knowledge, even though the novel still hinges on troubling stereotypes of the type of knowledge the laboring class excels at.

In the end, Maurice escapes with Alec to the greenwood, suggesting that social convention, like the community in the machine, has become

the distortion of what is natural. Homosexual desire can only be consummated in the woods, where nature, if not society, accepts it. As
Sandilands and Erickson point out, the shade of woods and parks, often
against the intention of the public design, has served as a place of queer
resistance: "A particular sexual sociality shapes physical nature-spaces –
parks, ravines, paths, empty lots – as part of a public challenge to
heteronormativity, and perhaps especially to the official heteronormativity of designated nature-space."[126] The playful though eventually tragic
encounter in "Arthur Snatchfold" occurs in just such a place. Using his
"easy out-of-doors voice"[127] Sir Conway intentionally plans to intercept
Arthur's usual delivery route by going to the wood where "there were two
paths through the bracken, a broad and a narrow"[128] until he hears "the
milk-can approaching down the narrow path,"[129] aligning the sexual
escapade both with a rejection of mainstream paths as well as the milk
exuded from a female yet phallic udder of a cow, and deliberately
commodified by the aspect of the delivery man. The story also exposes
the injustice of class in the material risks of queer identity; while the
milkman is imprisoned, one of the reasons Sir Conway escapes notice is
not only his lover's valiant silence, but also the prejudicial assumptions
that the other man must have come from the town's disreputable hotel
since the "little wood ... stretches up to the hotel, so he could easily
bring people in"[130] while no one apparently considered the other man in
the tryst as being the well-to-do visitor to the country mansion upon
whose very property the wood belongs. Unlike some of the earlier
pastoral short stories, Forster's critical approach to the privileged protagonist of Sir Conway, enjoying a weekend retreat at the country house of
another businessman, seems more aware of the injustice of class, featuring it as another kind of boundary or category that harmfully constructs
cultural prejudices that prevent "connection." In contrast to the small
stretch of "wood" between village and country manor in "Arthur Snatchfold," the greenwood Alec and Maurice retreat to is distinct from the
park space, and suggestively more aligned with pathless forests and a time
when England was itself more wild. Forster's terminal note for the novel
states that this is a "happy ending" in comparison to "a lad dangling from
a noose or with a suicide pact."[131] But also notes that by 1960, when he
was writing the terminal note, "it belongs to an England where it was still
possible to get lost. It belongs to the last moment of the greenwood,"
attributing its demise to the demands of war and science: "Two great
wars demanded and bequeathed regimentation which the public services
adopted and extended, science lent her aid, and the wildness of our island,

never extensive, was stamped upon and built over and patrolled in no time."[132] While these comments evoke a more traditional pastoral nostalgia and belief in a "happy" Arcadia, Maurice and Alec's abrupt disappearance and Maurice's dissemblance to Clive on the eve of departure also create a mood of furtiveness that, like the conclusion of *Howards End*, insert a sharp twang that disrupts pastoral harmony. As Gifford reminds ecocritics, this may simply illustrate one of those moments when a text can present a mixed application of both pastoral and anti-pastoral qualities.[133] Although Stuart Christie keenly critiques Forster's "happy" ending as "endors[ing] the homosexual silence"[134] of Arnoldian civic society, the novel's use of a complex anti-pastoral fantasy to communicate a discomfort and dissatisfaction in the reader adds another layer to the conclusion's affect. Indeed, Paul Peppis interprets the "greenwood" as a failed "happy" retreat because the epiphany is one that underscores social failure and injustice: "[Maurice] comes to understand his decision to take to the greenwood with Alec and live like homosexual outlaws as a profoundly committed, profoundly modern act: precisely because he refuses to subjugate his dissident sexuality to social regulation, accepting homosexuality as an inalienable part of his identity, and rejecting English society as irremediably unjust, Maurice completes his homosexual *and* modernist *Bildung*."[135] Further, for a sympathetic reader, the unlikelihood of the couple's happy future as outcasts and the ominous suggestion that they may be hunted as prey in the woods, rather than allowed any life of idyllic ease, provokes an anti-pastoral dissatisfaction. The "silence" Alec and Maurice are exiled to actively criticizes society's superficial ignorance.

Similarly, Leonard provides a stark, yet problematic, anti-pastoral critique of the upwardly mobile Schlegels. During the series of events that must take place for Margaret to eventually acquire title to Howards End, she is forced to realize the limits of her own liberal idealism. While she ardently professes the rights of women and a humanitarian responsibility toward the lower classes, she also comes to realize: "The very soul of the world is economic, and that the lowest abyss is not the absence of love but the absence of coin."[136] Despite their desire to disavow patriarchy and inequity, the ability to be outside of a monetary system of accumulation is inconceivable. Forster's work hints at the necessity to recognize the ways in which capitalist systems threaten the environment. Similar to the dangers elucidated by eco-Marxism, Forster implicitly critiques monetary value as at odds with the connective and pastoral ideologies he champions, seeming to agree with John Bellamy Foster that, "There is no conceivable capitalist economics compatible with a 'steady-state economy,' a system that abandons endless growth of the economy as its central feature."[137] Like-wise, Forster is sympathetic to the allure of ownership and the seeming futility of operating within any other system, yet still positions capitalism as a source of ecological danger. Margaret and her sister will enjoy the peaceful satisfaction that rural living offers, but the novel explicitly recog-nizes that pastoral harmony is still dependent upon the privilege of ownership material wealth makes possible. Consequently, Leonard Bast is haplessly manipulated and seduced by characters from the upper and middle class. Despite Helen Schelgel's love-for-love's-sake affair with him and his hope to better himself through long Thoreauvian walks in the country, his life is tragically cut short at Howards End. The ability to "see life steadily and see it whole, group in one vision its transitoriness and its eternal youth" demands Leonard's sacrifice. His death is required to finally allow punishment for Charles Wilcox's petty bourgeois selfishness and create a catalyst for Henry Wilcox's new-found humility. To see the characters in their rotundity, to "see it whole," relies on the "transitoriness" of Leonard's life and the "eternal youth" created by his early death.

The novels' ambivalent treatment of class is not surprising considering that Forster was also tinged with prejudices that colored his views of race and class. In a letter to an Anglo-Indian friend written in 1916 while Forster was in Alexandria, he shows a tormented awareness of his own fluctuating responses to racist attitudes: "I came inclined to be pleased and quite free from racial prejudice, but in 10 months I've acquired an instinctive dislike to the Arab voice, the Arab figure ... exactly the emotion that I censured in the Anglo-Indian towards the natives. What does this mean? ... It's damnable and disgraceful and it's in me."[138] What stands out about this acknowledgement is not only an admission of class and race prejudice but also a genuine attempt to root it out. It is this willingness for self-censure and individual change that must be considered in tandem with Forster's manifestations of class prejudice. In another letter written a year later, Forster proudly declares his affiliation with the lower class while in India, insisting that it is the "Middle class people" who "smell" on account of their snobbery toward "the lower class whom we love."[139] This is not to say that Forster consistently conquered the prejudicial underpinnings of his upbringing, but to show that he vocally and repeatedly endeavored against it. Actions he took in his own life bear out a pattern of resistance. Forster taught at the Working Men's College in London for twenty years or more, an experience that he drew on in constructing Leonard Bast.[140] Forster's first physical love affair was with an Egyptian tram-conductor, whom Forster continued to correspond with after the physical relationship was over. Furbank notes, "He had, or so he felt, broken through the barriers of class and colour."[141] Forster's long-term lover and friend, Robert (Bob) Buckingham, was a working-class policeman who "would attack Forster over class-attitudes."[142] Once again we see that while Forster overcame many class barriers his own social milieu still sanctioned, he continued to wrestle with the prejudices that remained.

This dilemma is evident when, confronted with the choice between preserving the countryside and building more homes to relieve London's working class from their cramped urban slums, he finds himself resisting the humanitarian side: "Well, says the voice of planning and progress, 'why this sentimentality? People must have houses.' They must, and I think of working-class friends in north London who have to bring up four children in two rooms, and many are even worse off than that. But I cannot equate the problem. It is a collision of loyalties. I cannot free myself from the conviction that something irreplaceable has been destroyed."[143] On one hand, the critical emphasis on Forster's liberal humanism eschews the significance of his biocentrism. One could argue that it is not that Forster thinks the lower classes aren't worthy of rural benefits; rather he chooses conservation over the influx of people in general, not necessarily a particular class. Wilfred Stone defends Forster's environmentalism: "That [conflicts between preservation and industry] often come down to conflicts between the haves and have-nots goes without saying, but they are not neat conflicts, with the bad guys on one side and nature on the other. . . . It is the same problem that every 'no growth' movement faces today and is inseparable from the environmental problem of a world filling up with people."[144] Stone is defending Forster's hedging as a reflection of an inevitable tension between humans and nature; but what Stone's assessment fails to recognize is that this conflict is not experienced equally by all humans. The environmental cause continues to have an adversarial relationship with certain *kinds* of people, frequently getting mired in issues of class prejudice, privilege, and the displacement of native people in favor of the protection of wilderness areas for the benefit of a distant, upper-class, white majority.[145] The environmental justice movement of the late twentieth and early twenty-first centuries has striven to bring attention to the ways in which toxic waste is often dumped in the backyards of those who cannot afford homes overlooking scenic areas.[146] Other ecocritics question preservation goals that work to the benefit of wealthy nations who used up their natural resources to get rich while continuing to deny economic opportunities to other nations.[147] But the champions of nature are still too often unaware of the economic privilege that enables their cause. Well-intentioned conservation efforts frequently perpetrate injustice against lower classes, minorities, or residents of other countries that have not been as voraciously developed. Forster's awareness of the issue, as evidenced in his quandary over the working class and their desire for better suburban housing in "The Challenge of Our Time," indicates that even though he still grappled with unresolved class prejudice, he was at least willing to bring this problem to the forefront of discussion.

Similarly, while his fiction betrays vibrations of deeper class prejudices – a form of the "goblins" that surface to threaten the pastoral symphony – Forster's texts just as frequently pluck out these problems and point them out for criticism. As in "The Story of a Panic" and "The Other Kingdom," the glib, narrow-minded English persona is often satirized in the form of a narrator that Forster cleverly sets up for ridicule. This technique is relevant to a Marxist ecocritical perspective, which "emphasizes the necessity of being particularly skeptical of assertions about the natural world when they conform to ruling class ideology";[148] it also suggests that the moments where the narrators of *Howards End* and *Maurice* seem to fuse with the author himself may be regarded as instances of self-deprecation and self-parody. Forster consistently monitors his own deficiencies as well as society's shortfalls. The rural value that nature is supposed to teach a greedy human species is that care is necessary toward all because everyone is interconnected: "Connect – connect without bitterness until all men are brothers."[149] While the abundant harvest and union of families in *Howards End* portends that this connection may be possible, Leonard's death, much like the "creeping" city Margaret observes in the distance, should unsettle the reader. Forster's jubilant final register in the midst of these harbingers draws attention to the depravity of civilized "progress" and intimates the unattainability of satisfying solutions to the problems of human solipsism and industrialization in modern culture.

Thus, Forster's idyllic pastoral conclusions should be read as part of the anti-pastoral effect of *Howards End* and *Maurice*. As Peppis explains, "most of Forster's literary works can be understood as national allegories that diagnose an ailing nation and offer literary cures for the malaise they anatomize."[150] The cures are "literary" because, as Peppis elaborates, "Forster uses . . . tools of melodrama and unexpectedly shifts generic gears, swerving between comedy, romance, and tragedy to maximize the likelihood of transforming readers."[151] The pastoral is another critical genre for creating dramatic shifts in mood. Forster's texts present ethereal, fantastical escapes that should prompt dissatisfaction in the reader. *Maurice*'s seemingly abrupt closure as the protagonists retreat to the greenwood, like the exiles "hiding in the mists and ferns" in "The Machine Stops" and the complicated pastoral gesture of *Howards End,* is another way of pointing out the solutions that English society seems incapable of achieving in the real world. In order to recognize the plight of others and live in a fully embodied way, one must cultivate an awareness that is based in the physical world and its organic processes. A Forsterian salvation from decayed urbanity is not a facile paradise; it exacts a heavy toll. Forster's natural world admits hardship, yet, as Margaret Schlegel ruminates: "Nature, with all her cruelty, comes nearer to us than do these crowds of men."[152]

Beyond the pastoral: *A Passage to India*

In *A Passage to India,* nature trumps imperial politics and exposes the hypocrisy of humanism. It antagonizes superficial efforts at uniting British, Indian, Muslim, and Hindu, reminding the reader that amity can only be achieved through an acceptance of unexpected meanings and inclusion of radically divergent forms of life.

Postcolonial criticism has focused primarily on how race and gender inflect Forster's vision of empire, while the landscape of India itself has been overlooked; or, if acknowledged, it has been relegated to the enigma of the Marabar caves.[153] Although the caves have been widely interpreted, the caves themselves are secondary to Forster's depiction of India as an entire environmental system. Indeed, Forster's representation of landscape and nonhuman life is the preeminent experience of *A Passage to India.* Environmental forces influence the direction of the plot and play a key role in the novel's complex resolution. Subsequently, Forster's alleged preoccupation with humanist values and the common identification of the story's "other" as native Indians glosses over the posthuman potential of Forster's text where the nonhuman is the primary "other."[154] Forster's India exerts a palpable presence embodied by heat and terrain. Moreover, it is endowed with the speech of its "hundred voices,"[155] including the central echo that communicates itself in a nonhuman language acquiring different valences of meaning as it radiates through the novel. Recent postcolonial ecocriticism has offered interpretations more attune to the representations of the nonhuman in Forster's text, but have generated opposing readings. For example, Serpil Oppermann's reading of the novel is rooted in Edward Said's well-known critical assessment that *A Passage to India* is "at a loss" because the novel form exposes "difficulties [Forster] cannot deal with" and "a locale frequently described as unapprehendable and too large."[156] She claims that:

> Not only the Marabar Caves but also the entire landscape reflects the anthropocentric set of values in the novel. There is 'nothing extraordinary' to the natural environment, even 'the very wood seems made of mud, the inhabitants of mud moving. So abased, so monotonous is everything that meets the eye' ... Using this type of negative environmental representation Forster was actually making a point about the Indian culture, in keeping with the anthropocentric colonialist conception of the environment and its inhabitants. Nature here becomes a symbolic inscription of the totalizing hegemony of the British and their culture over the colonized land and its people.[157]

It is true that the novel's narrative voice – which it is important to note is distinct from Forster himself and is often a voice he sets the reader up to critique – does espouse views that reflect the imperialist gaze; yet, this reading doesn't account for the ways in which the environment's power to resist human control is a major component of the novel's critique of a colonialist agenda. Further, as will be shown in more detail later in this chapter, Oppermann's own more recent theorizing of material ecocriticism ironically opens up avenues of interpretation that would contest the totalizing claims above. Another ecocritic, Yomna Al-Abdulkareem, identifies a very different role for the environment of *A Passage to India* more akin to my own, claiming that "nature reveals what people could not articulate: that India was resisting British rule, that the British were unable to understand India's differences"[158] and "the cave has given Indian's message: We are not open to strangers. The nature of India is fighting against external power through enclosing itself with strong will."[159] In this sense, the text records colonial resistance through its depiction of a landscape that many characters misunderstand or misinterpret, including Aziz, himself.

The depictions of India's forceful nonhuman agency may overwhelm the *human characters*, but it is the way Forster's *narrative style* acknowledges the limitations of the human imagination to comprehend an environmental "other" that constructs a successful critique of traditional Western knowledge. The unexpected result of Forster's nonhuman representations is that they propel the scope of his fictional critique far beyond condemning British and Anglo-Indian control – instead the novel more radically questions *all* anthropocentric assumptions of authority. Therefore, *A Passage to India* should be considered as a postpastoral text, subverting the pastoral formula in order to reassert the primacy of the material world and humble the human position within it.

Terry Gifford's six criteria for postpastoral literature would be didactic if they were methodically applied, but, as he suggests, simply using them as a set of possible vectors for inquiry helpfully reorients the novel's emphasis, thus clarifying how the colonial story of *A Passage to India* is dependent upon a larger ecological plot. Gifford identifies the following components as hallmarks of a postpastoral work: "an awe in attention to the natural world"[160]; "the recognition of a creative-destructive universe equally in balance in a continuous momentum of birth and decay, death and rebirth, growth and decay, ecstasy and dissolution"[161]; "the recognition that the inner is also the workings of the outer, that our inner human nature can be understood in relation to external nature"[162]; "to convey an awareness of both nature as culture and of culture as nature"[163]; "with consciousness comes conscience"[164] or, to paraphrase, the process of inhabiting a fuller, embodied awareness of the nonhuman world promotes an ethical sense of responsibility toward it; and lastly, "the realisation that exploitation of the planet is of the same mindset as the exploitation of women and minorities."[165] Certainly, Forster's descriptions of the sky's awing omnipotence, the multiplicity of cyclical references to life and death along the Ganges, the external weather of the trial linked to the storm of Adela's inner conflicts, the oscillations between personified hills and zooified human bodies, and the suggestion that the rocks and stones will not "yet" permit cultural reconciliation between Aziz in Fielding – in part, perhaps, because the violence humans enact toward wasps and caves has yet to be recognized – are all constitutive elements of the postpastoral ideologies described above. As Gifford has clarified, the postpastoral is distinct from other "post" terminology, such as "postmodernism," "postcolonial," or "posthuman" because, "'Post-'here does not mean 'after,' but 'reaching beyond' the limitations of pastoral while being recognizably in the pastoral tradition. . . . The post-pastoral is really best used to describe works that successfully suggest a collapse of the human/nature divide while being aware of the problematic involved."[166] Likewise, *A Passage to India* still involves obvious retreat and return motifs for its English characters as well as an expectation of leisure, whether it be Adela and Mrs. Moore's desire to "see" India or the "holiday" to the Marabar caves, both of which provide an opportunity for greater insight, even if that educational moment is elusive. Yet, the way the novel stages the experience "collapse[s]" the embodiment and agency of human and nonhuman characters.

These postpastoral features of *A Passage to India*, in addition to ecophenomenological analyses of Forster's depiction of embodied awareness, and postcolonial ecocritical insights, offer new perspectives on some of the more baffling or inscrutable moments in the novel. These theories also illuminate modernist aspects of Forster's writing techniques.[167] Specifically, Forster's emphasis on nonhuman subjectivity exhibits new methods of representing interiority, while his attention to the organic potential of language to change and gain a multiplicity of meaning as it is used, shared, and thereby transformed typifies a modern experimentation with language at the level of the word.

Forster acknowledges the novel strives toward a more ambiguous "poetic" or "philosophical" vision of humanity's relationship to the environment: "It's about something wider than politics, about the search of the human race for a more-lasting home, about the universe as embodied in the Indian earth and the Indian sky ... It is, or rather desires to be – philosophic and poetic."[168] His attention to the more-than-human world does encourage a critique of England's efforts to control India, but, as his statement suggests, Forster's novel also embraces many kinds of relationships – including a relationship with nature – which all grow out of humanity's fraught desire to subjugate what it should love more humbly. As Gifford articulates in his last postpastoral criterion, the exploitation of the planet is inextricably linked to mindsets that similarly sanction exploitation of humans. In *A Passage to India*, the physical interplay between human and nonhuman life resists the hierarchical rationalism of empire.[169] Yet, Forster's homage to the supremacy of nature's power proposes a vision of future reconciliation that is also more than political: a future transformed by an enlightened understanding of forces other than those of empire – connections and interdependencies that transcend individual desire or even nationhood.

Forster's India is a nation of contested human politics, but its terrain shows power dynamics operating on a much vaster scale. As postcolonial ecocriticism reveals, the axis and scope of human and natural history aren't always coconstitutive: "It must reckon with the ways ecology does not always work within the frames of human time and political interest. As such, our definition of postcolonial ecology reflects a complex epistemology that recuperates the alterity of both history *and* nature, without reducing either to the other."[170] As Forster's fiction records the British perspective during an era of colonialism, it also positions the environment as an entity that both shares in that story but also acts beyond it. Forster's India disregards the boundaries of human map-makers that audaciously conceive of land as inert and controlled by cultural divisions. Instead, Forster's landscape is imbued with a tactile physicality. The sky is omnipotent over humankind and vivifies the body of earth below:

> The sky settles everything – not only climate and seasons but when the earth shall be beautiful. By herself she can do little – only feeble outbursts of flowers. But when the sky chooses, glory can rain into the Chandrapore

bazaars or a benediction pass from horizon to horizon. The sky can do this because it is so strong and enormous. Strength comes from the sun, infused in it daily; size from the prostrate earth. No mountains infringe on the curve. League after league the earth lies flat, heaves a little, is flat again. Only in the south, where a group of fists and fingers are thrust up through the soil is the endless expanse interrupted. These fists and fingers are the Marabar Hills, containing the extraordinary caves.[171]

The "climate and seasons" dictate the action of the novel. Heat and fatigue play a role at the Marabar caves, in the departure and death of Mrs. Moore, the tense atmosphere of the trial, and the redemptive celebration of rain and fecundity in the final chapter. The prodigious power of the sky eclipses human efforts to control action. Moreover, the land's power is a dynamic living force, a nascent body that "lies flat, heaves a little, is flat again" in an image of inhalation and exhalation. The earth rests "prostrate" with "fists and fingers . . . thrust up," perhaps in a violent gesture of defiance against simple, superficial human attempts to see what is picturesque without comprehending larger patterns of meaning, or perhaps the embodiment of the force that reaches out in an effort to grip Adela as she tours the caves.

Jo Ann Hoeppner Moran has suggested that Godbole's association of the caves with Jainism admits the possibility that Adela harmed, or even enacted "a rape of the rock,"[172] when she struck the cave wall, which then merited her own thorny punishment in accordance with the Jainist belief that "all material is eternal, conscious, and subject to metempsychosis."[173] Here, Jainist philosophy, available to Forster, and articulations of post-colonial ecocriticism by Bonnie Roos and Alex Hunt within the new century overlap: "The rights of reproduction and the fact of rape are other important aspects of the language of both postcolonialism and environmentalism."[174] The environmental body, the sexual body, and the post-colonial efforts to interpret how to read the interstices between violence to land and humans cannot be separated. Forster's descriptions of India illustrate these complexities. While Forster's description employs components of personification, notably in the "fists and fingers" of the hills, Forster ultimately composes a landscape that retains a distinctly nonhuman sentience. As the episode at the caves will corroborate, the "voice" of India does not emulate human speech; it communicates in forms dissonant to human verbal logic. Although Forster's novel is a colonialist text, his techniques resemble strategies used by postcolonial writers as well; as postcolonial ecocritics explain, "These texts also suggest that since the environment stands as a nonhuman witness to the violent process of colonialism, an engagement with alterity is a constitutive aspect of postcoloniality."[175] The effort to understand acts of possession and brutality enacted against people and land simultaneously necessarily involves the inclusion of the nonhuman presence as another actor and witness within the same historical narrative. Yet, part of registering the environmental presence is representing it as an entity that disturbs human characters and challenges the reader to make sense of it. Forster's resistance to depicting humans in a romantic oneness with nature alludes to the fallacy of empathy that doesn't respect and acknowledge difference.

Forster doesn't merely overlay the land with human traits; he also shades his human characters with nonhuman attributes, complicating simple personification with the zooification or "terra-ification" of humans. This strategy disrupts the idea that the human is always the comparative standard. Just as the landscape is rendered as a bodily presence, human bodies are also transfigured as landscape. After Adela's flight from the caves, she becomes ill: "She had been touched by the sun, also hundreds of cactus spines had to be picked out of her flesh" and the doctor was "always coming on fresh colonies . . . She lay passive beneath their fingers, which developed the shock that had begun in the cave. . . . Everything now was transferred to the surface of her body, which began to avenge itself, and feed unhealthily."[176] Her body becomes a territory to be explored, where "colonies" are identified and brought under the control of western medicine. The "fingers" she lays "passive" beneath rhetorically recall the "cave" mentioned in the same sentence, fusing body and geography so that "everything" concerning the shock of her experience is mapped onto the surface of her body. The human body becomes a topographical territory dissolving the divisions between corporal flesh and physical terrain. This maneuver not only speaks to new postcolonial ecocritical discourses of alternative representations of violence and opposition, but it also implicates emerging theories of ecomaterialism. In studying the potent dynamism of the material object, Iovino's ecomaterialist philosophy relies on the transference and porosity of signification in the interplay of contact surfaces as the object becomes part of lived experience:

> Material agency as a field of emerging meanings is therefore epitomized by the physical maps of transcorporeality, a concept that "stresses the flow of substances and forces linking bodies and environments and whose ontological, cognitive, and ethical reverberations arise from an uncomfortable and perplexing place where the 'human' is always already part of an active, often unpredictable, material world" (Alaimo, *Bodily Natures*, 17). The idea of a semiotic flow of substances and forces, the very idea of using bodies as texts where the dynamics of actants and collectives are inscribed – in other

words, the idea of texts permeable to matters ('substances') and discourses ('forces') – is of crucial importance for a material ecocriticism.[177]

Forster's use of the surface of the cave and its obvious relevance to the imagery of the colonizing map of thorny demarcations on Adela's skin brings the material qualities of human and nonhuman flesh into stark relief while refusing the usual narration of the exact events that shaped the intimate encounter between place and person. Each substance is touched and transformed by the forces of the scene and the discourses used to express it. Thus, his formal inversion of personification and zooification not only refuses to make humans the basis for all other nonhuman comparison but also imaginatively figures a host of complex and reflexive interactions between humans and the environment.

The intercorporeality of human and environment that Gifford uses as an aspect of postpastoral texts is known in ecophenomenology as "the flesh of the world"[178] – a recognition of the reflexive interchange between an individual's tactile experience and the reciprocal sensory reaction of surrounding forces and objects that form the basis of humans' ability to know themselves within the world. *A Passage to India* is replete with images reinforcing the bodily interaction between humans and the impress of the world's "flesh": "The space between them and their carriages, instead of being empty, was clogged with a medium that pressed against their flesh"[179]; "If the flesh of the sun's flesh is to be touched anywhere, it is here, among the incredible antiquity of these hills"[180]; "The sun rose . . . touching the bodies already at work in the fields."[181] These examples of the open boundaries of the body of things heighten awareness of an interconnected whole; the mutation of ecological boundaries described in the opening pages of the novel, the meeting of races and cultures, the vibrant mesh of pulsating nonhuman life all overlap and affect each other.

The novel's emphasis on physicality extends beyond conventional humanism to encourage esteem for all forms of life, both human and nonhuman. Forster gives voice to the "pain that is endured not only by men, but by animals and plants, and perhaps by the stones."[182] As David Abram explains, the concordance of humans with other life forms a foundational tenet of ecocriticism: "Ultimately, to acknowledge the life of the body, and to affirm our solidarity with this physical form, is to acknowledge our existence as one of the earth's animals, and so to remember and rejuvenate the organic basis of our thoughts and our intelligence."[183] Acknowledging animals as equal members of the natural world makes them an indispensable "other" that must be incorporated into human life in order to fully invigorate humanity's own intelligence. Forster's belief that human forms of order and assumption must be disrupted is concisely communicated in a 1929 entry from his *Commonplace Book*: "'Give me Permanency!' says Man. And limits his intelligence by the request."[184] The abundance of animal life in *A Passage to India* – including alligators, snakes, birds, squirrels, flies, beetles, leopards, horses, and most significantly, wasps – adds another dimension of perspective illuminating how difference stimulates alternate forms of knowledge. Forster's use of the nonhuman resists simple anthropomorphism, which relegates animals to an inert mirror for human thought. Instead, nonhuman representations maintain an aspect of "otherness" of which the human characters remain ignorant – offering alternate insights to relationships of power throughout the text.

The nonverbal voices of the animals exemplify Forster's creation of a nonanthropocentric, nonhuman life consistently asserting itself as one of India's "hundred voices."[185] In one instance, as the squirrels occupy surrounding houses, a nonhuman language is intimated: "the squeals it gave were in tune with the infinite, no doubt, but not attractive except to other squirrels ... More noises came from a dusty tree ... another bird, the invisible coppersmith, had started his 'ponk ponk.'"[186] The squirrel's high-pitched "squeals" and the bird's "ponk" are not translated into language, nor are they necessarily harmonious to other ears, even though they are acknowledged as fellow-beings, also part of some larger "infinite" tune. Once this distance between human and nonhuman is established, Forster imagines that their ways of thinking might also contradict human assumptions: "Most of the inhabitants of India do not mind how India is governed ... the inarticulate world is closer at hand and readier to resume control as soon as men are tired."[187] The nonhuman does not serve the purposes of men in Forster's text; rather he privileges nature's power to vanquish all claims to human superiority. The expansive scale of environmental force diminishes political measures of control; power operates according to the dimensions of long-term natural history instead of the spasmodic timetables of national interests. Forster gestures toward a nonhuman dominion greater and more permanent than any political empire.

The wasp – an animal usually deigned to have little impact in the human world, but which is also capable of causing harm – is one of the most memorable instances of animal life in the novel and typifies Forster's ability to intermingle subjectivity and physicality while subtly critiquing colonialism . Early in the novel, Mrs. Moore finds a wasp resting on a peg where she had intended to hang her cloak. She chooses not to remove it, treating it with kindness, and calling it "pretty dear."[188] The encounter draws attention to the insistent presence of the nonhuman world but also shows how human relationships with the nonhuman lend new insight to relations between humans. The dormant wasp could represent the slumbering potential for violence in British and Indian relations. Although the wasp "did not wake," Mrs. Moore's "voice floated out, to swell the night's uneasiness"[189] as if her graciousness is not enough to prevent the impending swollen sting of colonial unrest. Simultaneously, the wasp serves as a reminder of nature's larger kingdom, carrying on without regard to human social structures. In fact, the wasp's disregard for human distinctions between the outdoors and built interiors indicates a certain mastery over human endeavors: "it is to [the wasps] a normal outgrowth of the eternal jungle, which alternately produces houses trees, houses trees."[190] Despite human activity and "advancement," the jungle is "eternal" and its animals still lay claim to its natural or reinvented territories. The doubling of "houses trees, houses trees" conflates the similarity by repetition; further, the comma separates not the individual words, but rather the word pairs, emphasizing "houses trees" as a singular noun or concept with one meaning that defies distinctions between built and natural places. The wasp's presence in the house as well as the tree contradicts the human belief, particularly British, in the stability of constructed boundaries and divisions, whether between Indians and British or humans and animals.

The episode at the Marabar caves illustrates the general ineffectiveness of western logic or human language to make sense of the multiplicity of India's nonhuman meanings. The caves are described in terms of absence throughout the text: "There is something unspeakable in these outposts. They are like nothing else in the world."[191] Notably, even Godbole, the character whose Hindu beliefs give him the perspective most aware of the nonhuman world, whose "whole appearance suggested harmony – as if he had reconciled the products of East and West, mental as well as physical,"[192] has difficulty finding words to describe the Marabar caves.[193] When asked about the cave's attractions, holy significance, or ornamentation, he replies "Oh no"[194] to any efforts to particularize their appeal. Some critics interpret such terms of absence as a literal expression of negation, or a sinister void that, as David Medalie describes it, "insidiously denies all meaning."[195] However, postcolonial ecocriticism is instructive in its emphasis on the significance of silences in depictions of colonial landscapes and their voices. Bonnie Roos and Alex Hunt explain: "Postcolonial ecocriticism must read for silences – because while ecological issues can be visible in postcolonial texts, they are often quietly in the interstices, inextricably bound within systems of language, justice, economics, and power."[196] Similarly, Benita Parry explicates the caves in terms of their "affirmative resonances" by pointing out the "circumlocutions of the opening paragraph" and Godbole's lines "Yet absence implies presence, absence is not a nonexistence."[197] She acknowledges that the inarticulability is based on a confounding multiplicity of meaning rather than its absence. Similarly, Godbole doesn't need to identify a single culprit in the Marabar caves, but understands the presence of good and evil as a concordance of a larger agency shared by all: "'It was performed by the guide.' He stopped again. 'It was performed by you.' . . . 'It was performed by me.' . . . 'And by my students. It was even performed by the lady herself. When evil occurs, it expresses the whole of the universe. Similarly when good occurs.'"[198] Acts of good and evil are "performed" by an individual yet concurrently implicated in the larger flesh of the world. Godbole's explanation assumes an integrated system of cause and effect where each act coalesces with others in a kinetic and ecological expression of the health of the organic whole. Thus, to expound upon Parry's analysis, describing the caves in terms of absence actually signifies an "affirmative" embedded potential. The communication of a more-than-human or other-than-human realm may thwart verbal meaning but doesn't indicate "nothing." Instead, it denotes the presence of a larger sensory world that cannot be contained by human language: "'Boum' is the sound *as far as the human alphabet can express it*, or 'bou-oum,' or 'ou-boum.'"[199] The echo is the utterance of the cave itself, created by the physical, tactile interaction of humans and stone, flame, shadows, and the press of unseen flesh.

The echo of the Marabar caves resonates with multiple valences of subjective human experience, nonhuman or prelinguistic communication, and alternate forms of knowledge. Mrs. Moore and Adela both leave with the echo still reverberating within their auditory senses – trapped inside the caverns of their own heads and bodies. The materiality of the experience in the caves is expressed through tenets of material ecocriticism, as explained by Serpil Oppermann, who draws on the work of Karan Barad:

> Agency is not restricted to human action, to human subjectivity and intentionality, nor is it something humans grant to nonhuman animals; rather agency signifies, to use Barad's words, "an enactment, not something that someone or something has" (*Meeting*178). It is not an attribute, but as she puts it "[a]gency is 'doing' or 'being' in its intra-activity" (178). Thus, matter is theorized as an actively formative and productive agent that shapes discursive practices, which in turn shape the way we interact with the world

showing their effects on materiality. In other words, discourse is always co-extensive with the material world.[200]

Similarly, the agency of the cave is expressed through the intra-activity of its resonances within Adela and Mrs. Moore, becoming a coextensive discourse between human memory, heard voices, and the site of shared physical trauma. The materiality of the experience at the cave becomes part of an embodied response that mingles with conscious discourse and logical comprehension, but remains a felt plurality of place and intersubjectivity that is not fully captured by language. As Mrs. Moore realizes after her experience, the sound of the echo encompasses many messages: "it had managed to murmur, 'Pathos, piety, courage – they exist but are identical, and so is filth. Everything exists, nothing has value."[201] Mrs. Moore interprets these murmurs as a reduction of value, but they also have the potential to magnify value. The qualities Mrs. Moore lists, "pathos, piety, courage," are attributes mired in Adela's false accusation of Aziz – her yearning for a sympathetic emotional bond with Ronny, her faithfulness to her own race, the community's belief in her courage – but they are also prognosticators of her ultimate acquittal of Aziz too – her compassion for his predicament, her piety toward her moral obligations to truth, and as Fielding attests, her courage in admitting her mistake. Similarly, "everything exists, nothing has value" has both negative and positive potential – it can articulate a nullifying reduction or an enlarged understanding of value, bolstering Godbole's claims that "nothing" does indeed *have* "value." Adela hears the echo resound in her head during a conversation with Mrs. Moore and thinks that Mrs. Moore has told her Aziz is innocent.[202] Although Mrs. Moore didn't actually verbalize this thought, she later confirms this conviction, suggesting the echo mediated a universal or more-than-human thought between the two women. Such nonhuman subjectivity pushes modernist concerns for interiority in new directions. Like other modernists, Forster represents internal subjective thought, but expands it beyond the consciousness of a single character to include the material agency and shared consciousness created between the intra-action of humans and nonhumans.

Forster's methods of representing physical encounters with place and nonhuman are also illuminated by the precepts of ecophenomenology. Maurice Merleau-Ponty's ecophenomenology presumes an attitude of open-minded questioning on the part of the perceiving human:

> The effective, present, ultimate and primary being[s], the thing[s] [themselves] ... offer themselves only to someone who wishes not to have

them but ... giv[es] them the free space they ask for in return ... [They are] not a nothingness the full being would come to stop up, but a question consonant with a porous being which it questions and from which it receives not an answer, but a confirmation of its astonishment. It is necessary to comprehend perception in this interrogative thought which lets the perceived world be rather than posits it, before which the things form and undo themselves in a sort of gliding, beneath the yes and the no.[203]

The formulation of meaning in nonhuman interactions comes when humans approach the encounter with the expectation of being taught something themselves – "to someone who wishes not to have them but ... giving them the free space they ask for in return." This attitude is akin to the difference between Adela's desire to know the "real" India on her own terms and Godbole's religious dance wherein he gives the world free space to speak to him: "scraps of their past, tiny splinters of detail emerged for a moment to melt into the universal warmth ... Chance brought [Mrs. Moore and the wasp] into his mind, he did not select [them] ... How can [an event] be expressed in anything but itself?"[204] Letting the "other" speak for itself may necessitate confusion and uncertainty, but ultimately, the effort offers inclusive insight.

The novel suggests that a more truthful relationship with the world requires acceptance of fluidity and flux. Simply because the experience resists verbal description does not mean it is a "nothingness" humans must "come to stop up"; rather, it becomes an encounter layered with potential discovery: "a porous being which it questions and from which it receives not an answer, but a confirmation of astonishment." The ability to know oneself in relation to other ecological and nonhuman life defies clear delineations; the relationship between human self and nonhuman "other" isn't a binary to be solved by "yes" or "no." Both modernism and ecocriticism overlap in their shared recognition that an ethical understanding of our relationship with the more-than-human world requires an openness to new forms and an acceptance of uncertainty. Only when one embraces the fracturing process of history and ecology as a means by which progress advances by "form[ing] and undo[ing]" can the gaps of difference be understood as spaces of potential. The landscape of Forster's India eludes any picturesque notions of it. Representing subjective streams of thought as well as exposing the limits of Victorian notions of faith and selfhood are primary concerns of modernists; Forster embraces such modernist practices as part of a realm of unknown possibility, rather than a frightening void.

This dialectic of positive and negative potential is seen in Forster's depiction of the nonlinguistic auditory experience of the caves. References to the cave and its echo continue to resurface, gliding between a premonition of evil and a nagging reminder of Aziz's innocence. Adela's conception of the Marabar caves undergoes a tremendous transformation from her initial reaction to her visualization of the episode at trial: "the double relation gave it indescribable splendour. Why had she thought the expedition 'dull'?"[205] The emphasis on cleaving oppositions, with potential left floating somewhere between the two proposed rifts of possibility reoccurs throughout the novel: Mrs. Moore exclaims of the Ganges, "What a terrible river! What a wonderful river!"[206]; Aziz's servant's failure to respond to Aziz's request is described as "Heard and didn't hear, just as Aziz called and didn't call"[207]; Godbole explains his expectation of God's answer to prayer as "Oh yes. Oh no, I do not expect an answer to my question now"[208]; Mrs. Moore remarks about herself, "'I am not good, no, bad'"[209]; God is construed "He is, was not, is not, was."[210] Like Merleau-Ponty's theory, the text does not resolve these straining oppositions. Instead it opens up both possibilities, leaving the reader to shuttle between them, "gliding, beneath the yes and the no" so that the tension of Indian relations, both human and nonhuman, remains always an uncompleted gesture. Akin to the binaries of "yes" and "no," the novel beats against the rhythm of question and answer in unexpected ways. Place symbolizes both question and answer: The arches of Fielding's house are "the architecture of Question and Answer" hinting that India embodies in its very structure the continuing rhythm of interrogation and response. Similarly, Adela's legal interrogation is imagined in spatial terms: "The court, the place of question awaited her reply. But she could not give it until Aziz entered the place of answer."[211] Ironically, the names "Quested" and "Aziz" may even suggest that the person of Miss Quested is the Question that must be answered by the person of Aziz. To extend the simile, "Aziz" may be interpreted as the response "as is," signifying that the quest to know India must finally be a quest to understand something as it is, not as one might want it to be. The dilemma Miss Quested presents and Aziz's response to her maltreatment of him again pose is the question and answer of the state of India's affairs and the future potential for equality between the races. Thus, Forster effortlessly slides the lexicon of "yes" and "no," "question" and "answer" through the permeable boundaries of places and bodies, breaking convention in new and unexpected ways.

Patterns, repetitions, and cycles, what Forster calls "rhythm" in *Aspects of the Novel*, provide the unifying formal undercurrent of the text. These patterns are intertwined with cycles of seasonal fluctuation and the necessity of death to propel new creation. The Ganges is both a symbol of holy life and a conduit for death. At the same time Mrs. Moore notes the "radiance" it participates in creating, she learns about the dead bodies released into its current and consumed by crocodiles, which Forster echoes when her own body is relinquished into another body of water, the Indian Ocean. The spiritual significance of the Ganges can't be divorced from the physical reality of the ecological system. Similarly, the water that flows throughout Chandrapore in a built system of tanks circulates through buildings and people like blood pumping through the valves of a heart: "A sudden sense of unity . . . passed into the old woman and out, like water through a tank."[212] And when the rains come after the stifling temperatures culminating in the heat of the trial, Aziz notes the change of season as a change in emotion that it would have pleased him to share with Mrs. Moore: "How I wish she could have seen them, our rains. Now is the time when all things are happy . . . the tanks are so full they dance, and this is India. . . .. Was the cycle beginning again? His heart was too full to draw back."[213] His heart, like the tanks, is racing and pulsating with energy and life; yet Aziz also recognizes the cycle of the seasons must twine with the cycles of life itself so that the disappointments of friendship or love and even the possibility of injustice and violence are always elements of the mixture which must resurface in time.

Forster's India insists upon change and fluidity in defiance of human desires for clear political hierarchies or cultural unity. Indeed, the human desire for constant harmony is *unnatural*: "Fish manage better; fish, as the tanks dry, wriggle into the mud and wait for the rains to uncake them. But men try to be harmonious all the year round, and the results are occasionally disastrous."[214] The ecological system that creates meaning in India relies on the interdependency of what humans often consider "negative" or "bad," but which actually contributes indispensably to the natural working order: "The signs of the contented Indian evening multiplied; frogs on all sides, cow-dung burning eternally; a flock of belated hornbills overhead . . . There was death in the air, but not sadness."[215] Thus, the presence of inevitable death and decay is folded into the process of constructive life. Or, as Gifford describes it in his definition of the postpastoral: "the recognition of a creative-destructive universe equally in balance in a continuous momentum of birth and decay, death and rebirth, growth and decay, ecstasy and dissolution."[216] In *A Passage to India* there is no singular, comforting identity; India thrives on its cyclical nature and its multiplicity. Difference creates a thriving whole: "The fissures in the

Indian soil are infinite: Hinduism, so solid from a distance, is riven into sects and clans, *which radiate and join*, and change their names according to the aspect from which they are approached."[217] The variety of cultures and people creates the beauty – radiating filaments that join the multi-hued pattern. The landscape mirrors the same sense of abundant variety: "the sister kingdoms of the north . . . stretched out their hands and sang as [Aziz] sang . . . and greeted ridiculous Chandrapore, where every street and house was divided against itself, and told her that she was a continent and a unity."[218] The context of relationships between landmasses creates new commonalities unique to Chandrapore. Subsequently, Chandrapore is part of a network of boundaries that unite into a continent containing the diverse ecotones and cultures of India.

The novel's most humanist character, Fielding, unlike Forster himself, remains confined by the limitations of his fidelity to the classic forms of antiquity and rational paradigms that sabotage his ability to appreciate India's divergent patterns of meaning. Fielding is arguably the character most sympathetic with the plight of the natives under colonial rule. His ease at hosting Indians in his home, his defense of Aziz during the trial, and his intimate friendship with Aziz set Fielding apart from other English characters. His deportment implies an equalizing personal philosophy and links him with favorable aspects of the humanist tradition. Consequently, that Fielding is still constricted by his own European modes of thinking bolsters the argument that Forster's novel expresses more than simple liberal humanism. Fielding's adherence to traditional forms hinders greater understanding: "The buildings of Venice, like the mountains of Crete and the fields of Egypt, stood in the right place, whereas in poor India everything was placed wrong."[219] Fielding's classical eye craves balanced, easily defined patterns; he fails to appreciate the divergent dissonance of India's patterns, patterns Forster emulates in his use of changing repetitive phrases and echoes that advance cyclically rather than linearly.

Forster's nonfiction account of his time in India, *The Hill of Devi*, is replete with descriptions that seem to have inspired the perception of place that he creates in *A Passage to India*, beginning with a deprecatory mention of "stone steps [that] led up to the dark cave of Chamunda on top" but "nothing detained the tourist there and the surrounding domain was equally unspectacular. No antiquities, no picturesque scenery, no large rivers or mountains or forests, no large wild animals."[220] What is "lacking" is defined by the standards of the English picturesque, a narrow gaze that Forster abandons as his appreciation of the country deepens and he recognizes: "The frivolity, the triviality goes on, and every now and then it cracks, as at our festival, and discloses depths. "'What am I', cries the poet, 'invested with a body of seven spans in a small part of this egg the world?' ... When the festival was over one was left with something inexplicable, which grows a little clearer with the passage of years."[221] Suggestive of Godbole's ambiguous epiphanies during the Hindu Birth Ceremony, the "cracks" and fissures are what provide the opportunity for insight that can only be apprehended with the passage between places and through time. As John Marx has noted, "imperial representation appears so discordant in *A Passage to India*: unsettling desires destablilize the carefully composed surface of the imperial picturesque, making that Victorian landscape disorderly and strange."[222] Forster privileges a more eclectic aesthetic of organicity, suggesting that the very absence of European expectations of "beauty" and proper order in a landscape are superficially deficient when compared to the wild proliferating diversity of India's terrain. As in *Maurice*, Forster's sexuality may have given him a personal stake in unsettling categories of what is "natural" or "proper" and what English values deem "unnatural" when writing *A Passage to India*. Stuart Christie has gone so far as to posit that the "unnamable" sensations provoked by an encounter with India constitute "the emergence of the obscene writing on the colonial text" to assert the latent presence of the homosexual "other."[223] While the exact role of sexual identity in the landscape is elusive, Christie's theory comports with the text's more overt goal of undermining assumptions of English superiority over the unknown and multifarious forces of nature. While gazing at the Marabar Hills from the Club veranda Fielding experiences a fleeting notion that we exist "not only for ourselves"[224] but in terms of each other. This insight grasps at Forster's famous motto from *Howard's End* – "only connect." However, in *A Passage to India* understanding and community doesn't hinge on a humanist connection between humans of different classes and national-ities; instead, the theme of reaching beyond oneself implicates the tenuous living filaments that connect and sustain a diverse range of living beings operating within a wider world largely ignored by humans.

From any individual human perspective, India's diversity doesn't reveal its larger patterns or holistic purpose. As Mrs. Moore prepares to leave, she begins to see other faces of India and worries whether she has seen "the right" places. But the land belies any singular human attempt to define it: "'So you thought an echo was India; you took the Marabar caves as final' [the palm trees] laughed. 'What have we in common with them, or they with Asirgarh?'"[225] The essence of a working organic system cannot be reduced to a single unit, just as the British colonies resisted homogeneous amalgamation to British culture. A healthy living system requires a web of diverse relationships – relationships that may not cohere from any individual perspective. When Godbole calls for the gods to "come, come, come," he receives a vision of the wasp and Mrs. Moore. His reaction expresses the frustration of unknowabilty: "This was all he could do. How inadequate!"[226] But within himself he knows that the reach from one living being to others must provide meaning: "'It does not seem much, still it is more than I am myself.'"[227] Yet the reader who experiences what just one character is unable to know can begin to understand the potential connections between the seemingly disparate images of Godbole dancing to the gods amidst a motley assortment of sparkling oddities, and the figure of Mrs. Moore who has reached out to the wasp and offered it graciousness. This divergent pastiche is a pattern of repeated possibilities of hope and empathy.

Just as notions of "ecological harmony" are suspect, the ending of *A Passage to India* does not simplify and eradicate differences in race and culture, whether they are between English and Anglo-English, Anglo-Indian and Indian, Muslim and Hindu, or human and nonhuman. *A Passage to India* manifests an interdependent system of relationships where the friction between races, cultures, and religions generates new possibilities for each and enlivens the multiplicity of cross-cultural meanings. Aziz and Fielding are denied an easy conciliatory embrace by the intervening nonhuman world: "But the horses didn't want it – they swerved apart; the earth didn't want it, sending up rocks through which the riders must pass single file; . . . the birds, the carrion, the Guest House, that came into view: they didn't want it, they said in their hundred voices, 'No, not yet,' and the sky said, 'No, not there.'"[228] It is not coincidental that the ubiquitous sky gets the final word. Further, the message, like other echoes, is not a complete negation; the animals, earth, and sky merely state that the season for such amity has not *yet* arrived.

Two earlier enactments of this same denial reinforce the promise of attachment not only between the two cultures, but also between humans and the "other" of the nonhuman world. In the first anticipatory invocation of the novel's conclusion Aziz tells Mrs. Moore's son, "'But you are Heaslop's brother also, and alas, the two nations cannot be friends.'" Ralph replies, "'I know. Not yet.'" But with a "swerve of voice and body that Aziz did not follow he added, 'In her letters, in her letters, She loved you.'"[229] Not only does this moment anticipate the ending and the "swerve" of the two horses, it also emphasizes the layers of relationships and the various modes of communicating love. Aziz's initial romantic notion of

Mrs. Moore is finally fulfilled. Even though it is doubtful she ever truly understood Aziz, the vision of her love and her secret understanding of his heart is somehow translated by her son to fruition. The bond of empathy is still possible – unexpected, misunderstood, but vital to the completion of the whole.

Yet the constitutive element suffusing the final "passages" of the novel with cohesive meaning is found in the ecological climax of the emblems of human Hindu ritual with the forces of nature. The moment before Aziz first recognizes the "small black blot" as the House Boat paddling out into the river, Forster describes the sky mirrored in the water of the Mau tank: "Reflecting the evening clouds, it filled the netherworld with an equal splendour, so that earth and sky leant toward one another, about to clash in ecstasy."[230] The two entities reaching out toward each other in an ecstatic union prefigures Aziz and Fielding precipitously rushing toward an intimate and suggestively sexual embrace. But the "about" suspends the union of cloud and sky as Aziz and Fielding were averted from joining. Moreover, the device of reflection allows Forster initially to present union as an illusion impossible to accomplish in reality. But Forster inverts the expectation – sky and earth may not meet in the lyrical, abstractly beautiful vision of the tank, but they do meet through the inconvenient burst of condensation into rain soaking the earth in a covertly sexual downpour. The bodies of amorous potential go far beyond the homosexual tension between Aziz and Fielding, but extend to the sexual ambiguity of the encounter in the cave, and the fertilizing potential of rain and human ritual which resonates with queer ecocriticism: "Scrutinizing and politicizing the intersections between sex and nature not only opens environmentalism to a wider understanding of justice, but also deploys the antiheteronormative insistencies of queer politics to potentially more biophilic ends than has been generally imagined."[231] As Aziz and Ralph's boat crashes into the boat containing Fielding and his wife, Mrs. Moore's daughter, Stella, "shrank into her husband's arms, then flung herself against Aziz" capsizing the entire party into the river with everything else; lightning and thunder "cracked like a mallet on the dome"[232] in a scene of unexpected physical embrace accompanied by echoing references of courtly "mallets" and cave-like "domes." All is coalesced in both body and language. The accomplishment of final ecstasy of union is expressed by the dramatic pent up release of lightning and thunder: "That was the climax, as far as India admits of one. The rain settled in steadily to its job of wetting everybody and everything through" carrying out the sexual analogy.

The nonhuman energies attain a union cemented not in cohesiveness but in the very wild fertility of unexpected and illogical chaos. Prior to the apocalyptic fusion, a beautiful woman descends into the sacred waters "praising God without attributes – thus did she apprehend him ... seeing Him in this or that organ of the body or manifestation of sky."[233] There is a lack of specificity, a confusing clutter of referents, but both human and nonhuman components create the "apprehen[sion]" of sought-after meaning. The rain, like the other earthly elements of horses, rocks, and sky that rise up to prevent Aziz and Fielding's embrace, interrupts the proceedings of the ceremony: "a wild tempest started ... Gusts of wind mixed darkness and light, sheets of rain cut from the north, stopped, cut from the south, began rising from below."[234] The drenching water accomplishes the blending of "darkness and light," another binary like "yes" and "no," "question" and "answer," but also connoting the combination of "dark" toned Indians and "light" skinned Britons. The geographical references are fractured and shifted from "north" and "south," above and "below" stressing the melding of all countries and all boundaries. Symbols of the festival are tossed into the river in a combination of forces that includes both the human agency of the participants and the driving strength of the storm: "baskets of ten-day corn, tiny tazias after Mohurram – scapegoats, husks, emblems of passage; a passage not easy, not now, not here, not to be apprehended except when it is unattainable."[235] "Not now, not here" is mimicked by the later command "No, not yet ... No, not there."[236] But in the passage quoted above "not now, not here" is given added meaning by "not to be apprehended except when it is unattainable." The very gulf between the emblematic gesture and the true attainment of understanding makes apparent the truth of what is professed to be accomplished by the gesture.

If the gesture or emblem was readily completed and consecrated it would not have as much worth, deflating the value of the ideal it professes to symbolize. Therefore, the "unattainab[ility]" of the representative gesture allows us to fully "apprehend" the larger significance of the goal, whether it be the true understanding between cultures that will sustain lasting relationships, or the search for affirmation that humans are indeed included in a larger system of meaning, a living ecology joining both humans and nonhuman "others" in a meaningful whole. The embrace between Aziz and Fielding is postponed because it emblematizes a greater understanding yet to be truly attained and practiced between Fielding and Aziz, Indian and Britain, human and nonhuman.

Just as the corn, tazias, and husks are representational "emblems of a passage; a passage not easy,"[237] *A Passage to India* is a challenging artistic and symbolic representation of a more universal voyage to unknown territories, a voyage controlled not by the intentions of human ritual, whether they are religious, political, or personal, but by realizations that extend beyond personal desires or quests for empire. In *Aspects of the Novel* Forster questions the traditional culmination of a story, asking, "Cannot it grow? . . . Cannot it open out? Instead of standing above his work and controlling it, cannot the novelist throw himself into it and be carried along to some goal that he does not foresee?"[238] *A Passage to India* contains rhythms that express "not rounding off but opening up"[239] by opening up a broader recognition of nonhuman agency and human humility. As other modernists foretell the demise of stable structures of empire and religion, Forster points to other cohesive possibilities – unions arising not out of planned expectations for logical coalition, but out of amalgamations of primeval nonhuman forces, portending alliances beyond cultural and political understandings. An enlightened perception of civilization and community must also include the environmental "other" before it can be consummated. *A Passage to India* offers possibilities for resolution, but they are arbitrated by ecological components twining animals and humans together not as one might expect, but in a moving jumble of confusion, a unique merger of its own form challenging us to see the gap we may yet reach across toward a better understanding of ourselves and the encompassing ecological world.

CHAPTER 2

The phenomenological whole
Virginia Woolf

Virginia Woolf's innovative formal strategies create an awareness of multiple animate beings within thick, sensory layers of earthly flesh. E.M. Forster was one of the first scholars to note the significance of Woolf's use of embodied perception. In a lecture he gave in 1942, only one year after she committed suicide, Forster pays tribute to Woolf's sensual descriptions:

> Food with her was not a literary device put in to make the book seem real. She put it in because she smelt the flowers, because she heard Bach, because her senses were both exquisite and catholic, and were always bringing her first-hand news of the outside world. Our debt to her is in part this: she reminds us of the importance of sensation in an age which practices brutality and recommends ideals.[1]

As Forster notes, Woolf's palpable depictions of bodily, gustatory life not only create vivid prose, they also subtly remind us of the primacy of the body, its ability to enrich meaning, its locus of joys, its susceptibility of pain, and the dangers we invite when we reject our knowledge of the embodied world in favor of a presumption of intellectual detachment. Forster also describes rereading her work as an experience that reminds him of organic profusion: "She is like a plant which is supposed to grow in a well-prepared garden bed – the bed of esoteric literature – and then pushes up suckers all over the place, through the gravel of the front drive, and even through the flagstones of the kitchen yard."[2] Here, Forster metaphorically aligns Woolf's writing with wild growth. Although Forster's assessment emphasizes the qualities of embodied perception and environmental awareness in her work, those attributes went largely unexamined by literary critics until the 1990s.

In recent decades, Woolf scholarship has shown a renewed interest in her representations of the natural world. Gillian Beer made the first significant foray in her book, *Virginia Woolf: The Common Ground*

(1996). Christina Alt's *Virginia Woolf and the Study of Nature* (2010), Bonnie Kime Scott's *In the Hollow of the Wave: Virginia Woolf and the Modernist Uses of Nature* (2012), and Derek Ryan's *Virginia Woolf and the Materiality of Theory* (2013) are also preeminent examples. Beer reminds readers of Woolf's interest in theories of evolution, prehistory, science, and physics – areas that directly impact her depiction of humans within a larger contiguous environment. Alt carefully traces how Woolf explored natural history as a child and later favored more life-oriented biological sciences over taxonomic classifications that promoted patriarchal models of categorizing knowledge. Merging biography, feminist studies, and ecocriticism, Bonnie Kime Scott unveils new details about how Woolf's family influenced her interest in the natural world and her own relationships with gardens and pets to suggest how Woolf breaks down the dualism of nature and culture. Ryan argues that Woolf enacts new materialism's theoretical precepts by "illuminating materiality as precisely the possibility of being: the becoming of the material world,"[3] using ideas articulated by Deleuze and Guattari, among others, and applying them to Woolf's representations of gender, nature, and the nonhuman. Louise Westling persuasively demonstrates how Merleau-Ponty's ecophenomenology elucidates Woolf's concern with the larger universe of human and nonhuman forces in her article, "Virginia Woolf and the Flesh of the World" (1999) and Westling's recent explication of the breadth of Merleau-Ponty's work in *The Logos of the Living World: Merleau-Ponty, Animals, and Language* (2014) fortifies many philosophical connections between Merleau-Ponty and Woolf. Even Alexandra Harris's illuminating exploration of nostalgia, nature, and creativity in *Romantic Moderns: Artists and the Imagination from Virginia Woolf to John Piper* (2010), a text that does not explicitly use ecocriticism as its theoretical basis, clearly has questions of environmental representation as its centerpiece, and Harris writes about Woolf with green in her ink. She reminds us of Woolf's "deep acquaintance with the Sussex landscape" and the significance of that relationship in understanding the tone of her final novel: "She delights in the naming of fields and villages, and in the rehearsal of local knowledge. For all its sadness, this novel is also Woolf's intense celebration of her countryside."[4] And, reprising Forster's assessment, Harris notices "She is often discussed in terms of ethereality, but she is a passionate food writer. Even her most abstract novel, *The Waves*, is set largely in restaurants, amid crumbs and greasy knives and the very physical paraphernalia of eating."[5] Using these readings as a starting point, my aim is to synthesize and add to them by highlighting an appreciation of how Woolf employs anthropomorphism, formal hybridity, shifting perspective, and fragmented language to create embodied representations that unsettle Cartesian duality and prioritize alternative modes of knowing that reorient human assumptions of power. As Woolf crafts her prose, it manifests the interrelated existence of humans and nature, creating an ecophenomenological representation of an embodied existence intertwined with a more-than-human sensory world. Animal studies and ecomaterialism also provide insight into the significance and effect of her representations of nonhuman subjectivity and agency. Woolf's interconnectedness is distinct from a nineteenth-century desire to become one with nature or transcend nature; nonhuman animals and the environment do not simply mirror human emotion in Woolf's fiction. Instead, they are in a shared relationship; the nonhuman world is given a voice with which to speak back to humans, frequently criticizing human actions and ideas.

Mark Hussey was one of the first to link Woolf with the philosophy of Merleau-Ponty in *The Singing of the Real World* (1986). While Hussey focuses more on how Merleau-Ponty intersects with Woolf's efforts to define the individual identity, rather than the environment, Hussey is also consistently emphasizing the way the self is defined by the crowding of forces, and, alternatively, the experience of "a lack, by a sense of an abstract 'gap' in being that cannot be directly referred to in language, but which is certainly a potential of human experience,"[6] implying the significance of a more-than-human world that the self defines itself against and within. For Hussey, Woolf's representation of the distance one feels which denies the fulfilling sense of complete knowledge or intimacy with another creates a fear and pessimism within her work – a dark and silencing "bewilderment in the face of human relations and a longing for knowledge and intimacy."[7] Yet, though his interpretive emphasis falls more on the down-beats than the up-swings of the pendulum of Woolf's phenomenology, he also acknowledges "Woolf's concern in [*Between the Acts*] is with the voice of the artist, and with the original 'song,' inspired by the natural world, from which literature, she speculates, is developed. She sees 'common emotion,' a unified source of common belief, as the heart of literature."[8] I would argue that it is the very meta-linguistic quality Woolf's art evasively glimpses which constitutes her representation of nonhuman consciousness–an effort to imagine the mind of matter as it courses through the text of our lives as weather, unfurling leaves, and the uncertain message of birdsong. For example, in *To the Lighthouse*, a line of a Tennyson poem, "We perished, each alone" is related to a mutilated fish at the end of a fisherman's line, both tugging at associations of violence in the human and non-human realms; and in *Between the Acts*, an airplane and a moo enact impulses of slicing and suturing the pageant's dialogue, all of which Woolf knits into prose that depicts a world alive with more-than-human actors. Thus, in Woolf's work, it is possible to understand the places where she inscribes the limits of understanding the human self or the moments of "failed" human community, as the invitation to recognize other nonhuman communities we already belong to, but don't allow to suffuse our sense of being. Hussey hints at the potential in the depictions of a gap or a rift: "thought folds back on itself when face to face with this metalinguistic 'reality'; it cannot be thought about; the circle cannot be escaped. It is perhaps Woolf's inability to put in actual terms what she means by 'reality,' beauty, and soul that gives the 'philosophy' implicit in the novels its essentially religious character."[9] Similarly, in a more recent essay, he links Woolf with Merleau-Ponty to show that she is "an artist of emptiness and silence who tries again and again to enact in her fiction the uncanniness of being . . . moments of interruption, stoppage, open-endedness" that are "enigmatic articulations that cannot be easily translated into narrative form."[10] I posit that this "religious character" or artistry of "silence" in "enigmatic form," which forms the basis of the experience of reading Woolf, is created by Woolf's experiments with an unexpected environmental consciousness infusing the material world with subjectivity that intermingles with representations of human experience and thought. The "other" the "self" is in relationship with is an animate world of multilinguistic potential. There is another layer of community available to human characters; one that may bring with it a shock of awareness evading perfect intimacy, but yet because of that very friction, fosters artistic efforts to bring the nonhuman world into dialogue with the human experience. Westling describes Merleau-Ponty's ecophenomenology in ways that uncannily resemble Hussey's description of Woolf, but, as I am developing, register it as a surfeit of awareness rather than a lack: "Human language intensifies this coiling back of self-reflection by allowing us to articulate the meanings we find sedimented in our experience, as language is itself a long cultural accumulation of significations, and "even the cultural rests on the polymorphism of the wild Being. All creatures without voices articulate their sedimented experiences in ways we only faintly understand."[11] Similarly, the exertion of reaching and striving across the barrier between nonhuman sentience and human language becomes a potential source of inspiration, sustaining Woolfian characters through the inevitable void of fears created by mortality and loneliness to suggest a new kind of potential for membership in a wider community of cyclical creativity. It is still a relationship of tension – recognition of the palpating world around us also requires giving up stable notions of the self as authoritative and authoring. As Gillian Beer has pointed out, Woolf engages with the loss of religion and permanence that Darwin's evolutionary science inaugurated, but the "need to discover origins" and the distress of was "*allayed* for Virginia Woolf by her awareness of the survival of prehistory. The continued presence of sea, clouds, leaves, stones, the animal form of man, the unchanged perceptual intensity of the senses, all sustain her awareness of the simultaneity in the present moment."[12] By reassessing the sensory aspects of her work – the same aspects that Forster celebrated in 1942 – we enrich our understanding of how Woolf manipulates images of unconscious felt connection, environmental stimuli, and the surge of natural forces. The nonhuman environment is registered not merely as a reminder of inevitable destruction and loss, but also as a stimulating, liberating space of potential transformation and continuance.

Woolf's personal diaries and nonfiction essays provide insight into her embodied renderings of the environment and its impact on her fiction. Woolf's autobiographical writings affirm how the larger natural world informs her self-identity and her literary imagination. Her diaries are replete with keen observations about the weather, which plant species are in bloom, and the habits of local birds. These passages are often the most lyrical sections of the entries. As she notes whom she has seen during the day or what she has done, the prose is often perfunctory; it seems to be rushed through like a list of chores in comparison with the way she lingers over her natural observations. The distinction is apparent in an entry dated March 3, 1920:

> Then there was Roger's speech at the Club and my first effort – 5 minutes consecutive speaking – all very brilliant and opening the vista of the form of excitement not before glimpsed at. Dined with Nessa and Duncan in Soho. Saw the woman drop her glove. A happy ending. Eliot and Sydney dine – Sydney righting himself after our blow about Suffield – not without a grampus sigh or so – Then off to Monks – and here I should write large and bright about the SPRING. It has come. It has been with us over a fortnight. Never did a winter sleep more like an infant sucking its thumb. Daffodils all out; garden set with thick golden crocuses; snowdrops almost over; pear trees budding; birds in song; days like June with a touch of the sun – not merely a painted sky but a warm one. Now we've been to Kew. I assure you, this is the earliest and loveliest and most sustained spring I remember. Almond trees out.[13]

The significance she awards "SPRING" in all capital letters makes it literally blossom out from the page. The profusion of adjectives and metaphors fully rounds out each image, suggesting her pleasure in this part of her daily experience. The final line is particularly sensual as the feel of the heat in a previous line, "not merely a painted sky but a warm one," brings out the scent of almond blossoms, "Almond trees out." These passages seem to have a direct correlation to the kinds of lush descriptions and sensory attention that distinguishes most of her literary work.

Indeed, some entries explicitly tie organic imagery to Woolf's conception of creativity: "What was I going to say? Something about the violent moods of my soul. How describe them, even with a waking mind? I think I grow more and more poetic. Perhaps I restrained it, and now, like a plant in a pot, it begins to crack the earthenware. Often I feel the different aspects of life bursting the mind asunder" (June 21, 1924).[14] The emotions she attempts to express through literary inspiration are likened to the wild growth of roots shattering the walls of decorative pots meant to neatly contain them. Similarly, Woolf was breaking free from Victorian prose by shattering old literary forms and by imagining a natural world that exists for its own sake, rather than merely to reflect a character's internal emotions. A comparable analogy is at work when she criticizes Arnold Bennett's prose in "Modern Fiction": "There is not so much as a draught between the frames of the windows, or a crack in the boards. And yet—if life should refuse to live there?"[15] The tight floorboards, like the pot that Woolf imagines breaking, suggests formal rigidity that must be loosened or broken. By contrast, Woolf's prose insists on the kinds of gaps and crevices that let life seep in.

Aware that she is in dialogue with the natural environment and other nonhuman voices, Woolf's writing leaves spaces of silence and questioning for those presences to be registered. She consistently values humans not as a superior species, but as a single component jostling in an undulating network of larger natural forces. Her openness to other forms of sentience indicates a willingness to listen and perceive with humility. Woolf's recollection of another particular afternoon as a young girl at St. Ives exemplifies the animate quality she perceives in the surrounding environment, particularly the living, changing skin of the apples and the interrogative mode of many "other than human forces":

> The lemon-coloured leaves on the elm trees, the round apples glowing red in the orchard and the rustle of the leaves make me pause to think how many other than human forces affect us. While I am writing this, the light changes; an apple becomes a vivid green. I respond – how? And then the little owl [makes] a chattering noise. Another response.[16]

Woolf writes "I respond – how?" as if the changing color of the apples was in itself a question posed by the natural surroundings. Merleau-Ponty's ecophenomenology explains that essential knowledge of an object or being can't be perceived by immobilizing the subject "as with forceps" into a fixed meaning; instead, a more fundamental understanding of another being is only achieved by "someone who therefore limits himself to giving them the hollow, the free space they ask for in return."[17] Woolf's attitude "comprehend[s] perception as this interrogative thought which lets the perceived world be rather than posits it."[18] Similarly, ecomaterialism demands that we reorient our position to the organic matter of the world. Serpil Oppermann, punning on the preconditions of ethical "responsibility" explains: "Agency is about response-ability, about the possibilities of mutual response."[19] Woolf's writing suggests our own innate awareness of these more recently theorized premises. Rather than representing the world as a static background, or using it as a literary symbol, Woolf depicts the environment as a dynamic, fully rounded character in its own right. Further, the "little owl" responds to nature's question before Woolf can frame her own response; the nonhuman presence reacts independently from and even more quickly than the human narrator. This kind of exchange resonates with ways Donna Haraway has defined the most productive kind of cross-species communication:

> The truth or honesty of nonlinguistic embodied communication depends on looking back and greeting significant others, again and again. This sort of truth or honesty is not some trope-free, fantastic kind of natural authenticity that only animals can have while humans are defined by the happy fault of lying denotatively and knowing it. Rather, this truth telling is about co-constitutive natureculture dancing, holding in esteem, and regard open to those who look back reciprocally. Always tripping, this kind of truth has a multispecies future. *Respecere*.[20]

Repeatedly, Woolf's narrators are recording not only their own view of the nonhuman world, but also giving space to or "greeting" how the trees, the wind, the horse, the moth, the cow, or the spaniel interjects and changes the course of that understanding, cocreating a sense of shared experience, even if the human narrator can't fully articulate or comprehend the nonhuman voice.

Yet Woolf and Merleau-Ponty both envision the potential of language to represent the embodied experience of a larger "whole" and the "dancing" "tripping" rhythms of its unexpected becomings. The words Merleau-Ponty claims most "closely convey the life of the whole" are not those with eloquently precise meanings, but rather the "brute," "wild" words that "energetically open upon Being" and "make our habitual evidences vibrate until they disjoin"[21] The parallel in Woolf's work is unmistakable; she also claims that a work of art is not a creation of certain, single-minded solidity, but rather "a symmetry by means of infinite discords ... some kind of whole made of shivering fragments."[22] Linking Merleau-Ponty's theories to modernist forms, Bourne-Taylor and Mildenberg affirm the potential of such ambiguity: "In the interstices of nothingness and meaninglessness there are vestigial moments of revelation. Negativity contains the seeds of liberation, and ultimately formulates its affirmative potential and creativity"[23] Moreover, depictions of momentary experiences of belonging and wholeness in Woolf's work are often associated with the nonhuman realm. In fact, in many instances, physical sensations of sound, light, birds, trees, and waves are the agents that create the oscillating shivers of contraction and expansion between separateness and community.[24]

Woolf as a green reader

Woolf's frequent and elaborate critical treatment of how nature is represented in the works of *other* authors offers useful signposts for understanding her own goal of rendering the natural world accurately and actively. Indeed, her analyses of other literary texts in *The Common Reader* essays resemble what one might now identify as ecocritical readings. In an essay titled "Outlines" Woolf spends several sentences discussing the variety of snow that one would have experienced in the eighteenth century, and remarks: "Sufficient attention has scarcely been paid to this aspect of literature, which, it cannot be denied, has its importance. Our brilliant young men might do worse, when in search of a subject, than devote a year or two to cows in literature, snow in literature, the daisy in Chaucer and in Coventry Patmore."[25] Following her own suggestion, she pays heed in "The Pastons and Chaucer" to Chaucer's ability to bring forth all of nature's vagaries: "Nature, uncompromising, untamed, was no looking-glass for happy faces, or confessor of unhappy souls. She was herself; sometimes, therefore, disagreeable enough and plain, but always in Chaucer's pages with the hardness and freshness of an actual presence."[26] Woolf's analysis is an apt description of the kind of representation of Nature she favors in her own fiction, particularly the cows that play such as significant role in expressing the emotion of Ms. LaTrobe's drama in *Between the Acts* and the way in which Woolf pronounces the mirror or looking-glass of Nature broken in *To the Lighthouse*.

In a similarly revealing review, Woolf claims that what makes Tolstoy "the greatest of all novelists,"[27] is that he proceeds, "as we are accustomed to proceed, not from the inside outwards, but from the outside inwards."[28] In other words, environmental and physical stimuli often prompt the internal thoughts of his characters. The "we" in the phrase "as we are accustomed to proceed" seems to embrace not only her audience of common readers but also modernist writers interested in recording daily experiences, as her fiction will also document. As Alexandra Harris notes, even in Woolf's unfinished drafts of "Reading at Random," intended to be a second chapter of her *Common History* book, she is attentive to the significance of how writers use daily interactions with nature to draw forth universal experience by "linking books back to the solid, daily world from which they grew. She imagined writers walking along the same paths as their readers, worried about the same things, looking out on the same view."[29] Thus, what Woolf finds interesting in Tolstoy is a sense of the embodied perception of ordinary experience. Thoughts are sparked by nudges received from the outside world of physical contact – a fire lit by the rub of sensation upon the flint of individual consciousness. According to Woolf, this kind of vivacity is particularly keen in the context of Tolstoy's use of nature within urban experiences of place:

> He is metropolitan, not suburban. His senses, his intellect, are acute, powerful, and well nourished. There is something proud and superb in the attack of him. Nothing glances off him unrecorded. Nobody, therefore, can so convey the excitement of sport, the beauty of horses, and all the fierce desirability of the world to the senses of a strong young man. Every twig, every feather sticks to his magnet.[30]

Such attention to the sensory impact of the environment on the thoughts and actions of characters similarly manifests itself in Woolf's work and recalls her admonition to modern writers in "Modern Fiction": "Let us record the atoms as they fall upon the mind, in the order in which they fall, let us trace the pattern, however disconnected and incoherent in appearance, which each sight or incident scores upon the consciousness." Every physical sensation, whether it is "every twig, every feather" or even the smallest measurable matter science has identified, every "atom," is part of the internal compositional score of the artist, created by the interplay of nature, perception, and thought.

The Second Common Reader is similarly illuminating. In "The Novels of Hardy" she describes Thomas Hardy as "a minute and skilled observer of nature; the rain, he knows, falls differently as it falls upon roots or arable; he knows that the wind sounds differently as it passes through the branches of different trees. But he is aware, in a larger sense of Nature as a force."[31] As she did with Chaucer, Woolf commends Hardy's representation of Nature as an entity that is not mastered by humans. His emphasis on Nature refuses to mold itself into the contours of classical pastoralism, which Woolf describes metaphorically as an "English landscape painter, whose pictures are all of cottage gardens and old peasant women."[32] Instead she distinguishes Hardy from the paint-by-numbers set, insisting, "And yet what kindly lover of antiquity, what naturalist with a microscope in his pocket, what scholar solicitous for the changing shapes of language, ever heard the cry of a small bird killed in the next wood by an owl with such intensity?"[33] What Woolf admires in Hardy goes beyond his deft language and his detailed knowledge of habitat and zoology. She reserves her most profound praise for his ability to evoke a feeling of sympathy with other creatures, a communal representation of anguish, grief, or pain that is shared across species. This resembles what Haraway would call "respecere" or Barad "response-ability," and what Merleau-Ponty might term the ability to "open upon being" but all of which turn on an insistence on reciprocity. Epiphanies of embodied perception are often a result of such moments of exchange and are vital to engendering such empathy. Hardy's own term for such flashes of inspiration in his work, "moments of vision,"[34] has a similar ring with Woolf's own interest in "moments of being." Woolf's term extends the emphasis on sight to a wider sensory experience, a more varied embodiment that she also found in Hardy's fiction. Woolf expresses Hardy's genius as "vivid to the eye, but not to the eye alone, for every sense participates, such scenes dawn upon us and their splendour remains."[35]

One of Woolf's goals for modern fiction is to render an atmosphere that is charged with sensory stimulation more felt than understood. In *The Visible and the Invisible*, Merleau-Ponty theorizes how unconscious embodied perception operates to imbue a sense of knowledge that can be shared and communicated, even if it can't be clearly enunciated: "'Private worlds' [of separate individuals] communicate . . . The communication makes us the witness of one sole world, as the synergy of our eyes suspends them on one unique thing. But in both cases, the certitude, entirely irresistible as it may be, *remains absolutely obscure*; we can live it, we can neither think it nor formulate it nor set it up in theses. . . . *It is just this unjustifiable certitude of a sensible world common to us that is the seat of truth within us*."[36] In other words, feeling sensations of interrelationship with the world affirms something at our core as embodied beings in an environment replete with other life, even if that experience evades articulation, and can only be hinted at in language – indeed the very elusiveness of the dynamic is part of its value. Woolf's pleasure in reading Hardy's best scenes stems from a similar sensation: "there is always about them a little blur of unconsciousness, that halo of freshness and *margin of the unexpressed which often produce the most profound sense of satisfaction*."[37] In Woolf's view, depicting an embodied attentiveness to surroundings and other sentient life forms is a pivotal component for representing the nebulous life force of modern fiction. As described in "Modern Fiction," it is the idea that "life is a luminous halo, a semi-transparent envelope surrounding us from the beginning of consciousness to the end."[38] The stream of one's consciousness is always already surrounded, coursing through banks of palpable matter our bodies interact with and made up of other life teaming within it, as the way we think is linked to the atoms of matter we ingest, absorb, and filter that make the "whole" of a being something that can't quite be grasped, of which our articulable sense of self is only one part.

However, it would be a facile and all too utopian vision to assume that what Merleau-Ponty and Woolf are describing amounts to a harmonious unity. It is the incompleteness – feelings of failure, frustration, and alienation – that make these revelations about the glimpses of shared meaning so poignant. Merleau-Ponty's concept of the "flesh of the world" has often been misunderstood as metaphor for seamless unification. Louise Westling corrects this oversimplification by referring us back to the way he describes the flesh as two hands:

> And yet this reversibility is "always imminent and never realized in fact," so that there is no coincidence or merging but instead a divergence or "incessant escaping" (*écart*) that prevents the exact superimposition on one another of "the touching of the things by my right hand and the touching of this same right hand by my left hand." Similarly the relation of any creature to others within the flesh of the world is never fully realized or identical; this dehiscence or *écart* generates differentiation even as the intertwining of things and creatures ensures their kinship.[39]

The chiasm and intertwining Merleau-Ponty describes as the basis for ecophenomeonlogical awareness is echoed by recent ecomaterialist philosophy. As Serpil Oppermann describes, ecomaterialism seeks to construct a sense of more-than-human interconnectivity while still pointing to the spanner that resists full coalescence and insists on the presence of difference: "Considering the material and the discursive together does not mean, according to [Karen] Barad, 'collapsing important differences between them,' but means 'allowing any integral aspects to emerge.' This is diffractive thinking – thinking concepts and matter through one another – that material ecocriticism holds crucial in bridging the divide between matter and its social constructions, and in positing the co-presences and coevolution of humans and nonhumans."[40] This manifestation of doubt and amazement that is not readily filled – as it all too often *is* in the annals of human history and fictional narrative, with the authoritative voice pronouncing, defining, and claiming – forms a crucial aspect of Woolf's ecocritical analysis of others and her own writing techniques. The literary practice of allowing room for the not-fully-understood in descriptions of palpable interaction with the nonhuman world – affirming it without erasing its evasiveness, and honoring the uncertainty without negating its meaning – nurtures an environmental consciousness based in ethical relationships. Woolf's fascination with nature and her enthusiasm for sensory renderings of the nonhuman in the work of other authors solicits a green reading of how this environmental ethic is achieved in her own work.

Humans and nonhumans in "Kew Gardens," *Flush*, and "Thunder at Wembley"

In some of Woolf's work, nonhuman animals assume key roles, with a status equivalent to their human counterparts. Thus Woolf implies their independent agency and a lateral, rather than hierarchical, relationship to the human species. As Hardy rendered the plaintive anguish of the small bird facing its predator, Woolf incisively describes the emotional responses of other animate beings. Her depictions of their delight, terror, anger, and affection entreat the reader to value nonhuman experience as diverse and meaningful. As a result, her representations of nonhuman life create a larger sense of community with animals while also critiquing presumed rights of dominion over "others" inherent in British culture.

"Kew Gardens" (1919) is one of the works by Woolf that has been consistently noted for its unique treatment of the nonhuman, as represented by this assessment of John Oakland: "The fusing processes, particularly that of human with non-human, break down differentiation in the establishment of inter-related harmonies."[41] Yet early environmental appraisals such as Oakland's have sometimes teetered on an overly celebratory peak: "There is nothing in the text to suggest that this qualitative movement towards unity is anything but harmonious and optimistic."[42] While the story does evoke unity, it also recalls the First World War and reveals tensions in gender relations. The theme of balance and Woolf's formal experimentation in prose are anticipated by the story's original cover art. The first edition copy of "Kew Gardens" at Washington State University's archive, which resembles many of the first-edition Hogarth prints of "Kew Gardens," is a small pamphlet with a hand-painted paper cover. It has a solid black background that has been brushed over the entire cover, a reminder of the story's backdrop of war. The black paint is topped with splotches of bright cobalt blue, orange, and a shade of purple made from a combination of the other two colors. The presentation of the cover suggests the story's prose technique, which features a fragmented style and opposes clear, realist representation. Similarly, references to the flowers at Kew are splashed throughout the prose with reappearing descriptions of their light and color. This first edition also contains a woodcut by Vanessa Bell mingling figures of people with flowers, presenting the figures slightly elongated and askance, as if from an unfamiliar vantage point. The perspective of the story is also unexpectedly skewed as the action of human characters is presented from the point-of-view of a snail. This unlikely protagonist is attempting to resolve the conflict of how to make its way through an oval flowerbed. Between segments focusing on the snail, the reader is introduced to four sets of couples strolling past the snail's garden plot. Edward Bishop has convincingly argued that the four couples represent middle, upper, and lower class, maturity, old age, and youth, as well as relations between husband and wife, male companions, female friends, and young lovers,[43] emphasizing the way in which both the flora one finds at Kew Gardens and humanity itself are organized into classification systems.

Postcolonial ecocritics reference Kew Royal Botanical Gardens in asserting the significant link to the "language of taxonomy, discipline, and control" and cultural traditions of ranking organic and human species: "Just as the British Museum and Kew Gardens were constituted by the flora, fauna, and human knowledges extracted from the colonies, the discourse of natural history was articulated in terms of biotic nations, kingdoms, and colonists ... contributing to biologically determinist discourses of race, gender, and nature."[44] In "Kew Gardens" Woolf seems aware of this propensity, denying the experience of Kew as a colonial display-case of sanctioned movement and classification by reclaiming it as a site of overlapping intersubjectivity using imagistic parallels that highlight gradations of similarity, rather than hierarchies of difference. Woolf's rendering of Kew Royal Botanical Gardens as an abstraction of fused color, light, and water, with zooified representations of people and prominent nonhuman characters, directly subverts the usual cultural depictions of such a highly ordered, hierarchical place. Bonnie Kime Scott clarifies that Woolf's early experiences with gardens as prescribed therapy, before Kew became a regular feature of her life with Leonard in Richmond, might have made it a site for considering dynamics of ordered control in contravention with experiences of organic entanglement and transformation: "assigned gardening as a form of therapy, she could also use the garden to express ways that she felt coerced or regulated," suggesting that Woolf "learned that gardening was largely a matter of control, and that this struggle among genders, plants, and animals was part of what she wanted to record."[45] Similarly, in "Kew Gardens" fractured language and miniature plots playfully trick logical conformity and traditional literary practice as the omniscient narrator only presents what goes on within the snail's vicinity and human voices are reduced to bits and scraps of conversation.

The reader enters the snail's world with dramatic shifts in scale. Initially, the flowers are described as if the reader was him or herself walking past, admiring the summer blooms: "From the oval-shaped flower-bed there rose perhaps a hundred stalks spreading into heart-shaped or tongue-shaped leaves half way up and unfurling at the tip red or blue or yellow petals marked with spots of colour raised upon the surface."[46] The reader's gaze is then drawn down deeper, beneath the petals, which are now appreciated from overhead: "The petals were voluminous enough to be stirred by the summer breeze, and when they moved, the red, blue, and yellow lights passed one over the other, staining an inch of the brown earth beneath with a spot of the most intricate colour."[47] Just as Woolf sought to record "an incessant shower of innumerable atoms" in "Modern Fiction," here she follows the pattern of dappled light as it illuminates the tissue of living matter:

> The light fell either upon the smooth grey back of a pebble, or shell of a snail with its circular veins, or, falling into a raindrop, it expanded ... The light now settled upon the flesh of a leaf, revealing the branching thread of fibre beneath the surface, and again it moved on and spread its illumination in the vast green spaces beneath the dome of the heart-shaped and tongue-shaped leaves.[48]

Alt notes how Woolf "is drawn from classification to observation" in stories such as "The Death of the Moth" and "Kew Gardens"; reflecting Woolf's increasing interest in an account of nature that incorporates ethology's awareness that "the significance of any creature is most fully realised when it is observed as a living thing within its natural surroundings."[49] Here, that approach is exemplified in the way the snail is embedded within a fully animate environment and operates as a moving, living creature, rather than an inert being. The literary application of this intense form of lived observation changes the perception of scale and creates a new consciousness of the lived, bodily sensorium. In terms of ecophenomenology, an attentiveness to perspective and the senses prompts embodied awareness:

> To learn to see colours is to acquire a certain style of seeing, a new use of one's own body: it is to enrich and recast the body image. Whether a system of motor or perceptual powers, our body is not an object for an "I think", it is a grouping of lived-through meanings which moves towards its equilibrium. Sometimes a new cluster of meanings is formed; our former movements are integrated into a fresh motor entity, the first visual data into a fresh sensory entity, our natural powers suddenly come together in a richer meaning.[50]

Again, the echo of these ideas in ecomaterialist theory is striking:

> Like taste, or sound, or smell, color results from the combination of physics and physiology. Therefore if "grey is the fate of colors at twilight," (qting. "Grey" by Cohen) color, generally taken, is the fate of light when it meets the eye. It is the fate of physics meeting physiology. It is the way waves of energy get hybridized with hybrid layers of biology, stepping from the unseen to the visible.[51]

By twining these two, old and new, theories with Woolf's fictional devices, the way they all "point at" a similar philosophy orienting us to see our "reality" as a fabric of matter that participates in creating the "meaning" we read into ourselves and the world becomes more apparent. Woolf uses prose to evoke an artistic aesthetic that brings together a "fresh sensory entity" of garden and a new "richer meaning" of a shared organic world. Her writing moves away from the "'I think'" by encouraging the reader to "acquire a certain style of seeing" uniting images, light, and associations that require the reader to integrate "the first visual data into a fresh sensory entity."

The play of light, atmosphere, and matter is linked to the very basis of thought through Woolf's suggestive comparison of verdant undergrowth and active, embodied brain. She describes the light as it traces patterns in "flesh" and "veins," of succulent green tissue that also resembles a circuited mind in its "branching thread of fibre beneath the surface." The multiple references to the leaves that are "heart-shaped and tongue-shaped" with "throats" also correlates organic and human flesh, and refers subtly to language, specifically the kind of words that "reveal the flickerings of that innermost flame which flashes its messages through the brain."[52] Similarly, the thoughts of the human characters will be illuminated in seemingly random patterns of revelation and memory. The human body and the organic matter are coalesced in these images. It is the variants of this interactive play of light, flower, scale, and sensory memory that becomes story. Or, as Serenella Iovino describes it, "Material ecocriticism takes matter as a text, as a site of narrativity, a storied matter, a corporeal palimpsest in which stories are inscribed."[53] The garden as a text of colonial classification reclaimed by a renewed awareness of the vibrancy of over-looked life and the interconnected narratives of human and nonhuman beings makes embodied knowledge and minute matter meaningful. The fact that Woolf was representing such understandings in tandem with Merleau-Ponty's philosophy or prior to new materialism's theoretical arrival is not as important for its chronological coup as it is for how it reminds us that environmental consciousness is always already part of us, and is carried forth through our continued efforts to make it culturally visible.

Changes in perspective and scale emphasize that all beings are embed-ded in the thickness of the physical world. Using a stone wall as his example, Merleau-Ponty explains what happens to the body when we allow our gaze to be absorbed by a close object: "There is no longer even a stone there, but merely the play of light upon an indefinite substance."[54] Woolf's morphing description of falling light in "the vast green spaces" beneath the leaves enacts this kind of engrossed gaze. However, when one's body moves through space, one's understanding of visual objects also shifts. Woolf's description of light moves upward again from the dappled caverns of the undergrowth: "Then the breeze stirred rather more briskly overhead and the colour was flashed into the air above, into the eyes of the men and women who walk in Kew Gardens in July."[55] The reader is shunted from an absorbed view of the undergrowth back to the perspective of the humans walking above the flowers, fostering a recognition of the depth and space of world we move within and the variety of lives that experience it from differing subjective planes. Thus, in one opening paragraph, Woolf destabilizes the reader's sense of scale, suggesting that there is life worth recording not only from our own perspective, but also from the viewpoint of insects and snails, all interlaced within the world's thick flesh.

Woolf identifies humans and language with natural phenomena throughout the story. The first couple who meander past the flowerbed is a husband and wife who recollect their first encounters with love.

The man is caught in a reverie about Lily, the woman who refused his proposal of marriage years earlier; her name is another mingling of humans/flowers. The man encapsulates his memory of the rejection with the image of Lily's impatient "square silver shoe-buckle and a dragon fly,"[56] an image that stresses form and organicity. Although this memory interjects another woman between the married pair, the wife seems past any jealous provocation. Whether the wife's equanimity is the product of serene security or tired indifference is uncertain: "Why should I mind, Simon? Doesn't one always think of the past, in a garden with men and women lying under the trees ... ghosts [of] one's happiness, one's reality?"[57] Woolf affirms the power of setting to inspire self-reflection, illuminating the layers of self-identity and sentiment brought up from the muddy depth of memory and suddenly flashed into consciousness. The wife shares her own emblem of love and happiness, which is also pointedly not part of the past she shares with her husband. Hers is a childhood joy, a memory of "the mother of all my kisses of all my life"[58] – the unexpected kiss of a grey-haired art instructor on the back of her neck when she was only a girl. While the recollections are not about each other, sharing them renews a sense of the couple's intimacy. The pattern of their movement changes correspondingly. At the outset of the interlude the man is walking "six inches in front of the woman,"[59] a distance he maintains "purposely,"[60] but as they depart the woman calls the children to them and they walk "four abreast." They are physically reunited as they are blended back into the story's canvas and reduced to figures that reenact the previous description of the snail: "[They] soon diminished in size among the trees and looked half transparent as the sunlight and shade swam over their backs in large trembling irregular patches."[61] Embodied awareness of environmental stimuli pricks memory, the characters communicate this to each other, and then they are absorbed back into the larger communicative efforts of the story's themes of balance. Indeed the "irregular patches" describe bits of human dialogue as well as the moving pools of sunlight.

Thus while Oakland is correct in his assessment that the story evinces unity, it would be unnecessarily reductive to equate this blending of human and organic life with a denial of human (and nonhuman) hardship or loss. These aspects are also present, although their threat is folded into the other unifying impulses of the garden so that these darker tones have their place in the balance of the whole. Even the snail's progress is impeded by difficulties of circumventing "crumbs of loose earth" or "vast crumpled surfaces of a thin crackling texture."[62] Although the snail finally decides to go under rather than atop or around a major obstacle, the story doesn't allow the reader to see the snail reach its goal. The snail's decision-making during its journey may have been influenced by Frederick Gamble's claims about animal consciousness in *The Animal World* (1911), a book the Woolfs owned. "Above all," wrote Gamble, "there is in a [non-human] being not only a certain awareness, but a certain power of choice, a certain independence when faced by a multitude of alternatives."[63] Woolf's depiction of the snail's independent agency might therefore not be solely fictional, but rather based on scientific descriptions of the possibilities of animal behavior. Woolf's world reflects that both humans and nonhumans have the capability for rational thought.

Like the snail, humans encounter difficulties too. Though the somber note of marital regret was only lightly sounded in the married couple's conversation, the two men who come along next recall the trauma of war. An old man is operating under delusions that recall shell-shock and grief. His conversation with "spirits of the dead" is punctuated by a cry of, "Women! Widows! Women in black – ."[64] His excitement is prompted by seeing a woman wearing a dress "which in the shade looked black."[65] Whether or not this refers to the two working women dressed in black who will saunter into range after this pair leaves is uncertain, just as a reference to an "old man" in the two women's dialogue will ambiguously recall the war veteran. Whether the characters are actually referring to each other doesn't prevent the association for the reader, however, who is continually provoked to make patterns from the apparent randomness. The old man's younger male companion "touch[es] a flower with the tip of his walking cane in order to divert the old man's attention."[66] Yet the flowers prove to be a diversion for several characters, not just the mentally unstable old man. The old man begins talking to the flower as if he could "answer a voice speaking from it."[67] The shape of the flower may resemble a conical earpiece that hangs on an upright receiver, suggesting that the man is imagining another human speaker. In any event, his experience of a direct, sentimental voice that can be understood as if one was speaking to a flower over the phone is initially made to look foolish. The reader only gets half of the old man's delusional conversation, but the experience of this kind of dislocation and fragmentation becomes normalized in the context of the story, which is replete with vague and unfinished dialogue. Unlike Septimus Smith, whose trauma is confirmed by shell-shocked visions of dogs and trees becoming figures of the risen dead in Regents Park, in "Kew Gardens" the mutability of human and nonhuman voices, and the ability of others to hear flowers or become flowers, is normalized as a common phenomenon, one that may sometimes be expressive of trauma, but is not necessarily a sign or harbinger of mental distress as much as a daily experience of a world that is refracted and experienced in a multiplicity of ways. The possibility of shared communication between environment and perceiving human is not disparaged, but rather revised, by the next couple.

The idea of nonhuman communication is taken up again as another woman is engrossed by the flowers; but here the play of language renders dialogue as sensory, rather than literal. In the interlude that gives the reader the conversation of two working women, the pattern of the prose is meant to communicate a feeling rather than a precise or lucid meaning:

'Nell, Bert Lot, Cess, Phil, Pa, he says, I says, she says, I says, I says, I says'
'My Bert, Sis, Bill, Grandad, the old man, sugar,
    Sugar, flour, kippers, greens
    Sugar, sugar, sugar'[68]

The "flour," a homophone for "flower," and the multiple connotation of "greens" as both salad leaves and the green color of the garden, mix the setting of Kew gardens into the woman's rhetoric. The repetition of "I says" creates rhythm. The mere sound produced by the movement of the tongue, "say[ing]," like the tongue of the flowers, is emphasized over the direct narrative intelligibility of their discourse. This new sketch revises what seemed insanity in the old man and shows how disconnected thought, time, memory, and language are convoluted in "ordinary" ways as well. Meaning is sensually communicated through movement, sound, memories of people carried in the litany of names, and a certain sense of happiness created by the repetition of "sugar" and its associations with sweetness. One of the women even becomes a kind of flower as she looks at the flowerbed and listens to the friendly prattle: "The ponderous woman looked through the pattern of falling words at the flowers standing cool, firm and upright in the earth, with a curious expression. . . . She stood letting the words fall over her, swaying the top part of her body slowly backwards and forwards, looking at the flowers."[69] The words become the "incessant shower" ("Modern Fiction") "falling over her" to produce an unconscious lull in her attachment with the human world, allowing her to hear the pattern of words, and to express the physicality of the flowers as she sways her stalk-like body with the breeze.

Forms, both in language and human figure, are protean. As Westling explains, this idea is central to Merleau-Ponty's ecophenomenology as well: "It is in [*The Visible and the Invisible*] that he extended the embodied, gestural definition of speech from the earlier works into an ontological description of language bubbling up from silence and reaching back into the Invisible to articulate meanings that are the lining and depth dynamically woven into the texture of social life with all its cultural accumulations, in a chiasmic overlapping with the visible world."[70] Woolf's writing makes these potential connections immanent. Woolf experiments with this understanding using language as a manifestation of traces of pre-reflexive experience, cultured thought, and intersubjective perspectives of shared world, not just in these bits of dialogue in "Kew Gardens" but as a recurring image of creativity and the "singing of the world" in other stories as well: the warbling voice of an old woman conflated with the bubbling of water from earth in *Mrs. Dalloway* or Miss La Trobe feeling the beginning of words for a new play effervescently surface as she drinks the fermenting malt of her beer toward the end of *Between the Acts*, for example. Miss La Trobe drowsily, drunkenly contemplates the origins of inspiration as "words of one syllable sank down into the mud ... The mud became fertile. Words rose above the intolerably laden dumb oxen plodding through the mud. Words without meaning – wonderful words."[71] For Woolf, language, itself, is embedded in environmental sensations, a manifestation of humanness generated from a rich layered potential of communications that don't (yet) have human meaning, but are still innately part of more-than-human meaning-making. Personified and zooified descriptions, dialogue as rhythmic poetry, and sudden shifts in scale represent the "lining and depth" of experience "woven into the texture of social life" and consciousness. Just as Woolf was inspired by physics to consider the fluidity of world and matter, contemporary theorists of ecomaterialism use physics to remind us that "the universe of materiality is a crossroad of compound bodyminds" whose "copresence" is a kind of agency that "discloses concretely the internal relations in a storied world."[72] Today, we might think of this coauthored material agency of world-making as the determinism of single-cell organisms, the swarming capacity of small fish, or the ability of photons to act as wave or particle or both, according to the presence of an observer, as shown in the double slit experiment.

In "Kew Gardens" the overlapping imagery, poetic dialogue, and the mesh of interwoven human and nonhuman narratives is achieved in tandem with controlled samples of gender, age, and class, as well as the central axis of the circular snail inside an oval flowerbed. Like the nest of Chinese boxes in an imperial garden, in turn enclosed by London, control and organicity productively tussle in a world that continues to move through time and memory, or stroll out of the range of local space. The patterns themselves are a product of flux – the cyclical change of life as it is lived and the protean quality of shared thoughts as they struggle to find expression.

Embodied perception of the environment propels a back and forth of corporeal interplay between the last couple of young lovers. The two insinuate physically what they cannot yet verbalize or even consciously realize: "The couple stood still on the edge of the flower-bed, and together pressed the end of her parasol deep down into the soft earth. The action and the fact that his hand rested on top of hers expressed their feelings in a strange way."[73] The symbolic union of their hands and coinciding penetration of fertile loam hints at the marital and sexual potential of their relationship, provoking them to think of concealed "precipices" and "something loom[ing]" behind their words. The sense of bodily awareness taps undercurrents of weighty thoughts; there is a physical sensory interaction with the environment and each other. The young man's response is to withdraw from the natural encounter – "he pulled the parasol out of the earth with a jerk and was impatient to find the place where one had tea with other people, like other people"[74] – whereas the woman wishes to engage the nonhuman world more fully – "trailing her parasol; turning her head this way and that way forgetting her tea, wishing to go down there and then down there, remembering orchids and cranes among wild flowers."[75] Their intercourse with the environment instigates a form of nonliteral communication.

The flowers and the atmosphere have combined to pollinate not only the implied sexual urges of the pair, but also the reader's awareness of the text's unique mode of perception. This short story has no linear narrative, no plot, and no clear climax; instead, as Edward Bishop points out, "the experience of reading ["Kew Gardens"] initiates, in the sensitive reader, a growth of perception."[76] The young couple exchanges vague words with unclear antecedents that nevertheless have meaning within the pattern of the story. The woman brushes aside her suitor's comment on the price of admission saying, "Isn't it worth sixpence?" to which he asks "What's 'it' – what do you mean by 'it'?"[77] The woman's response is unclear as she struggles to find words for the mood created by the garden: "O anything – I mean – you know what I mean."[78] But just as the woman resists putting a price on the experience, Woolf doesn't depreciate the value of ambiguous, half-formed language: "These short insignificant words also expressed something, words with short wings for their heavy body of meaning, inadequate to carry them far and thus alighting awkwardly upon the very common objects that surrounded them."[79] Likening the small words to a bee laden with pollen, Woolf seems to suggest that these half-sensory, half-literal gesticulations of communication approximate the gaps and pauses of illumination that pollinate or give creative meaning to ordinary experience. These fissures in form and language are what allow growth. Further, that growth is the development of an interplay of images and atmosphere rather than a clear narrative trajectory.

Woolf's modernist experiments with language invest language with a life of its own. In her essay "Craftsmanship" Woolf expresses the vivacious nature of her working material of words. Words, which she proclaims are "the wildest, freest, most irresponsible, most unteachable of all things,"[80] take on an independent life. They "live in the mind ... variously and strangely, much as human beings live, by ranging hither and thither, by falling in love, and mating together."[81] She playfully acknowledges the limits of her own ability to pin (or pen) words down. She allows them the potential to have meanings beyond her immediate control as an author by depicting the tendency of language to change and develop as it lives in the mind of the writer as well as language's transformation when those words are read and absorbed into the minds of readers who may have a multitude of associations and meanings that "mate" and join with those words. Woolf recognizes the charge of this reciprocal openness to being not only in her own vivification of words, but also in the ability of the *words* to leave space for her to engage with *them*: "The test of a book (to a writer) [is] if it makes a space in which, quite naturally, you can say what you want to say. . . . This proves that the book itself is alive: because it has not crushed the thing I wanted to say, but allowed me to slip it in, without any compression or alteration."[82] Woolf allows language to form spontaneous or unexpected meanings, and in an equivalent sense a book is most "alive" by allowing her to engage with it and add her own words to the evolving product. Recent material ecocritical theorists such as Serenella Iovino recognize that this kind of interplay between an object and its lived experience creates a collaboration of meaning that is part of an environmentally aware perception: "Just as discourses might have material effects (e.g., in concepts and practices of marginalization, exploitation, or segregation), so matter discloses properties that prepare for the insurgence of discourses."[83] As a result of this kind of embodied knowledge, ideas and conceptions of our own "being" change: "The knower and the known are mutually transformed in the process of knowing, and new levels of reality emerge. Whether it involves cells or social practices, knowing is a material-discursive becoming. It transforms both the individuals and the world."[84] While I don't follow new materialists so far as to grant consciousness to inanimate objects, the interplay of material that itself undergoes processes of transformation and impacts the processes of ecological growth and beings – both human and nonhuman – that do have consciousness can remind us of the coconstitutive significance of matter on both macro and micro scales. Woolf's work invites us to reorient our position in terms of flowers, insects, color, and even the pages we hold between our hands so that our own understanding of self in relation to these other subjects and objects is transformed, and new interpretations, new knowledges, perhaps some Woolf may not have even consciously intended, emerge. In some respect, all literature participates in this kind of process, but Woolf not only directly acknowledges the fluidity of such cocreation, but also attempts to find forms that open the "greeting" for new engagements with being to be made visible. As a result, Merleau-Ponty's brand of ecophenomenological perception and ecomaterialism provide another possible theory for the reflexive, participatory qualities that make modernist narratives uniquely "new."

Language is often identified as the dividing line separating humans from other animals. In "Kew Gardens" Woolf deemphasizes human language as the *sine qua non* by extending communication to include the exchange of nonverbal meanings. However, in other texts she bestows the power of human speech on animal characters. For some literary scholars such devices of personification constitute a pathetic fallacy, the term Ruskin invented to signify any attribution of human characteristics to "*in*animate natural objects."[85] More often, conferring human language on animal characters is labeled anthropomorphic. As Lorraine Daston and Gregg Mitman identify, anthropomorphism is "usually applied as a term of reproach, both intellectual and moral."[86] Several scholarly works are dedicated to challenging this assumption. It is crucial to distinguish "anthropocentrism" – the assumption that human interests have a higher priority than those of nonhumans – from "anthropomorphism." According to Lawrence Buell, "anthropomorphism" is a more complex term wherein "an anthropocentric frame of reference," including personification, can "dramatize the claims or plight of the natural world" rather than merely projecting human desires upon nature.[87] The human author is still a mediating presence, but literary devices can be used to undermine and complicate human control.

Respecting the life of another living being in part depends upon a capacity for imaginative empathy – a variety of anthropomorphism that is not anthropocentric. Donna Haraway insists on a similarly open and empathetic engagement when she suggests what Jacques Derrida's philosophical inquiry into the gaze of his cat, described in *The Animal that*

Therefore I Am, lacked: "Derrida failed a simple obligation of companion species; he did not become curious about what the cat might actually be doing, feeling, thinking, or perhaps making available to him in looking back."[88] It is just that additional turn – extending to the nonhuman a sense of mutual respect and curiosity, provoking a dialogue that reaches toward understanding other forms of communication, emotion, and meaning – that distinguishes anthropomorphism from anthropocentrism. Lorraine Daston and Gregg Mitman justify some forms of personification in writing about nonhuman animals. They note a shift away from representing animals as a group, both in literature and in other real-world contexts of science and animal activism, repudiating the practice of transposing onto species of animals symbolic human attributes such as bravery, cunning, or loyalty. Instead, the current trend is toward personifying individual animals. Thinking of particular animals as having personal idiosyncrasies is "the way naturalists who knew most and cared most for the animals discussed them" even in documentaries of experienced field biologists.[89] To take this approach is to consider "what it would be like to be that animal" in a way that "roughly parallels that between an introspective approach to human thought, in which the psychologist turns inward and examines the contents of his or her own consciousness as data for understanding the workings of human consciousness."[90] Or, as Caroline Hovanec has documented, how subjective psychologists of the modernist era attempted to get at a better understanding of the questions they should ask about animal consciousness by a kind of cognitive ethology that was "attempting to articulate the experiences associated with sensory stimuli and instincts in animal minds,"[91] including imaginative renderings: "[J.B.S.] Haldane and Woolf light on similar tropes as they continue to grapple with the question of how our own biological senses and mental structures determine the way in which we understand the world."[92] Despite the fact that we are now in the Anthropocene, our willingness to use the human capacity for thought and sensory experience to attempt to enter into a more ethical relationship with nonhumans is still a crucial device to advancing knowledge in literature, science, and philosophy.

Eileen Crist argues that an emotional continuum between humans and animals was a major piece of Darwin's evolutionary biology, the particulars of which he elaborated in his 1872 work *The Expression of Emotions in Man and Animals*, a text Woolf likely read. Darwin argued that human and animal domains were no longer separated by "essential difference."[93] *The Expression of Emotions in Man and Animals* furthers his view of an evolutionary continuity by showing that "evolutionary common descent entails the probability that subjective phenomena are not the sole province of human beings."[94] Crist explains that Darwin even goes so far as to argue that some "animals have powers of imitation, attention, memory, imagination (seen in animals' dreaming), and reason."[95] Notably, Darwin's own pet dog is one animal frequently used as an example of how emotions are manifested through the dog's gait as well as particular movements of the tail and mouth. Darwin notes how hair, posture, and ears change when the dog is approached by a stranger versus when it is approached by its master and "the body sinks downward or even crouches, and is thrown into flexous movements . . . his hair instantly becomes smooth; his ears are depressed and drawn backwards, but not closely to the head; and his lips hang loosely."[96] Darwin uses specific observations of several species of animals in various circumstances as proof that many animals have voluntary physical movements that are used as gestural communications of emotion, similar to the way humans express feelings of despair, anger, or elation.

This same acute sensitivity to detail is apparent in Woolf's biography of Elizabeth Barrett-Browning's spaniel, Flush. The canine biography is based on Woolf's historical research about Flush gleaned from Elizabeth and Robert Barrett-Browning's letters. The factual information is, of course, generously padded with Woolf's own fictional license. This is apparent even in the novel's pictorial representations. Pinker, the dog Sackville-West gave Woolf in 1926, was used for the frontispiece photograph of Flush.[97] The dog is poised and alert across the period-costumed lap of a sitter whose face does not appear in the photograph. This staged portrait of Flush is presented along with other paintings of the real Miss Mitford and Mrs. Barrett-Browning. Genre-blending is a familiar tool in Woolf's oeuvre. In *A Room of One's Own* she imagined the life of Shakespeare's sister to round out a polemical critique of a very real gender inequality. A similar amalgamation of realism and fantasy is pertinent to Woolf's activist critique in *Flush*.

On one hand (or paw), *Flush* is a playful novel that amused a large reading audience when it was published in 1933.[98] The mass acclaim was dubiously received by admirers of her previously published novels and all but extinguished close critical scrutiny of *Flush* for several decades.[99] However, the expanding field of animal studies led many scholars to give this slim novel a second sniff in the early years of the twenty-first century. Criticism gravitates toward two concerns often discussed as if they are competing claims. One approach attempts to get past the "comedy"[100] of the canine aspects of the text in order to rehabilitate what is seen as the novel's primary interest in using a dog's life to allegorize weighty issues related to gender, class, and race.[101] Another common reading explicitly sets aside the human social implications of the text, prioritizing instead how the novel depicts "the actuality of an animal's consciousness."[102] I am indebted to both of these approaches, but propose they should be considered as interrelated rather than interpretations that are at odds. *Flush* resists settling into taking either humans or animals as its primary subject, but rather romps through the contact zone of the relationship between them, tracking what humans should learn about their limited subjective understanding of all "others," as well as how to respect and value difference.

In the oft-quoted passage when Flush and Elizabeth Barrett Browning are first introduced to one another, Woolf represents the scene as one of mutual acknowledgment – an open perceiving of one another with the intent to truly experience the resulting sensations and emotions:

> 'Oh, Flush!' said Miss Barrett. For the first time she looked him in the face. For the first time Flush looked at the lady lying on the sofa. Each was surprised. Heavy curls hung down on either side of Miss Barrett's face; large bright eyes shone out; a large mouth smiled. Heavy ears hung down on either side of Flush's face; his eyes, too, were large and bright: his mouth wide. There was a likeness between them. As they gazed at each other each felt: Here am I – and then each felt: But how different! . . . Could it be that each completed what was dormant in the other? She might have been – all that; and he – But no. Between them lay the widest gulf that can separate one being from another. She spoke. He was dumb. She was woman; he was dog. Thus closely united, thus immensely divided, they gazed at each other. Then with one bound Flush sprang on to the sofa and laid himself where he was to lie for ever after – on the rug at Miss Barrett's feet.[103]

The reciprocity of their gaze is initially rendered as an assessment of equal curiosity on the part of woman and dog. Merleau-Ponty explains that "the tactile palpitation where the questioner and the questioned are closer, and of which the palpitation of the eye is a remarkable variant"[104] is the kind of intense, interrogative looking that promotes understanding between two beings. Donna Haraway, writing more specifically about the relationship between humans and the animals they live with, explains the mutual exchange as learning about a being we will come to love: "We are training each other in acts of communication we barely understand. We are, constitutively, companion species. We make each other up, in the flesh. Significantly other to each other, in specific difference, we signify in the flesh a nasty developmental infection called love. This love is a historical aberration and a *naturalcultural* legacy."[105] The third person narrator resists attributing recognition to one or the other, but allows the comprehension of physical similarity and spiritual sympathy to be shared by both. The way the prose stutters after the thought that one might "complete" the other implies a romantic rhetoric of love that is abandoned, or perhaps replaced by a courtly version with all the trappings of chaste virtue. They are "closely united" in sympathy but separated by an "immense divide" of difference. In this way the natural sympathies and cultural tropes of romance are part of the "natureculture" bonding moment without discarding the "divide" that merits a respectful acknowledgement of the limitations of understanding, despite kinship. As Derek Ryan notes, the syntactical function of the semicolon supports this reading: "The use of the semi-colon too is important in signaling an openness to the boundaries between them, and the possibility that what they are 'divided by' is not essential and finally determined."[106] Although the scene ends with Flush "on the rug at Miss Barrett's feet," suggesting the superiority of human over dog, Woolf gives Flush an agency in acquiescing to bind himself to human company as if it were his own individual desire motivated by mutual affection rather than a master–pet hierarchy. This complicates readings of Flush as simply an instrument of social critique. The feminist opposition to patriarchal control of education and politics in *A Room of One's Own* and *Three Guineas* indicates that Woolf would not assume that another human being would so jauntily choose to be stationed below another person. Scott attempts to reconcile this potential conflict by comparing this moment in *Flush* to the narrator's recognition in *A Room of One's Own* "that the beadle is throwing her off the turf of Oxbridge. It repeats received order rather than achieved understanding," an order that will ultimately be shown up as a false cultural construction when "as the book proceeds, it emerges that Flush has unique abilities, agency, and capacity to adapt."[107] Ryan suggests a similar satirical purpose: "The aim of this approach is not to empty Woolf's text of humour, but rather to ask whether the humour is not aimed at the ways in which we take our own human position too certainly – an effort, in Woolf's words, to 'caricature the pomposity of those who claim that they are something.'"[108] Yet, Woolf may also be wrestling with some of her own conflicted ideas about domestic servants, as Alison Light has suggested in *Mrs. Woolf and the Servants*.[109] Pamela Caughie takes up this question and posits that the nonhuman character offers Woolf "a way out of the double bind of the modernist writer who would write across class lines without making her character – whether Lily Wilson or Mrs. McNab – a representative figure of the working classes."[110] Yet, rather than offer a way "out" of such entanglements, the uneasy conflations may only serve to point out the problematics of power in multiple kinds of labor relations since questions of domesticity and power are also part of animal studies, which illuminates the history of domestic non-human animals meant to serve our needs as pets or sources of agricultural labor. Woolf conflates problems of class and human and non-human relations in other parts of the novel too by using zooifying words for humans "herded together" and highlighting the correspondence of terms related to humans and animals in referring to human dwellings as "Rookeries" and "cells."[111] Thus, at times, *Flush* underscores the differences between humans and other animals, particularly pets, with results that productively reveal the history of human–animal–class ensnarement, rather than negate the complexities of the bonds between them. Woolf's novel points out how the nested hierarchies of assumed systems of power trouble our inability to develop a consistent awareness of ethical and economic codes of behavior as they relate to servants and leisure class, women and patriarchy, human and nonhuman. *Flush* heightens our prismatic sensitivity to the pluralistic and competing roles we all assume within these nested power dynamics. Combining and blending them challenges our awareness of how inequity is sometimes only recognized from one position, rather than encompassing an understanding of how one may be *both* victim and oppressor within these interlocking social systems of daily life and culture.

However, in considering how Woolf treats hierarchy and classification in *Flush*, it is important to note that the traits that distinguish the canine species are just as often described as superior to the qualities humans possess. As a result, the novel not only plays within the vertical hierarchies of these roles, but also eschews quantitative positions of "better" or "worse" by reminding us of qualitative distinctions which defy such cultural assumptions. Woolf imagines Flush as having an appreciation for the phenomenal world that far exceeds the poetic powers of Britain's most renowned writers:

> Here, then, the biographer must perforce come to a pause. Where two or three thousand words are sufficient for what we see ... there are no more than two words and perhaps one-half for what we smell. The human nose is practically non-existent. The greatest poets in the world have smelt nothing but roses on the one hand, and dung on the other. The infinite gradations that lie between are unrecorded. Yet it was in the world of smell that Flush mostly lived. Love was chiefly smell; form and colour were smell; music and architecture, law, politics and science were smell. ... To describe his simplist experience with the daily chop or biscuit is beyond our power.[112]

A similar passage bears out the pervasiveness of Woolf's insistence on Flush's superlative senses:

> He knew Florence in its marmoreal smoothness and its gritty and cobbled roughness. Hoary folds of drapery, smooth fingers and feet of stone received the lick of his tongue, the quiver of his shivering snout.... In short, he knew Florence as no human being has ever known it; as Ruskin never knew it or George Eliot either. He knew it as only the dumb know. Not a single one of his myriad sensations ever submitted itself to the deformity of words.[113]

Flush's animal body allows him to experience an enthralling array of sensations. Woolf's analogy of smell to architecture, law, politics, and science is not mere hyperbole. Dogs know whether a place is safe for sleeping or whether it houses danger by its scent. Similarly, habits of interaction with other dogs – whether to play, fight, retaliate, or put a tail between the hind legs – a dog's governing codes for behavior – are bound up with cues that are particular to other canines. Even the exploratory snuffle of a canine nose performs something akin to empirical investigation.

And yet, Woolf also imagines a canine appreciation of beauty too. As Barrett-Browning records reveling in "the exquisite, almost visionary scenery of the Apennines, the wonderful variety of shape and colour," Woolf notes that both the baby and Flush "felt none of this stimulus,"[114] refusing to make the distinction one of merely human versus nonhuman, but instead the capacity of each body in relation to vision, whether it be the baby's near-sightedness or Flush's primary perception of scent over sight. Yet while maturity may be needed to improve the baby's appreciation of beauty, the mature Flush already possesses it, just within his own realm:

> Beauty, so it seems at least, had to be crystallised into a green or violet powder and puffed down the fringed channels that lay behind his nostrils before it touched Flush's senses; and then it issued not in words, but in a silent rapture.[115]

Accurately describing the anatomy of the dog's highly developed olfactory lobe with its great interlaced or "fringed" network of over two-hundred and twenty million sensory receptors in comparison to the mere five million possessed by the human body, Woolf translates the appreciation of smell to a synesthetic painter's palate of artistic odor. There is no "superior" appreciation of beauty here, but rather different yet equally analogous modes of registering it.

Paradoxically, Woolf's analogies are rooted in a biological understanding of difference. This approach is evident in her earnest efforts to distinguish Flush's perceptions of events from how they would be ascertained through the more limited sensory capacities of her human characters. Dan Wylie, one of the critics interested in Woolf's rendering of animal consciousness, demotes these references as instances where experience "still has to be translated in human terms,"[116] as if this constitutes a defect. Yet it is the effort of the translation that highlights the inadequacy of human language. Her assertion, "Not a single one of his myriad sensations ever submitted itself to the deformity of words"[117] like the "words with short wings for their heavy body of meaning"[118] in "Kew Gardens," betrays the limit of language to delve into the full pungency of embodied life, whether it be human sensory experience or what she imagines is a dog's richly odiferous world. Derek Ryan, who follows the markers of different theoretical paths, investigating how "Miss Barrett's becoming-animal is not a matter of her growing a tail, nor is Flush's becoming-other a matter of walking on two legs"[119] still arrives at a similar conclusion: "In emphasizing the inadequacies of language and suggesting that it is not a necessary component of close companion species bonding, Woolf posits the animal's apparent lack of speech as not in fact a lack at all."[120] To put this in literary terms described by Daston and Mitman, she isn't enacting anthropomorphism as much as striving for zoomorphism: "The yearning to understand what it would be like to be, say, an elephant or a cheetah scrambles the opposition between anthropomorphism and zoomorphism, that is between humanizing animals and animalizing humans."[121] Woolf's nephew, Quentin Bell, denotes an imaginative effort on Woolf's part that exemplifies the best kind of anthropomorphism: "*Flush* is not so much a book by a dog lover as a book by someone who would love to be a dog."[122] Woolf only has human words, but she juxtaposes them in unexpected ways with how she might imagine culture or society and personal interaction were she in a dog's skin. In this way, the blending of fiction and biography becomes an interdisciplinary method for exploring possibilities of consciousness and subjectivity through embodied knowledge and information that touches the boundaries of what humans know. David Herman considers this hybridity of genre central to what he calls "zoonarratological"[123] writing: "Woolf thus uses modernist methods of narration to resituate the practice of biography in a transspecies context, revealing the extent to which life writing necessarily becomes entangled with the broader endeavor of writing life – the endeavor of documenting and engaging the nonhuman as well as human ways of encountering the world."[124] From this perspective, the novel is therefore less about satirizing the nonhuman animal than it is about revealing the restrictive conventions upon which human communication hinges. And with those differences acknowledged, making a human attempt at imagining what might be behind that door-flap of canine subjectivity.

Remarkably, Flush's better qualities are not limited to his physical attributes of scent and touch. Woolf fictionalizes a heightened capacity for empathy on the part of Flush in comparison with her human characters. Describing Flush's attentiveness to his first owner, she writes:

> Flush, as his story proves, had an even excessive appreciation of human emotions. The sight of his dear mistress snuffing the fresh air at last, letting it ruffle her hair and redden the natural freshness of her face, while the lines on her huge brow smoothed themselves out, excited him to gambols whose wildness was half sympathy with her own delight.[125]

The ruffled "hair" and smoothed wrinkles are features that could be equally recognizable as an expression of canine pleasure and release, but there is no hint that either of Flush's human companions is sensitive to his manifestations of emotions. Although Ryan argues that Miss Barrett's "becoming-animal" allows her to "recognise and respond to the violence enacted against her companion species"[126] when Flush is dognapped, my reading of her reaction is quite the opposite. When Flush is stolen by fanciers who specialize in bribing wealthy pet owners, Woolf stresses Barrett's inability to appreciate what Flush might be going through. Flush's captivity is terrifying: "The room was dark. It grew steadily hotter and hotter; the smell, the heat, were unbearable; Flush's nose burnt; his coat twitched. And still Miss Barrett did not come."[127] Miss Barrett's capacity for empathy seems limited in comparison to Flush: "Miss Barrett lay on her sofa at Wimpole Street. She was vexed; she was worried, but she was not seriously alarmed. Of course Flush would suffer; he would whine and bark all night; but it was only a question of a few hours."[128] Five days of starvation and dehydration pass before a proxy (not Barrett) finally arrives to collect Flush. When he gets back home, he experiences something that resembles human shellshock as his mind throws him back to the sounds of his frightful abduction: "As he lay dazed and exhausted on the sofa at Miss Barrett's feet the howls of tethered dogs, the screams of birds in terror still sounded in his ears."[129] Barrett's disappointment at Flush's less than enthusiastic response at being released back to her shows a similar inattentiveness to the dog's own needs. Woolf's fictional narration offers another reason for Flush's inattention to her that the character of Barrett doesn't consider – the dog's basic thirst commands his first priority upon return. In the words of Craig Smith, this shows how "the conventional human expectation of creatures who are created for our pleasure is unmasked here as a failure of human empathy."[130] Yet the real Barrett-Browning's literary career attests to her concern for others; "The Cry of the Children" is devoted to exposing the cruelty of child labor practices and rails against the horrors she empathetically imagines they experience. Further, as Barrett-Browning's letters indicate and Woolf dramatizes, she defied not only her father, but also Robert Browning in deciding to meet the thieves' demands and pay the ransom for Flush's life. Woolf sympathized with the personal challenges that Barrett-Browning faced,[131] so it is doubtful that she would intend to malign her personally. Instead, by using such a well-intentioned human subject, the inability to fully extend empathetic reasoning to the motivations and intentions of nonhuman animals in this crucial moment of need seems less attached to Barrett-Browning as an individual, and more indicative of a shortcoming of humans in general.

However, these human and nonhuman dynamics, while not merely extended metaphors for relationships between humans, do bear on similar patterns that are embedded in the infrastructure of human relations. The class structure of society and the superficial assumptions of cultural bias are factors that play a prominent part in the novel's critique not only of how humans treat nonhuman animals, but also of how they regard other humans. Flush, who is both a dog and an aristocrat due to his breeding, participates in social stratification:

> Dogs therefore, Flush began to suspect, differ; some are high, others low; and his suspicions were confirmed by snatches of talk held in passing with the dogs of Wimpole Street. 'See that scallywag? A mere mongrel! . . . By gad, that's a fine Spaniel. One of the best blood in Britain!'[132]

This passage enacts a hierarchy that is culturally conditioned rather than biologically determined. Anna Snaith comments, "By attributing the 'bestial' view of Whitechapel to an aristocratic *dog*, Woolf exposes the ridiculousness of the hierarchies."[133] Revealingly, the clues Flush uses to assess how status is ascertained – "Some take their airings in carriages and drink from purple jars"[134] – are the same kind of shallow monikers that stuff the society columns. Although I disagree with Jutta Ittner's assessment that Flush has "no agency of his own" and "all the different layers of this anthropomorphic construct are human,"[135] her attention to the way in which Flush's oppression is a particularized critique of

Victorian society is keen: "Miss Barrett's efforts to 'refine and educate [the puppy's] powers' comments on a society that tried to turn little 'savages' into obedient citizens. Like a young child, the eager puppy measures himself against the idealized parent, yet even the most talented animal will never make the grade."[136] Woolf does seem to aim her satirical bite on the rigid gender, class, and race constructs of Victorian society. Even Elizabeth Barrett, who in some ways lives an upper-class life of ease in comparison to those living just a few streets away and thus is in a position of power and privilege in regards to class, is still herself a victim of oppression in other measurements of Victorian paternalism and gendered expectation: "Elizabeth's life may not look problematic, living as she does in a rich house on Wimpole Street, yet she is in actuality stifled in the dark."[137] In other passages Woolf likens her confinement to that of a pet on a leash or a caged animal: "She could not go out. She was chained to the sofa. 'A bird in a cage would have as good a story,' she wrote, as she had."[138] Woolf also draws a comparison between farm animals and humans forced to live in squalor: "Yet how could one describe politely a bedroom in which two or three families lived above a cow-shed, when the cow-shed had no ventilation, when cows were milked and killed and eaten under the bedroom?"[139] The problem of human indifference toward both other humans and animals of other species is criticized. The degradation of humans has historically been reinforced through comparison to nonhuman animals:

> Arguments for human specialness have regularly been utilized by human groups to justify the exploitation not just of other organisms, but of other *humans* as well (other nations, other races, or simply the 'other' sex); armed with such arguments, one had only to demonstrate that these others were not *fully* human, or were 'closer to the animals' in order to establish one's right of dominion.[140]

Making these parallels in the context of a novel about a dog, however, has the effect of deriding, rather than reinforcing, assumptions of superiority. If the reader can readily appreciate how Flush is harmed by Barrett-Browning's erroneous presuppositions about his life, the deliberate silencing of the suffering of humans who can communicate through shared language becomes shamefully acute. *Flush* discerns the ways in which the upper class is often mistaken in their assumptions about their servants. In a note to the text, Woolf quotes one of Barrett-Browning's letters praising the bravery and boldness of her maid, Wilson, in coming with her to Italy in defiance of her father. Woolf surmises that Wilson may have had little choice but to follow her employer:

It is worth, parenthetically, dwelling for a second on the extreme precariousness of a servant's life. If Wilson had not gone with Miss Barrett, she would have been, as Miss Barrett knew, 'turned into the street before sunset,' with only a few shillings, presumably, saved from her sixteen pounds a year. And what then would have been her fate?[141]

Snaith astutely points out that the class dynamics have implications for Woolf as well: "[Woolf] has the power to bring lives up from the basement: to make lives for Flush and Wilson."[142] Although Woolf conscientiously draws attention to Wilson's plight, and remonstrates that "The life of Lily Wilson is extremely obscure and thus cries out for the services of a biographer,"[143] Woolf seems to beg the question of why she chose to write this biography about Flush instead of Wilson.

One possible rejoinder is that the nonhuman focus allows for a more persuasive assessment of discrimination as a cultural construction. Both Flush and Barrett-Browning thrive in the more democratic atmosphere of Italy. In Florence, "Flush faced the curious and at first upsetting truth that the laws of the Kennel Club are not universal. . . . He had revised his code accordingly. . . . He was the friend of all the world now. All dogs were his brothers."[144] Flush's previous illusion regarding the fixed status of particular breeds is shattered – such hierarchies among and between species are not innate, they are the creation of a particularly English sense of social propriety. Haraway underscores the significance of the kennel pure-breed within human market systems:

> The state, private corporations, research institutions, and clubs all played their roles in moving practices for controlling animal reproduction from pockets of memory and local endeavors of both elites and working people to rationalized national and international markets tied to registries. The breeding system that evolved with the data-keeping system was called scientific breeding, and in myriad ways this paper-plus-flesh system is behind the histories of eugenics and genetics, as well as other sciences (and politics) of animal and human reproduction. [145]

The ways in which interactions between humans and nonhumans have both been shaped by human cultural systems and have been used to justify the suppression of humans within the system as well are inextricably bound; Woolf's text, while playful, still represents the traces of these shared narratives.

Not only are dogs liberated from the strictures of breeding class in Italy, but Flush also shows signs of enjoying personal freedoms in relation to humans: "He had no need of a chain in this new world; he had no need of protection. If Mr. Browning was late in going for his walk – he and Flush

were the best of friends now – Flush boldly summoned him."[146] All
hierarchies, including the gulf between humans and "lower" animals, have
been turned on their heads as Flush now "summon[s]" the human. These
are the same attributes of a more fully inflected reciprocal relationship
between humans and domesticated animals as described by Vicki Hearne
as she envisions mutual calling and teaching within the pet–owner relationship. The effect of the shared trajectory of Barrett-Browning's liberation and Flush's independence is simultaneously to model a better form
of mutual respect and companionability between species and to pose a
challenge to the entrenched conviction that humans, particularly the
British ruling class, are automatically entitled to priority over any econom-
ically stratified, racialized, or nationalized "other," human or nonhuman.
Yet, as Haraway reminds us, this correspondence should not be mistaken
for equivalency: "I resist the tendency to condemn all relations of instru-
mentality between animals and people as necessarily involving objectifica-
tion and oppression of a kind similar to the objectifications and
oppressions of sexism, colonialism, and racism."[147] As she defends the
productivity of certain kinds of systems and instrumentalities that construct human and nonhuman relations, she also implies that inequalities
between humans demand a more wholesale condemnation of any oppres-
sive prejudices. Yet, while it would be egregious to reduce all oppression to
direct equivalency, the nodes of correlation between different ways mastery
and oppression are enacted on humans, nonhumans, and landscapes is
relevant to deepening our understanding of the complexity of these
cultural practices and their impacts: "Sustainability is a mutual enterprise
that pertains as much to human social well-being as to the health of the
physical world. If they are at odds, it is only because of our failure to
consider their interdependencies."[148] The shared aspects of all forms of
oppression are significant to understanding the cultural biases and assumptions that underlie overlapping systems of control. As Scott even-handedly
notes, both problematic animal representations and more posthuman
moments of "think[ing] like a tree, thus crossing over green margins of
the species barrier"[149] exist in Woolf's biographical experience with and
literary treatment of different types of animals, including hens, horses,
pets, and fish, insects, and birds. Modernism's experimentation with ways
of representing interior subjectivity, here exemplified in Woolf's fiction,
complete with the messiness of its divergences within and between both
human and nonhuman characters as they move within and around the
same physical world – sometimes in shared commonality of feeling and
perception, and other times in misunderstanding and isolation – offer a

new form of manifesting the empathies and antagonisms that permeate the more-than-human world, whether it be in potent silences, shared glances, or the twittering sounds of intermingled human and nonhuman vocalization.

In Woolf's work it is not just the humans who get to analyze and claim dominion over the environment; nonhuman forces are equally capable of examining and hypothesizing about the human animal. The suggestive commonalities Woolf establishes between humans and nonhuman nature is often foundational to her political critique of empire. In "Thunder at Wembley" Woolf's subject is the dynamic interaction between humans, animals, and weather during the spring Exhibition of Empire in London, which she and Leonard toured in May 1924. The exhibition was a miniature version of the British empire that constructed a fiction of its own stewardship and benevolent interest in foreign territories, exemplifying DeLoughrey and Handley's observation that in many colonial representations, "naturalized others were likened to a construction of nature that was increasingly seen to require masculine European management."[150] Specifically, as Scott Cohen's research describes, the Exhibit of 1924 featured:

> A map of the world that could be strolled in a well-planned afternoon or over several days, as the official guide recommended. Every territory that could afford to build a pavilion had one at the exhibition. Along with the Palaces of Industry, Engineering, and Science, the largest structures were reserved for pavilions representing India, Canada, and Australia, each occupying about five acres. Wembley allowed visitors to inspect their empire, either while strolling the fifteen miles of roads named by Rudyard Kipling or riding in one of eighty-eight carriages circling the park on the Never-Stop Railway.[151]

Insidiously evocative of current amusement parks, the deliberate entertainment and story-telling function is evident in employing a famous adventure novelist and defender of the empire to name the exhibit's roads.

In contrast, Woolf is interested in narrating what *isn't* in the exhibit. Her story highlights England's solipsistic exclusion of all that doesn't programmatically reflect its unquestioned control. From the outset of "Thunder at Wembley," anything associated with nature is at odds with authority: "It is nature that is the ruin of Wembley; yet it is difficult to see what steps Lord Stevenson, Lieutenant-General Travers Clarke, and the Duke of Devonshire could have taken to keep her out."[152] Woolf satirically muses that "they might have eradicated the grass and felled the chestnut trees."[153] The verbs "eradicate" and "fell" suggest the violent action of war and overthrow, a prerequisite for the imperial control the exhibit is designed to exalt. DeLoughrey and Handley suggest the significance of subverting the rhetoric of colonial power by noting that "the self-conscious process of renaming and revisioning is a subversion of the colonial language of taxonomy, discipline and control."[154] Here, Woolf uses wild nature – moving freely within and across the exhibition as an agent of disruption – to recontextualize the assumptions of British superiority based on human notions of labeling and demarcation. Likewise, ecophenomenology and ecomaterialism rebuff the traditional view of human hierarchy; instead of being apart from or above other animals, humans are, as David Abram succinctly describes, "in the midst of, rather than on top of this order,"[155] a realization that must, as Serpil Oppermann puts it, "dehierarchize our conceptual categories that structure dualisms to reconfigure our social, cultural, and political practices."[156] While humans are in the process of observing and passing judgment on the life around them – as the British citizens are doing at the Exhibition of Empire – other animals are also scrutinizing human behavior. Consequently, the human species becomes the animal to be examined.

A crucial question about the British citizens in "The Thunder at Wembley" is posed by a bird: "And what, one asks, is the spell it lays upon them? How, with all this dignity of their own, can they bring themselves to believe in that?"[157] The bird is the agent questioning how these people could believe in "that," the supposed glories of imperial conquest. Woolf writes, "But this cynical reflection, at once so chill and superior, was made, of course, by the thrush."[158] Woolf endows the thrush with sentience and an ability to critique the human species. The choice of the thrush, in particular, has both literary and ecological relevance. As Hubert Zapf has pointed out, "birds especially are frequent dialogic others of poets and incarnate the transformative power of poetic discourse" as Woolf would know Keats so famously did in "Ode to a Nightingale." But the thrush also has a more particular ecological resonance as well. *Birds In London*, a book the Woolfs owned that was published the year Woolf was writing "Thunder at Wembley," details the precarious survival of the thrush as a result of human activity in the parks and the importation of exotic plants: "Of all these vanishing species the thrush is most to be regretted, on account of its beautiful, varied, and powerful voice.... In these vast gardens and parks ... there should be ample room for many scores of the delightful songsters that are now vanishing or have already vanished" due in part to planting "so many unsuitable exotic shrubs."[159] While Christina Alt does not mention this work specifically, she documents that its author, W.H. Hudson, was an influence on Woolf's depiction of the natural world: "Hudson's intermingling of the roles of ethologist and novelist suggested to Woolf the way in which the study of nature might serve as an analogy for the representation of life in fiction."[160] His influence here might have been more literal; the fact that this species is at risk due in part to the British importation of foreign plants – an act of power and domination that was done without full understanding of the wider ecological relationships involved and potentially motivated by a desire to use the "exotic shrubs" as objects displaying the reach of the British empire – makes the thrush a particularly appropriate commentator on the threat of the British colonial mindset to all its enterprises in controlling and placing plants and animals, both human and nonhuman. Furthermore, the "superior" thrush disrupts the chain of human hierarchy by articulating an insight that most people have not yet recognized about themselves. As Cohen notes, the people at the exhibit are both "readers" of the exhibit's tale of conquest, but they are also "characters"[161] manipulated by its carefully constructed layout as they walk through and play the role of gawking tourist. The titled authorities may think they can encapsulate the world in an exhibit based on English supremacy, but nature and the nonhuman can't be kept out. Other animals are equally, if not more perceptively, cognizant of the human specimens on display.

Woolf's empathy for the nonhuman perspective both reveals a resonant more-than-human world, and emphatically stresses the folly of humanity's exalted notions of its own importance. For Woolf, being in conversation with nonhuman creatures acknowledges collective community and expands literary representations of daily life. As Abram explains, "Ultimately, to acknowledge the life of the body, and to affirm our solidarity with this physical form, is to acknowledge our existence as one of the earth's animals, and so to remember and rejuvenate the organic basis of our thoughts and our intelligence."[162] Woolf's ability to make visible what often goes unseen and unspoken in the surrounding environment distinguishes her attempts to render a meaningful experience of human life.

The meaning of a more-than-human life in *To the Lighthouse*

Virginia Woolf's *To the Lighthouse* is traditionally understood as an elegiac commentary on the apocalyptic crisis of the First World War. An ecocritical reading of the novel shifts this tonal emphasis, acknowledging the dark impulses of death, but revealing the ever-present tension of isolation and community posed by the invigorating potential of embodied interaction with the encompassing environment. Embodied encounters with the natural world spur her characters' thoughts about their place in the larger world and reveal the unconscious bonds that sustain them. Indeed, Woolf's depiction of embodied life in a shared organic world generates the novel's ultimate affirmation, the creation of Lily Briscoe's art. The culmination of Lily's painting depends on an embodied participation in the "dictates" of the environmental forces that surround her. Throughout the novel, Nonhuman creatures and nature are depicted as having distinct lives, not necessarily invested in human concerns, and yet they participate in and respond to the same events and stimuli. *To the Lighthouse* rejects a romantic "oneness" – a belief that nature exists to serve humans or mirror their emotions – in favor of this kind of intertwining. An ecophenomenological reading of *To the Lighthouse* complicates conventional readings of the novel that treat nature as primarily antagonistic to humanity, or as an agent of apocalyptic destruction; instead environmental presences in the novel also compete with these registers to suggest the creativity and rejuvenation that come from acknowledging humans as creatures embedded in a more-than-human world.

Critical appraisals of the "Time Passes" section of the novel – which informs the reader of the death of primary characters by means of bracketed asides while the organic changes taking place in the neglected seaside home constitute the main action – commonly assume that despair and ruin are the primary themes. Christine Froula's analysis claims that "Time Passes" "evokes a world emptied of life," "a world lapsed out of meaning," and "foreshadows death's oblivion"[163] and that only the human presence of the narrator and Mrs. McNab can "make stay against destruction and beckon the seeker back to a life that is enough, an art that arrests nature's flux."[164] An ecocritical reading adds another interpretive layer to these readings, suggesting that the imagined destruction of the Ramsay home, had it not been rescued by Mrs. McNab, offers several images that can be seen as comforting or beautiful and that rather than human art arresting nature's flux, nature's flux is sometimes crucial to the very formation of the human creative act. Froula acknowledges that Woolf and Lily's art reveres the natural world and seeks to record the mystery of its everyday significance, but assumes artistic creativity is ultimately separate from and oppositional to the rhythms of nature: "rather than copy nature, abstraction strives to evoke the (imperceptible, unrepresentable) 'thing itself' as it exists beyond the organic world of time, death, and decay."[165] Similarly, Julia Briggs declares, "'Time Passes' is a rhapsody upon time, death and endings."[166] Though death, emptiness, and a grief over human mortality are certainly important aspects of the novel, ecocritical attention to Woolf's efforts to depict the nonhuman world in this section of the novel suggests that those impulses are simultaneously infused with the potential for nonhuman life to provide alternate conceptions of continuity and joy. Although Louise Westling writes primarily on *Between the Acts* in "Virginia Woolf and the Flesh of the World," she offers a provocative contrasting analysis of "Time Passes" by pinpointing the source of "tragedy" as emanating from a realization that "centuries of humanist assumptions are overturned."[167] This revelation may be startling for readers, but it is ultimately productive for ushering in a new appreciation of other diverse forms of life. I contend that Woolf's vision of human experience depends on a dialectic that has despair and loss as one pole, but unity and hope as the other. The positive register requires readers to embrace an embodied life that presumes humans have value not only for their individual accomplishments deemed important by human society, but also as part of a larger community of daily miracles, fluctuation, change, and continuation. Laura Doyle has helpfully pointed the way toward acknowledging the importance of embodiment in *To the Lighthouse* arguing, "Woolf corporealizes the spaces rendered empty by patriarchal culture and thought" and "situates the mother strategically at the center of this power-inflected intercorporeality."[168] However, Doyle's emphasis on the tension between patriarchal philosophy and maternal phenomenology in the novel is too constrictive. First, it obscures how Lily Briscoe revises Mrs. Ramsay's perspective by unifying light and dark, a detail that suggests that the mother is not the most important figure in the text. Second, it neglects Mr. Bankes' capacity for embodied appreciation, a trait that resists gendering phenomenal awareness. My reading builds on Doyle's recognition of embodiment in the novel, but extends beyond her interest in gender codes to suggest ecophenomenology's significance for understanding the novel's larger theme of embracing the potential of change and uncertainty as a source of creativity and renewal.

Although Woolf's interest in eulogizing her own family lends biographical credence to the novel's darker impulses,[169] biography also hints at a balance between loss and rejuvenation. Woolf's relationship with Vita Sackville-West was ongoing while she was writing *To the Lighthouse*. Sackville-West's *Country Notes* (1939) express a belief in renewal that correlates with Woolf's representations of nature's persistency:

> I suppose the pleasure of the country life lies really in the eternally renewed evidences of the determination to live. That is a truism when said, but anything but a truism when daily observed ... The small green shoot

appearing one day at the base of a plant one had feared dead, brings a comfort and an encouragement for which the previous daily observance is responsible. The life principle has proved unconquerable, then, in spite of frost and winds? The powers of resistance against adversity are greater than we thought; the germ of life lies hidden even in the midst of apparent death. A cynic might contend that nothing depressed him more than this resoluteness to keep going; it depends on the angle from which you regard this gallant tenacity... If you have a taste for such things, no amount of repetition can stale them; they stand for permanence in a changing world.[170]

Sackville-West's "angle" on the world offers a perspective that recasts "permanence" as the promise of perpetual change – the months of noting the absence of the "small green shoot" are necessary for creating the ensuing feelings of "comfort" and "encouragement" when it breaks the ground again. The "tenacity" Sackville-West's essay affirms in these natural cycles of the "life ... hidden in the midst of apparent death" resemble the "thistle thrust[ing] itself between the tiles of larder" in "Time Passes."

Woolf's own memories on the anniversary of her mother's death are capped by an immersion in an embodied consideration of nature's capacity for stimulating something new. A diary entry from May 5, 1924, the 29th anniversary of Julia Stephen's death, describes Woolf's recollection of herself as a thirteen-year-old girl in the presence of her mother's dead body, laughing uncomfortably behind her hand as the nurses sobbed. The entry transitions from this memory to a contemplation of life and nature:

> But enough of death – it is life that matters. We came back from Rodmell 7 days ago, after a royal Easter which Nelly survived heroically. After weeding I had to go in out of the sun; and how the quiet lapped me round! and then how dull I got, to be quite just: and how the beauty brimmed over me and steeped my nerves till they quivered, as I have seen a water plant quiver when the water overflowed it. (This is not right, but I must one day express that sensation).[171]

The movement from a consideration of death to writing about a quietness that bursts unexpectedly into beauty that "steeped [her] nerves till they quivered" like a plant receiving water expresses a tight oscillation between the impulses of loss and life. The "life that matters" still comes through. The way it makes itself known comes from a submersion into stillness, a giving over to the atmosphere of solitude around her that rewards her patience with inspiration. In terms of Merleau-Ponty's ecophenomenology, one might say that Woolf "obtains [from embodied reverie] not an *answer* but a confirmation of its astonishment."[172] The fact that she can't find the right words to express the experience attests to the difficulty of capturing embodied revelation in prose, yet doesn't negate the sensation of being subsequently renewed by the unexpected encounter.

Similar instances of embodied revelation comprise many pivotal moments of silent communication in *To the Lighthouse*. Lily acts "with all her senses quickened as they were,"[173] and "Mr. Bankes was alive to things which would not have struck him had not those sandhills revealed to him the body of his friendship" with Mr. Ramsay.[174] Merleau-Ponty explains that consciousness is always filtered through our physical experience of being bodies in the world: "As for consciousness, it has to be conceived, no longer as a constituting consciousness and, as it were, a pure being-for-itself, but as a *perceptual* consciousness, as the subject pattern of behavior, as being-in-the-world or existence."[175] The inner consciousness isn't solipsistic or enclosed, but exists in relationship with the physical environment. Or, as Karan Barad puts it, "[w]e do not obtain knowledge by standing outside of the world; we know because 'we' are of the world."[176] Woolf composes long passages to put these links between world and mind into words, as in this scene describing Lily Briscoe and Mr. Bankes' shared experience of the seaside:

> They came there regularly every evening as if drawn by some need. It was as if the water floated out and set sailing thoughts which had grown stagnant on dry land, and gave to their bodies even some sort of physical relief. First, the pulse of colour flooded the bay with blue, and the heart expanded with it and the body swam, only the next instant to be checked and chilled by the prickly blackness on the ruffled waves. Then, up behind the great black rock, almost every evening spurted irregularly, so that one had to watch for it and it was a delight when it came, a fountain of pure water . . . They both felt a common hilarity excited by the moving waves; and then by the swift cutting race of a sailboat, which, having sliced a curve in the bay, stopped; shivered; let its sails drop down; and then, with a natural impulse to complete the picture, after this swift movement, both of them looked at the dunes far away, and instead of merriment felt come over them some sadness – because the thing was completed partly, and partly because distant views seem to outlast by a million years (Lily thought) the gazer and to be communing already with a sky which beholds an earth entirely at rest.[177]

This passage explicitly engages the minds of Lily and Mr. Bankes, who are "drawn" to the vibrant scene through their perceiving bodies. Looking and feeling together in simultaneous rhythms with the landscape, their shared thoughts are set in motion in accordance with the movement of the ships on the water. The blueness of the sky "expands" the "heart" yet in the next instant the cold sea-salted air "checks" and "chills" the body. The description is unique, as Abram reminds us, "Even today, we rarely acknowledge the local presence of the atmosphere as it swirls between two persons" but instead relegate it to "empty space."[178] Woolf insists on the fingering "airs" both here and in "Time Passes" as well as their ability to "expand," lift and carry, or "check," disturb and disintegrate. These varying responses to divergent environmental prompts are also seen when the characters react with "hilarity" to the thrill of erratic bursts of water and then experience feelings of sadness produced by gazing toward the dunes. The view of the dunes isn't necessarily at odds with the "merriment" of the sea scene. Instead, it is "a natural impulse to complete the picture" that prompts the viewers to look toward the distant dunes. This swaying of perspectives will recur when Mr. Ramsey, James, and Cam sail to the lighthouse in the third section of the novel, causing Lily to muse upon the effects of distance and individual perspective. Both of these poles are necessary for a "complete" understanding of place and people.

As with Woolf's diary entry, the sensations produced in Lily and Mr. Bankes don't lead to a resolution as much as they provoke wonder. In the words of Merleau-Ponty, this kind of embodied participation in viewing the natural world and appreciating its palpable presence suggests the potential of the environment to exist in and for itself, beyond human control, even as it is perceived through the human body:

> As I contemplate the blue of the sky I am not set over against it as an acosmic subject; I do not possess it in thought, or spread out towards it in some idea of blue such as might reveal the secret of it, I abandon myself to it and plunge into this mystery, it 'thinks itself within me', I am the sky itself as it is drawn together and unified, and as it begins to exist for itself; my consciousness is saturated with this limitless blue. But, it may be retorted, the sky is not mind and there is surely no sense in saying that it exists for itself. It is indeed true that the geographer's or the astronomer's sky does not exist for itself. But of the sky, as it is perceived or sensed, subtended by my gaze which ranges over and resides in it, and providing as it does the theatre of a certain living pulsation adopted by my body, it can be said that it exists for itself.[179]

The fact that the sky, or the view, acts upon the human attests to the agency of the nonhuman world. The reaction is registered both physically through the "living pulsation adopted by my body" and mentally as the sky "thinks itself within me" and "saturates" human thought. Eco-materialists Serenella Iovino and Serpil Oppermann similarly describe the experience of color as a complex nexus of body and physics – "Resulting from the coevolution of organism and light, the eye is a biological prism. Like in all things biological, this interaction is organized differently in all living species. We humans see a spectrum that dogs perceive less vividly, and bees see colors that we humans can only imagine"[180] – as contact surfaces of light and reception remind us that our understanding is always only a partial register of a constantly present world of matter and material. This same nonhuman agency and intertwined body–mind response characterizes Woolf's depictions of human characters reacting to their environment.

The way impulses and moods ripple across the water, land, and Lily and Mr. Banks are suggestive of a shared consciousness not stimulated by any one being, but cocreated. Wendy Wheeler explains, "We learn that 'mind' cannot be understood simply as mental events going on inside individual heads; it is, powerfully and *really*, in our bodies, in the world, and in other people. Subjectivity is intersubjectivity."[181] Woolf composes such rhythms of intersubjectivity throughout her fiction, such as *Between the Acts* where Woolf directs the reader to "Look and listen. See the flowers, how they ray their redness, whiteness, silverness and blue. And the trees with their many-tongued syllabling, their green and yellow leaves hustle us and shuffle us, and bid us, like starlings, and the rooks, come together, crowd together, to chatter and make merry while the red cow moves forward and the black cow stands still,"[182] or in "The Death of the Moth" where "The same energy which inspired the rooks, the ploughmen, the horses, and even, it seemed, the lean bare-backed downs, sent the moth fluttering from side to side of his square of the window-pane."[183] Indeed, one might even stitch these moments of intersubjectivity to intertextuality as the leaves' "many tongued syllabling" recalls how Mrs. Ramsay intuits the lyrics, "And all the lives we ever lived and all the lives to be are fully of trees and changing leaves" as arising from some logos of the world mingling with the song: "The words (she was looking out the window) sounded as if they were floating like flowers on water out there, cut off from them all, as if no one had said them, but they had come into existence of themselves," perhaps not recognizing, as Lily will when she completes her painting, that the dictates are emanating from the impulses of the organic environment, which are not "cut off" or "no one," just as the atmosphere between Lily and Mr. Bankes is not "empty." Additionally, the significance of the moth's participation in the impulses to movement and stillness in the swells of energy that roll from the plough and the animals outside, suggest the frame for the lives that beat against invisible thresholds that may open upon understanding in "The Window" section of *To the Lighthouse*.

Repeatedly, Woolf's representations invest the environment with its own agency, a sentient power that human characters only occasionally sense in their own "moments of being" – the reverberations made manifest in art, song, and language, when humans take the time to look, listen and let the sky "think itself within me."

Part of humanity's experience in a world not fully regulated by human control is the pull between alternating surges of loss and joy. The novel's phenomenal aspects create the positive tensions that many critics overlook. Mrs. Ramsay's response to the pulsing beams of the lighthouse illuminates the novel's revolving emotions of loss and discovery. Woolf depicts Mrs. Ramsay's embodied perception – based on "sound" and "sight" – of the lighthouse and the sea:

> Always, Mrs. Ramsay felt, one helped oneself out of solitude reluctantly by laying hold of some little odd or end, some sound, some sight. She listened but it was all very still; cricket was over; the children were in their baths; there was only the sound of the sea. She stopped knitting; she held the long reddish-brown stocking dangling in her hands a moment. She saw the light again. With some irony in her interrogation, for when one woke at all one's relations changed, she looked at the steady light, the pitiless, the remorseless, which was so much her, so little her, which had her at its beck and call (she woke in the night and saw it bent across their bed, stroking the floor), but for all that she thought, watching it with fascination, hypnotized, as if it were stroking with its silver fingers some sealed vessel in her brain whose bursting would flood her with delight, she had known happiness, exquisite happiness, intense happiness, and it silvered the rough waves a little more brightly ... It is enough! It is enough![184]

Once again, stillness and attentiveness precede revelation. Mrs. Ramsay questions, an "interrogation," but receives differing impulses or "answers," the result of "when one woke" or the state of becoming conscious of surrounding stimuli in a new way. She identifies with the light, but also distances herself from it, acknowledging that it is still somehow different from her. The light alternatively inspires reflections of that which is "pitiless" or "remorseless" and that which gives, through a direct physical interaction of "stroking" the brain, an intense "delight." As Laura Doyle notes, the image is infused with female sexual innuendo,[185] a point which, I argue, also emphasizes the intimacy of the human and nonhuman interaction. Further this physical and "phenomenological interaction with the expanse of that which is beyond the human" can prompt "inquisitive openness to new pleasures."[186] Patricia Morgne Cramer reminds readers that Woolf's use of lesbian imagery derives from her appreciation of earlier romantic conventions: "Like Plato, Dante, and other authors of idealist love traditions, Woolf aims to reshape the collective (female) erotic imagination, not to retell or even reinvent lesbian-love plots about couples"[187] One of the ways Woolf reframes collective lesbian desire is through imagining alternative modes of erotic encounter with nature. As Derek Ryan also surmises, "Where the sexual politics of Woolf's novels are concerned, then, the lines of becoming shared between human and non-human are crucial."[188] Mrs. Ramsay's surrender to the stimulus presented by her surroundings – the crickets, the sea, the light across the floor – stirs new impulses of desire and satisfaction.

This understanding of the world as an agent that interacts with humans on an embodied level, rather than something inanimate that humans control, expresses the divergence between the other characters' experiences of reality and Mr. Ramsay's adherence to a philosophical reduction of reality. Mr. Ramsay's quest to get from "Q" to "R" in the scheme of human achievement represents a methodological hierarchy that can be teleologically comprehended as a predictable progression. It assumes that knowledge exists on a mental plane manipulated by human thought and detached from embodied experience. The epitome of this detachment is expressed in Andrew Ramsey's efforts to explain his father's philosophy to Lily by giving her the following directive: "Think of a kitchen table ... when you're not there."[189] The ridiculousness of this kind of philosophy is exposed when Lily imagines the table: "with a painful effort of concentration, she focused her mind, not upon the silver-bossed bark of the tree, or upon its fish-shaped leaves, but upon a phantom kitchen table, one of those scrubbed board tables, grained and knotted, whose virtue seems to have been laid bare by years of muscular integrity, which stuck there, its four legs in air."[190] The upside-down table is a bit farcical, or as Westling writes, "thoroughly satiric."[191] Its position is completely at odds with the function of a table. Lily's thoughts gravitate toward the kinds of details that make the table a physical entity – it is "scrubbed," "grained and knotted," and possesses a structural "integrity." While it is unclear exactly what Andrew's instructions were meant to make Lily comprehend, Lily tries to place the table in the material world. By seeing it in a tree, she implicitly associates the table with its natural source – not the human mind, but the organic life of the tree's living wood. Lily interprets the kitchen table as a new materialist might "in which all life forms and matter exhibit a kind of incipient self-articulation that communicate via internal relations."[192] As Lily comprehends it, the image of the table still expresses its origins and the process by which it was metamorphosed into a structure that humans use to chop, recombine, and prepare to feast on other, edible, matter. Mr. Ramsey imagines the tree as an implement of thought, while Lily, thinking through the perspective of the wood, sees written in the grains and knots, the thing "entire." While at least one critic has used Woolf's skeptical view of philosophy to argue that any application of a philosophical theory to her work is deleterious,[193] Merleau-Ponty's embodied philosophy is also at odds with the kind of philosophy that Woolf mocks in *To the Lighthouse*. Abram explains how Merleau-Ponty's philosophy relies on an engagement with the world rather than a detachment from it:

> By disclosing the body itself as the very subject of awareness, Merleau-Ponty demolishes any hope that philosophy might eventually provide a complete picture of reality (for any such total account of 'what is' requires a mind or consciousness that stands somehow *outside* of existence, whether to compile the account or, finally, to receive and comprehend it). Yet by this same move he opens, at last, the possibility of a truly authentic phenomenology, a philosophy which would strive, not to explain the world as if from outside, but to give voice to the world from our experienced situation *within* it, recalling us to our participation in the here-and-now, rejuvenating our sense of wonder at the fathomless things, events and powers that surround us on every hand.[194]

Embodied phenomenology, in fact, affirms the values inherent in Woolf's retort. The "complete picture of reality" that ecophenomenology rebuffs coincides with the image of an alphabet, discrete units that can be known from beginning to end, or A to Z. Both Merleau-Ponty and Woolf reject totalizing theories. The mind can't be severed from reality or understood by visualizing an object without any relation to the human perceiver. Instead, Merleau-Ponty and Woolf advance an understanding of humans "within" the world – a coexistence that "rejuvenat[es] our sense of wonder" at that which remains undefinable and dynamically evasive.

Communal awareness and interconnectivity are key themes in one of the novel's most memorable scenes, the dinner party. Ecophenomenological awareness of the atmosphere creates an undercurrent of unity in these passages – bodies sharing the same space participate in a positive moment of connection between individuals. Initially, everyone is separate and feels acutely isolated: "Nothing seemed to have merged. They all sat separate";[195] "Lily felt that something was lacking; Mr. Bankes felt something was lacking. Pulling her shawl round her Mrs. Ramsay felt that something was lacking."[196] Mrs. Ramsay feels a responsibility to draw these individuals together, and so "giving herself the little shake that one gives a watch that has stopped, the old familiar pulse began beating, as the watch begins ticking – one, two, three, one, two, three. And so on and so on, she repeated, listening to it, sheltering and fostering the still feeble pulse as one might guard a weak flame with a newspaper."[197] Here Woolf's prose also participates in the merging by fusing together a myriad of symbols. She combines the watch (a potential patriarchal object of measured control in the form of Paul Rayley's pocket-watch that Mrs. Ramsay admires), a symbol of individual human lives passing, with the three pulses of the lighthouse. The lighthouse, in turn, is also associated with the feeble flame of protection that Mrs. Ramsay has felt as a fleeting joy that makes the effort of life worthwhile. However, the flame also alludes to the lighting of the centerpiece candles, which inaugurate an atmosphere of unity:

> Now all the candles were lit up and the faces on both sides of the table were brought nearer by the candlelight, and composed, as they had not been in the twilight, into a party round a table, for the night was now shut off by panes of glass, which, far from giving any accurate view of the outside world, rippled it so strangely that here, inside the room, seemed to be order and dry land; there, outside, a reflection in which things waved and vanished, waterily. Some change at once went through them all, as if this had really happened, and they were all conscious of making a party together in a hollow, on an island, had their common cause against that fluidity out there.[198]

The atmosphere of the room is changed by the flames waving against the black windowpanes. Now there is a unity among the individuals at the table, forming a kind of protective center, but the word "island" also recalls the unity of Britain itself. This is the kind of stability that Mrs. Ramsay wishes to keep, the promise of a center of light that doesn't disappear and reappear in rhythmic beats, but rather emanates, through the power of human effort, light without end. The room itself is described as the lamp of the lighthouse: the candles are the source of focusing light "compos [ing]" the party and shining out through panes of glass that "rippled," creating "a reflection in which things waved and vanished, waterily." Thus, the dinner scene is transformed into one of the novel's visions of the lighthouse. However, this vision of solidarity will be challenged by the proliferation of other perspectives on the lighthouse and its significance. Transitoriness is fundamental to the dinner party – perishable food is consumed, candles burn down, everyone will finally rise and depart. Yet these diminishments are part of what gives the meal its poignancy and value.

The presence of a variety of points of view on the same object is also a unifying feature of the scene, as we will see at the end of the novel with multiple perspectives on the lighthouse itself. The glow of the candles illumines another artistic bringing together, Rose's fruit arrangement, making shadows and hollows of color on the table "like a world in which one could take one's staff and climb hills [Mrs. Ramsay] thought."[199] She notices Augustus Carmichael looking too, but "plunging in" and "breaking off a tassle there," which was "his way of looking, different from hers. But looking together united them."[200] Merleau-Ponty elucidates the alchemy of such unity: "Private worlds communicate" because each is "a variant of one common world."[201] It is only though our shared experience in the same phenomenal world that we can begin to identify truths that can be shared by all: "It is the same world that contains our bodies and our minds ... which connects our perspectives, permits transition from one to the other."[202] The shared experience of eating the food, being encompassed in the light emanating from the center of the table, and gazing upon the creations placed on it, are part of the atmosphere that allows for the "private worlds" of each individual to "communicate."

Between "The Window" and "The Lighthouse" sections of the novel, Woolf inserts "Time Passes," a narration of the changes that occur to the summer home during ten years of the family's absence, including the timespan of the First World War. Yet even the presence of war is alluded to in the first section of the novel. While Mrs. Ramsay is reading to her son James, she hears:

> Suddenly a loud cry, as of a sleep-walker, half-roused, something about
> Stormed at with shot and shell
> Sung out with the utmost intensity in her ear, made her turn apprehensively.[203]

The line "Stormed at with shot and shell" creates a break in the prose, appearing off by itself, as if a bomb has ripped through the paragraph. It anticipates visually the shelling that will kill one of the Ramsays' sons during the war: "[A shell exploded. Twenty or thirty young men were blown up in France, among them Andrew Ramsay, whose death, mercifully, was instantaneous]."[204] Like the offset type above, the brackets segregate this section of text, encapsulating the sentences in a way that both treats them as an insignificant aside and also emphasizes the suddenness of disaster – the explosive revelations are packed into the casing of the brackets. "Stormed at with shot and shell" is a line from a Tennyson poem that Mr. Ramsay is reciting, "Charge of the Light Brigade." So this evocation of a Victorian colonial military disaster ironically presages the carnage of the First World War. These textual repetitions create an ecophenomenological sense that humans are already synchronized with a larger repeating rhythm of the world:

> Every sensation carries within it the germ of a dream or depersonalization such as we experience in that quasi-stupor to which we are reduced when we try to live at the level of sensation . . . Each time I experience a sensation, I feel that it concerns not my own being, the one for which I am responsible and for which I make decisions, but another self which has already sided with the world, which is already open to certain aspects and synchronized with them.[205]

Mrs. Ramsay's apprehension at hearing her husband's unexplained shout of interruption is not only a reaction to the moment, but also an instinct of fear that goes beyond herself in the present moment and carries with it an awareness of some impending potential harm. The reference to "a loud cry, as of a sleep-walker, half-roused" also foreshadows Mr. Ramsay's grief at the death of his wife, another event revealed in "Time Passes": "[Mr. Ramsay, stumbling along a passage one dark morning, stretched his arms out, but Mrs. Ramsay having died rather suddenly the night before, his arms, though stretched out, remained empty.]"[206] Mr. Ramsay's shout, heard by Mrs. Ramsay through the window, is out of context and unexplained, exemplifying not only the modernist style of fragmented prose, but disrupting the narrative, as the war will tear into a generation of lives, leaving them without the context of satisfying explanations or meanings. The awkward, disjointed sentence describing Mr. Ramsay's arms with tripping dependent clauses thrust in at odd intervals replicates the sensation of his stumbling, confused, sleep-walking grief. The sleep-walking state of mind further creates a sensation of anonymity, an anonymity repeated in the phrase "twenty or thirty young men . . . among" which was Andrew. The chilling vagueness as to the exact number of lives lost, and the obscurity of Andrew within this group suggests a collective grief, not exclusive just to these individuals, or this family, but a wider, anonymous sharing in the experience of death and war. Sounded in a summer day years before the war would actually happen, these experiences would eventually be repeated again in a second world war, and in other deaths yet to come. Stimulated by an awareness beyond her own individual understanding, Lily too will act from the same instincts; this synchronicity with the world doesn't only register doom or peril, but also inspiration, continuation, and hope.

By sinking these revelations about her characters into a section devoted primarily to nonhuman life, Woolf shifts the focus of experience to a larger host of sentient beings living within the spectrum of human politics and history. In this sense, decay and transformation don't perpetuate despair as much as they offer alternatives for life different from usual human expectations. Westling's reading of the "empty" barn in *Between the Acts* is instructive. The barn empty of human characters is still full of scuttling animal life, suggesting "the proper context for rethinking human destiny: a giddy tangle of forms and beings within each kind dances its own rhythm, irrepressibly intertwined."[207] Similarly, in "Time Passes" the suffusion of moist green decay and animal life invades the Ramsay home:

> A thistle thrust itself between the tiles of the larder. The swallows nested in the drawing-room; the floor was strewn with straw; the plaster fell in shovelfuls; rafters were laid bare; rats carried off this and that to gnaw behind wainscots. Tortoise-shell butterflies burst from the chrysalis and pattered their life out on the window-pane. Poppies sowed themselves among the dahlias; the lawn waved with long grass; giant artichokes towered among roses; a fringed carnation flowered among the cabbages; while the gentle tapping of a weed at the window had become, on winters' nights, a drumming from sturdy trees and thorned briars which made the whole room green in summer.[208]

This is a house where life wants to live. It is teeming with creatures making it their home, and filling it with sound, color, and beauty. Just as Mrs. Ramsay is the central figure of the first section of the novel, "The Window," and passes away with brief mention during "Time Passes," a butterfly, too, patters and expires in the same window, equating the life cycles of the resident insects and animals with the previous human occupants. Wildness proliferates in "giant artichokes," "fringed carnations," and other organic forms that make music by "tapping" and "drumming." The "whole room [is] green" with summer's unvanquished ardor. The absence of humans in "Time Passes" isn't necessarily dismal or dreadful. In fact, this representation of heretofore overlooked nonhuman life is the epitome of the kind of unexpected, unacknowledged, ordinary life that Woolf's "Modern Fiction" champions. As Doyle explains, "Woolf and Merleau-Ponty interlace life with death, trace the intertwining of emptiness and fullness, and in this different way 'triumph' over the finality of death."[209] When the narrator imagines what would happen if the house were completely overtaken by nature, its structural transformation has beauty even for other humans who might come there: "In the ruined room, picnickers would have lit their kettles; lovers sought shelter there, lying on the bare boards; and the shepherd stored his dinner on the bricks, and the tramp slept with his coat round him to ward off the cold."[210] This imagined fate of the "ruined" house still insists on life residing there. Even if it loses its identity as an upper-class vacation cottage, the home would still shelter other lives. It would witness other joys, other meals, and other sleepers.

Thus, while erosion and loss are present in "Time Passes," interpreted ecocritically, they represent more than what Julia Briggs describes as "a sense of nature as impervious to human suffering, blind and silent, a sadly familiar theme in twentieth-century literature."[211] It includes this theme, but the narrative in "Time Passes" also moves beyond it into something more inclusive and hopeful, as Adrienne Bartlett illuminates:

> The understanding that humanity will not ever fully grasp the truth or meaning or temperament of the world's natural forces is not a wholly pessimistic point of view, if considered within the proper context. Small connections, such as those made by Mrs. Ramsay, are nonetheless markedly insightful when achieved. Rather, such a viewpoint puts life into a healthier perspective for many human beings; it is one that greatly humbles.[212]

Additionally, the novel as a whole doesn't make nature the only agent "impervious to suffering." In "The Lighthouse" section, another death occurs in brackets: "[Macalister's boy took one of the fish and cut a square out of its side to bait his hook with. The mutilated body (it was alive still) was thrown back into the sea.]"[213] The repetition of the brackets encapsulating just two sentences narrating extreme and sudden suffering references the human deaths in "Time Passes." Some of the soldiers who fought in the war may have been similarly punctured by shrapnel that exploded holes in their bodies. They were sacrificed as military bait for a larger political (not environmental) agent. But while Andrew's death "mercifully, was instantaneous," the fish is thrown back "mutilated" but "alive still" in a gruesome image of pain and torture. Nature is not the only agent, or even the primary agent, of suffering. Nature exists for itself in this novel. It is not at the service of humans; but it isn't an enemy either. Rather, Woolf renders the lives of humans and nonhumans as consistently intertwined. Merleau-Ponty explains that "far from opening upon the blinding light of pure Being or of the Object, our life has, in the astronomical sense of the word, an atmosphere."[214] That atmosphere is comprised by the same elements that Woolf integrates into her rhythmic structure:

> It is constantly enshrouded by those mists we call the sensible world or history, the *one* of the corporeal life and the *one* of the human life, the present and the past, as a pell-mell ensemble of bodies and minds, promiscuity of visages, words, actions, with between them all, that cohesion which cannot be denied them since they are all differences, extreme divergences of one same something.[215]

Human and nonhuman characters are distinct, but Woolf provides evidence that there is a tremendous enveloping presence of many different kinds of beings that are all born, create nests, confront peril or interference, perish, and persist.

Nonhuman life exists in the house even when the Ramsays are still in residence. It is referenced in Mrs. Ramsay's reflections on what the children (the next generation) talk about:

> Anything, everything: Tansley's tie; the passing of the Reform Bill; seabirds and butterflies; people; while the sun poured into those attics which a plank alone separated from each other so that every footstep could be plainly heard and the Swiss girl who was sobbing for her father who was dying of cancer in a valley of the Grisons, and lit up bats, flannels, straw hats, ink-pots, paint-pots, beetles, and the skulls of small birds, while it drew from the long frilled strips of seaweed pinned to the wall a smell of salt and weeds, which was in the towels too, gritty with sand from bathing. Strife, divisions, difference of opinion, prejudices twisted into the very fibre of being, oh, that they should begin so early, Mrs. Ramsey deplored. They were so critical, her children. They talked such nonsense.[216]

While Mrs. Ramsay may not fully appreciate the significance of her children's debates – the new mode of talking about "anything, everything" – her eclectic list represents the kind of conglomeration of everyday life experiences, human and nonhuman, divergent yet shared, that form the stuff of modern fiction. The planks don't separate rooms and lives into hierarchies of upstairs and downstairs; they let sound and light pass through, allowing often overlooked people and things to be known. The presence of another's grief for a lost family member is part of the atmosphere. Bats and beetles live there. The sea is also there, brought in by human activity, but also anticipating the natural erosion of the house in "Time Passes." As Merleau-Ponty elucidates, a representation of embodied life reveals that there is no "pure Being"; it is "a pell-mell ensemble" of entities that have their own unique divergences, yet also share a common space of experience that "twist[s] into the very fibre of being," the very essence of an embodied life.

The novel rejects the belief that nature and humans are "one," or that the nonhuman functions to reflect human experience; instead it privileges an intertwined relationship between the two. Mrs. Ramsay indulges in an older form of pathetic fallacy: "She thought, how if one was alone, one leant to inanimate things; trees; streams; flowers; felt they expressed one; felt they became one; felt they knew one; in a sense were one; felt an irrational tenderness thus (she looked at that long steady light) as for oneself."[217] The paratactic style emphasizes simplistic correlation in its short repetitive clauses. Mrs. Ramsey's sentiment expresses a desire for nature to always be in sympathy with human existence. But it isn't, as the narrator reminds us in a description of the "perfectly indifferent chill night air."[218] "Time Passes" marks the repudiation of the pathetic fallacy: "Did Nature supplement what man advanced? Did she complete what he began? With equal complacence she saw his misery, his meanness, and his torture. That dream, of sharing, completing, of finding in solitude on the beach an answer, was then but a reflection in a mirror . . . the mirror was broken."[219] Woolf creates a nonhuman representation that functions not merely to define the human characters, either as antagonistic foil or sympathetic mirror. These other lives exist for themselves within a shared world. Rendering the environment through embodied perception creates an awareness that nonhuman life is distinct from human concerns and yet participates in and responds to the same events and stimuli.

Mrs. McNab's song toward the end of "Time Passes" expresses this paradox of fragmentation and cohesion – lives that share similarities, but are not identical. Mrs. McNab acts as the airs that fingered and wore the walls of the house. As she "rolled from room to room, she sang. Rubbing the glass."[220] Eroding and cleaning are given a similar feel. The song she sings to pass the time as she works combines light with dark, optimism with despair, "as if, after all, she had her consolations, as if indeed there twined about her dirge some incorrigible hope."[221] Who or what is producing the song becomes unclear:

> And now as if the cleaning and the scrubbing and the scything and the mowing had drowned it there rose that half-heard melody, that intermittent music which the ear half catches but lets fall; a bark, a bleat; irregular, intermittent, yet somehow related; the hum of an insect, the tremor of cut grass, disservered yet somehow belonging; the jar of a dorbeetle, the squeak of a wheel, loud, low, but mysteriously related; which the ear strains to bring together and is always on the verge of harmonizing, but they are never quite heard, never fully harmonized, and at last, in the evening, one after another the sounds die out, and the harmony falters, and silence falls.[222]

Here is the mosaic of life experience. Importantly, Woolf offers no ecstatic union, but an effort, a "half-heard melody," which in its repeating patterns "is always on the verge of harmonizing." This verge, the strain to understand, creates a tension between order and chaos that never lapses into either, but offers suggestive fragments of an alternate conception of the world – it is sensory and perceived only when one is fully listening to the phenomenal world. As Melba Cuddy-Keane puts it, "the effort is to perceive a pattern in 'worldly sound' rather than to create a humanly constructed pattern."[223] This idea of another form of coherence and composition that still retains within it gaps and flux symbolizes both the new prose of the modern artist and a new relationship between humans and the environment. It is made of sounds both mechanical ("mowing," "the squeak of a wheel") and organic ("a bark," "a bleat," "the hum of an insect," "the jar of a dorbeetle") as well as the sounds of products of both human and natural making ("the tremor of cut grass, dissevered yet somehow belonging"). When war and grief have shattered forms of traditional knowledge – the assurance of Mr. Ramsay's brand of hierarchical and human-centered philosophy – humans are left to listen to the phenomenal environment. Humans stop positing, and begin questioning. The lapse into silence isn't failure; it is merely the newness of exercising unused sensory muscles. It represents the struggle to find words that go to the depths of our emotions and most profoundly disturbing revelations of human fragility. Woolf depicts a hitherto unperceived reality that exists beyond but not completely outside of human experience.

Merleau-Ponty associates artistic process with the effort of "bringing truth into being" so that the inner experience of sensation is made visible. He asserts that ecophenomenology "is not the reflection of a pre-existing truth, but, like art, the act of bringing truth into being."[224] The effort of rendering physical instinct and emotion into a visible representation is always an act of translation, and it is the effort of transference, imperfect and fluctuating rather than direct and comprehensive, that best expresses the polymorphous state of being. Or, as Merleau-Ponty explains this link between inner sensation and outward sign in another book, "the tactile palpitation where the questioner and the questioned are closer, and of which the palpitation of the eye is a remarkable variant."[225] Expressing one's vision through art is one way to communicate the complexities of embodied experience through the medium of hand and eye. This is the new perception that Lily also strives to make visible in her abstract painting of Mrs. Ramsay. Ariane Mildenberg has shown that several modernists are interested in this pre-reflective moment: "Woolf, Stein and Stevens promote such a phenomenological sense of the real as the foundation for expression and creative production alike. All of them step back into *epoché*, seek to expose the world in its pre-givenness and bring to light a pre-conceptual, unmediated experience of this world," and the character of Lily Briscoe in particular "longs to capture a state of pre-objective freshness on the canvas in front of her."[226] This longing, however, is not easily fulfilled. Upon returning to the Ramsay summer home after war and death have intervened, Lily has difficulty identifying and articulating her feelings: "What did she feel, come back after all these years and Mrs. Ramsay dead? Nothing, nothing – nothing that she could express at all."[227] But what might be taken for an evacuation of sensation actually anticipates Lily's own journey toward illumination, her own voyage to the lighthouse. As Bourne-Taylor and Mildenberg note about modernist literature more generally, "In the interstices of nothingness and meaninglessness there are vestigial moments of revelation. Negativity contains the seeds of liberation, and ultimately formulates its affirmative potential and creativity."[228] Similarly, Lily begins with a feeling of nothingness but translates that emotion into embodied creativity that is not just of her own making, but in concert with the logos of the world. Her memories, the figure of Mrs. Ramsay, and the significance of the lighthouse, both as a symbol and an actual journey toward a specific place, must be filtered through the sensations she feels standing on the lawn where she stood ten years ago and where now she watches the progress of James' long-promised trip to the lighthouse. Lily makes her first effort to put brush to canvas:

> The brush descended. It flickered brown over the white canvas; it left a running mark. A second time she did it – a third time. And so pausing and flickering, she attained a dancing rhythmical movement, as if the pauses were one part of the rhythm and the strokes another, and all were related; and so, lightly and swiftly pausing, striking, she scored her canvas with brown running nervous lines which had no sooner settled there than they enclosed (she felt it looming out at her) a space. Down in the hollow of one wave she saw the next wave towering higher and higher above her. For what could be more formidable than that space?[229]

The first three rhythmical strokes of her brush resemble the three strokes of the lighthouse. The "nervous lines" connote both painting and writing, linking Woolf's creative efforts with Lily's. The pauses, blank spaces, and "hollow" of the waves have their place in the pattern of the whole in which "all were related." The rhythm of the prose loosely suggests a pattern of cohesion with alliteration ("pauses were one part," "brown running nervous lines") and repeated grammatical endings ("lightly and swiftly pausing striking," "no sooner settled there than they enclosed"). The metaphor of the waves makes Lily part of the experience of those in the boat, too; they are alone, parted by growing distance, but still connected to her in sight and thought. Dipping into her color palette, Lily saturates herself in embodied perception:

> She began precariously dipping among the blues and umbers, moving her brush hither and thither, but it was now heavier and went slower, as if it

had fallen in with some rhythm which dictated to her (she kept looking at the hedge, at the canvas) by what she saw, so that while her hand quivered with life, this rhythm was strong enough to bear her along with it on its current.[230]

Lily is directly reacting to the surrounding environment. She is "looking at the hedge" that "dictated to her" the movements of her hand. The hedge, itself, has symbolic significance as a contact zone for human desires to demarcate boundaries or "lines" in landscape and nonhuman habitats that take over and claim hedgerow spaces, making them a lush example of the complicated nexus between human and nonhuman, where the ostensible human purposes of ownership become transformed and enriched by the abundance of nonhuman animals and plants that grow within them. Yet, Lily doesn't create an image of the hedge on her canvas; rather, the hedge makes itself known to her so that she can be caught in the current of ambient life around her and learn how to express it. The outer world is not the product of her own conscious thought; instead, it is what inspires her thought and action. As Doyle notes, this form of artistic expression differs from the style of previous generations: "Art herein 'takes its place among the things it touches' and, in this way more than any other, art is political. Redefining art in this way, Lily and Woolf avoid the Romantic model of art-making in which the artist engages in materiality only to transcend it."[231] Contrary to the art of the Romantics, Lily's embodied perception guides her art and "thinks itself within her." Wendy Wheeler's explanation illuminates this key moment in the novel: "Nature isn't just 'out there', but is *in us all.* This is a different way of thinking about humans as being 'in place', in which we discover ourselves as being in place, not only in virtue of social role, but in virtue of our being placed as processes of being in a processual web of natural, social and cultural life. . . . It is the semiotic of ethic responding: both responsibility and responsiveness."[232] Lily hears the dictates of the hedge within herself and responds. Lily allows a space for the hidden hollow from which she translates how the world "rays" its colors and expresses the "many-tongued syllabling" of leaves, birds, and other comingled lives within the hedge. She gives expression to the latency that had been "nothing" she could translate, rendering it visible. Similarly, Merleau-Ponty uses Proust to describe how the "little phrase" of remembered music is "only 'bare values substituted for the mysterious entity he had perceived, for the convenience of his under-standing.'"[233] The full complexity of the idea it represents is necessarily veiled, which:

give[s] us the assurance that the 'great unpenetrated and discouraging night of our soul' is not empty, is not 'nothingness'; ... The carnal texture [of other invisible presences] presents to us what is absent from all flesh; it is a furrow that traces itself out magically under our eyes without a tracer, a certain hollow, a certain interior, a certain absence, a negativity that is not nothing.[234]

For Lily, the hollows of the wave, the invisible presence of Mrs. Ramsay, and the silent ambient world are "a negativity that is not nothing." They animate her hand and she creates shapes from their impulses. Difficult to articulate, more felt than understood, they nonetheless form the basis of the outwardly visible creation of her painting. Merleau-Ponty aids our understanding of how the painting paints itself within her:

> We do not possess the musical or sensible ideas, precisely because they are negativity or absence circumscribed; they possess us. The performer is no longer producing or reproducing the sonata: he feels himself, and the others feel him to be at the service of the sonata; the sonata sings through him or cries out so suddenly that he must 'dash on his bow' to follow it. And these open vortexes in the sonorous world finally form one sole vortex in which the ideas fit in with one another.[235]

As with Mrs. McNab's song in "Time Passes," sound and sight are part of a shared sensory engagement with the environment. What one produces, either intellectually or physically, is a visible register not of one's own sole accomplishment, but of how the multiple forces of the ecophenomenological field filter "through" the instrument of our being. Object and subject, nature, human, creativity, are part of a larger material transformation: "Everything in the physical environment enacts a complex dynamic between social subjects and material processes not reducible to a subject-object binary."[236] Whether music, painting, or prose, the creative act is achieved in concert with the "invisible" dictates of the material and ecophenomenological world.

In terms of grief and loss, this understanding is transformative. If the bringing into being of an experience relies on the presence of what isn't there – the kinetic energy of absence and the metamorphosis of matter – to give form and substance to what remains, then even death is part of life's energy. Lily's body registers her grief, but also shows how it can make Mrs. Ramsay's memory gain in meaning and significance:

> How could one express in words these emotions of the body? express that emptiness there? (She was looking at the drawing-room steps; they looked extraordinarily empty.) It was one's body feeling, not one's mind.

> The physical sensations that went with the bare look of the steps had become suddenly extremely unpleasant. To want and not to have, sent all up her body a hardness, a hollowness, a strain ... Oh, Mrs. Ramsay! she called out silently , to that essence which sat by the boat, that abstract one made of her, that woman in grey, as if to abuse her for having gone, and then having gone, come back again. . ... Suddenly, the empty drawing-room steps, the frill o the chair inside, the puppy tumbling on the terrace, the whole wave and whisper of the garden became like curves and arabesques flourishing round a center of complete emptiness.[237]

The steps, the chair, and the puppy are all part of a material reality that draws attention to the figure that is no longer there. Visible and invisible mingle through the perceiving artist's body. The "curves and arabesques" are suggestive of not only painted arcs demarcating the boundaries of blank space and painted object, but also handwriting that curves and loops to form words. These lines demarcate emptiness, but the blank space also allows the viewer to see the marks. They both work together. Emptiness and death are infused with memory, creating the upsurge of life. There is something palpable in the hollows left behind that actually produces signification. In this regard, death is, to borrow a phrase from Merleau-Ponty, the "secret blackness" that makes life significant.[238]

This may not be the response the characters desired to find in their repeated questioning of what makes life worthwhile or whether their life has meaning, but it is an answer Lily's experience offers her. She contemplates the surprising paradox of momentary permanence:

> The great revelation perhaps never did come. Instead there were little daily miracles, illuminations, matches struck unexpectedly in the dark; here was one. This, that, and the other; herself and Charles Tansley and the breaking wave; Mrs. Ramsay bringing them together; Mrs. Ramsay saying 'Life stand still here'; Mrs. Ramsay making of the moment something permanent (as in another sphere Lily herself tried to make of the moment something permanent) – this was of the nature of a revelation.[239]

Lily recognizes that the illuminations of truth, like the lighthouse beams that pulse in and out of sight, are ephemeral revelations. There is no single, lasting truth, but a series of flickering moments that offer meaning for our lives. Daily experience is the great revelation meekly waiting to be recognized. Such epiphanies are ignited by overlooked material forces, or as Serpil Oppermann explains it, the daily "storied matter" that is "inseparable from the storied human in existential ways" that converge on a "fusion of horizons" where "we find creative materiality encoded in the collective poetry of life."[240] A poetry both artists, Lily and Mr. Carmichael, seem to somehow share when they stand together at the moment of the Ramsay's presumed arrival at the Lighthouse: "They had been thinking the same things and he had answered her without her asking him anything."[241]

This acknowledgement, far from causing Lily despondency, offers a more positive interpretation of the "somethingness" inherent in the "nothingness" of darkness or silence. Lily remembers Mrs. Ramsay's silences and praises the potential of the unknown, the expressiveness of feeling that isn't neatly captured in human discourse:

> Who knows what we are, what we feel? Who knows even at the moment of intimacy, This is knowledge? Aren't things spoilt then, Mrs. Ramsay may have asked (it seemed to have happened so often, this silence by her side) by saying them? Aren't we more expressive thus? The moment at least seemed extraordinarily fertile. She rammed a little hole in the sand and covered it up, by way of burying in it the perfection of the moment.[242]

This "lack" of sound, this silent hollow, is full of meaning. The richness of silent experience may even be "spoiled" by reducing it to a visible or auditory communication. The text moves back and forth between times when characters yearn for someone to speak – Mrs. Ramsay with her husband at points, Lily with Augustus Carmichael on the lawn – and other moments when the characters prefer a silence nevertheless replete with understanding. The parenthetical "(it seemed to have happened so often, this silence by her side)" encapsulates a thought that does not directly participate in the sentence it is within, enacting a kind of alternative aside that replicates the potential of what may not be communicated directly. Similarly, Lily encapsulates a bubble of silence in the earth itself, covering it in a hole hollowed out in the sand: "The moment at least seemed extraordinarily fertile. She rammed a little hole in the sand and covered it up, by way of burying in it the perfection of the moment." This gesture has connotations of both death and life embedded within it. The verb "bury" might make the act an effort to inter the revelation, but the word "fertile" competes with it. Suddenly, the burial becomes a planting, the seed of an idea about the power of silence and uncertainty as a promise of potential. Ecomaterialism challenges us to see such metaphors as a medium for ecological consciousness. In the words of Hubert Zapf: "As in biosemiotics, metaphor emerges as a mode of biological, mental, and textual-semiotic operation that translates these processes into language and cultural discourse."[243] The gap of signifier and signified, like the empty space that allows the stroke to become apparent, or functions simultaneously as grave and planting, is the human way of writing a world so replete with more-than-human narrative it can only be expressed with the abstract, which gestures toward the multifarious potential of what exceeds direct representation.

The novel's final pages insist on multiplicity as a type of truth. Distance and one's situated perspective become crucial to understanding the "whole" or full meaning of a moment, person, or object. Both distance and subjective perspective are embodied perceptions: "The relations between things or aspects of things hav[e] always our body as their vehicle."[244] Our body's situatedness in relation to the world allows us to know how distance and perspective function: "Lily stepped back to get her canvas – so – into perspective."[245] Lily creates distance between herself and her painting to see it more clearly. Woolf's prose also enacts this process as the dashes create distance between the two halves of the sentence, the "so" in the center representing the moment Lily's clarity coalesces. Lily remembers Mrs. Ramsay gazing out to the sea asking, "'Is it a boat? Is it a cork?'... 'Is it a boat? Is it a cask?' Mrs. Ramsay said. And she began hunting round for her spectacles."[246] Mrs. Ramsay, as one should now expect, desires to identify accurately what she sees as a fixed solid object. Lily's memory at this moment also invokes another kind of perspective – her perspective through time. Remembering this moment as she herself is standing at the water's edge – taking note of the progress of the boat containing Mr. Ramsay, James, Cam, and the fishing boy, which appears small against the horizon – makes Mrs. Ramsay's statement anticipate the present moment that Lily recalls her into. She and Lily are in the same place, noting the same sensation. Perspective and distance are not just a matter of space, but also a matter of time. Yet in contrast to Lily's revelations concerning momentary truth, Mrs. Ramsay wanted to know if what she saw was one thing or the other – which is true and which is false. But the section's third example of distance and perspective replaces objective truth with subjective truth. James is also contemplating his past desire to see the lighthouse with his present approach as he finally nears the monument that had so occupied his imagination as a child:

> The Lighthouse was then a silvery, misty-looking tower with a yellow eye, that opened suddenly, and softly in the evening. Now –
> James looked at the Lighthouse. He could see the white-washed rocks; the tower, stark and straight; he could see that it was barred with black and white; he could see windows in it; he could even see washing spread on the rocks to dry. So that was the Lighthouse, was it?
> No, the other was also the Lighthouse. For nothing was simply one thing. The other Lighthouse was true too.[247]

As James gets closer to the lighthouse, both through time and through distance, he perceives it differently. From the faraway and nostalgic perspective, the lighthouse has appeared another animate being gazing at him, but now, in the present moment of his educated older self, he sees the close-up details that render it more concrete and less idealized. Unlike his mother's desire to determine if what she saw was a cork or a boat, James affirms that an object can be more than one thing. Moving to a different place, either in time or space, allows us to know more about the subject. It doesn't deny the prior understanding, but contributes to it, ultimately multiplying the subject's meaning and significance. In the words of Merleau-Ponty, "We do not think then that the dichotomy of Being and Nothingness continues to hold when one arrives at the descriptions of nothingness sunken into being.... Could we not express this simply by saying that for the intuition of being and the intuition of nothingness must be substituted a *dialectic*?"[248] To know what the lighthouse means does not require choosing between the physical presence of its "being" in the present and the "nothingness" of its felt atmosphere that was his past perception of it. Indeed, it is an entity only recognized in the tension of dialectic that sustains both understandings. In a similar fashion, Woolf has continued to rework and reimagine the lighthouse as a reoccurring symbol throughout the novel. The lighthouse's ability to carry multiple meanings for multiple characters doesn't negate its effectiveness, but rather enriches its power to communicate a variety of emotions to the reader.

A variety of revisions allows us to gain a deeper appreciation of not only material objects, but also people. Lily imagines Mrs. Ramsay from multiple perspectives in an effort to understand her better: "There must be people who disliked her very much, Lily thought . . . People who thought her too sure, too drastic. Also her beauty offended people probably."[249] Lily's indulgence in a variety of imagined perspectives doesn't diminish Mrs. Ramsay as much as round her out so she is seen from all sides, the light and the dark. She does this when considering Mr. and Mrs. Ramsay's marriage too: "But it would be a mistake, she thought, thinking how they walked off together, arm in arm, past the greenhouse, to simplify their relationship. It was no monotony of bliss – she with her impulses and quicknesses; he with his shudders and glooms."[250] Indeed, the idea of sustained perfection is a "monotony" and a reduced "simplif[ication]" of the truth, which must admit a more nuanced and fluctuating existence. Although it might expose something "dark" to acknowledge that the marriage has had its difficulties and disappointments, those perspectives are necessary to complete the picture of the Ramsays and to reach a full understanding of the "truth" of their lives together. Mr. Bankes' comments on Lily's initial attempt at the painting in the first section of the novel points toward this process: "A mother and child might be reduced to a shadow without irreverence. A light there required a shadow there."[251] Forms that are more abstract than concrete, which balance light with shadow, are the very forms Lily is after; they are the most expressive. Indeed, these are also the techniques Woolf employs in her modernist prose.

To take Mrs. Ramsay's perspective as the main or singular viewpoint of the novel is reductive and obscures the work's larger significance. Julia Briggs argues that "Mrs. Ramsay has struggled to make 'Time stand still,' to create pools of tranquility in the midst of flux, and for this she will be remembered by her children, by Lily in her painting and by the novel itself, for the art of holding back time's swift foot, the recurrent theme of Shakespeare's sonnets, belongs as much to Mrs. Ramsay as it does to the artist Lily Briscoe or the novelist Virginia Woolf."[252] While this perspective is certainly one of the prominent views voiced in the novel and Briggs's analysis of it is insightful, the quote suggests that it is the primary attitude endorsed by the work as a whole. Yet Woolf presents Mrs. Ramsay's desire to make life and love forever happy or to make an object "stand still" as a potentially outdated mode of thinking that gets reworked as the novel culminates in a wider proliferation of meanings. Lily's perspective of multiplicity, in concert with James and possibly even the silent artist, Mr. Carmichael, is at least equally persistent. The impulses of stasis and flux interact dialectically. However, as I have shown, the novel moves toward the revelation that joy is temporal and truths are multiple. Uncertainty – the twisting together of various fibers that never settle into one fixed meaning – is relished. As in "Time Passes," the fissures in language throughout the novel admit life and the potential of new meanings that reside in what is left unsaid. As the novel progresses, the kaleidoscopic angles on various themes fall into new patterns. They gain in vitality. Flux isn't merely the moving sea within which humans drown; it nurtures the very beginnings of human life in its most basic forms and carries humans along in its current.

When Lily makes the final stroke on her canvas, she is no longer concerned with the likelihood that the finished piece will be forgotten. Instead, what gives it value is her own experience in creating it, the effort it produced, the journey she took in recording her sensations:

> Quickly, as if she were recalled by something over there, she turned to her canvas. There it was – her picture. Yes, with all its greens and blues, its lines

running up and across, its attempt at something. It would be hung in attics, she thought; it would be destroyed. But what did that matter? she asked herself, taking up her brush again. She looked at the steps; they were empty; she looked at her canvas; it was blurred. With a sudden intensity, as if she saw it clear for a second, she drew a line there, in the center. It was done; it was finished. Yes, she thought, laying down her brush in extreme fatigue, I have had my vision.[253]

The vision is her own. It doesn't need to be valued by others to have value for her. The "attempt at something" matters, not the thought "it would be destroyed." Her vision is momentary, but she is alert for it. She is "recalled" into her body and her work by some outside stimuli and achieves unity in a match-like flash of intense illumination. The line in the center of the short declarative sentence "There it was – her picture" expresses the brief, concentrated force of her inspiration. Her impulse to finish by "dr[a]w[ing] a line there, in the center" is replicated in the horizontal dash in the center of the sentence. The "line" once again connotes the shared project of painting and writing. Part of the reader's pleasure is in the teeming potential of the "line" that unifies the work. Its significance is uncertain. Does it represent the upright line of a tree, which Lily visualized in the tablecloth during the first scene? Is it Mrs. Ramsay? Does the line's presence through the center of the painting indicate that unification is found through acknowledging division? Does it symbolize the lighthouse that radiates from the center of the novel?[254] Perhaps, as James discovers, it is all this and more. That multiplicity of significance gives it a meaning that is uncertain and yet more complete than any single answer. The idea of interconnection extends to the generations of readers who come after Woolf, with their own subjective perspectives. The uncertainty of the concluding image in *To the Lighthouse* challenges readers to have their own personal moments of vision – we must contribute to the ongoing meaning of Lily's final stroke and of Woolf's novel as a whole. This is what makes the text live on.

CHAPTER 3

Brute being and animal language
W.H. Auden

Despite Auden's bold assertion "a culture is no better than its woods,"[1] ecocritics have been surprisingly disdainful of Auden's poetry. A critical reviewer of three foundational ecocritical studies severed Auden from the realm of environmental literature by quoting, "Poetry makes nothing happen,"[2] a line from Auden's "In Memory of W.B. Yeats," and then caustically rejoining, "Ecocriticism believes otherwise."[3] One ecocritical anthology covertly blames Auden for importing a contaminated, urbane English pastoral poetry to America: "The self-proclaimed 'postmodernism' of Randall Jarrell, John Berryman, Robert Lowell, and Richard Wilbur – sanctioned for American poetry by Auden's move to New York in 1940 – revitalized the 'smooth walks' and 'trimmed hedges.'"[4] This conception of environmental poetry as focused on pristine "wilderness" is a regrettably narrow formulation of ecocritical poetry.[5] Even so, the conspicuousness of Auden's depiction of unstable human systems of ordering and poetic appropriations of natural figures demonstrates his poems' active engagement with the environment and frustrates facile labels of solipsism; these traits are especially apparent in his later poems, composed after leaving England.[6]

Building on an earlier generation of poets who advocated for changes in human attitudes toward nature by following Thoreau's dictum to "speak a word *for* Nature," many of Auden's later poems strive to work under, over, and across this barrier of language, consciously questioning whether any human can ever speak "for" Nature. Instead, Auden accentuates the way humanity is inextricably tangled within any lines that attempt to capture a nonhuman voice. While these poems aren't "nature" poems in any straightforward sense, they expose how animate Nature (writ large, in the Thoreauvian idea of its personified largess), and particularly the sentient animals within it, is often diminished, demonized, or anthropocentrically caricatured in human culture and literary tradition. As Cary Wolfe has noted, "the traditional humanist subject finds this prospect of the animal other's knowing us in ways *we* cannot know and master *simply unnerving*. And in response to that 'skeptical terror,' we have mobilized a whole array of prophylactics."[7] Auden's work begins to separate those latex barriers of anesthetized scientific rhetoric and cultural purity, making them visible, daring us to get in touch with our own fears and the truths of our own animality. Auden's ability to embrace a sexual identity scorned by the cultural majority may have emboldened him to see through the artificial cultural stereotypes that tightly constrict so many notions of "otherness" and separate the world into dialectics of "natural" and "unnatural."

Throughout the later poems, Auden cannot resist plucking at the tension in the line that connects human and nonhuman interests. Yet he does not reduce the problem into a neat postulate; instead, he voices concerns that arise and resolve themselves in diverse forms of sympathy and alterity. In this way, Auden is relevant to Wolfe's inquiry into how language "rather than simplifying the question of ethics by securing the boundary between human and the rest of creation, instead now re-opens it – permanently as it were – by embedding us in a world to which the human is subject."[8] Even though Auden was not writing in an era of posthumanism, his poetry makes a significant intervention into assumptions about the Cartesian dualities that separate animal body from human mind by playfully sliding along slippery interspecies exchanges. "Natural Linguistics" states "Every created thing has ways of pronouncing its own-hood," and poems titled "Talking to Dogs" and "Talking to Mice," as well as "New Year's Greeting," addressed to the variety of unseen microscopic life forms that live on the body of a human host, acknowledge conversations that occur across the species divide. And while Auden's libretto *Paul Bunyan* and play *The Dog Beneath the Skin* feature singers and actors thinly disguised as anthropomorphic and comedic figures, the dramatization of humans as trees, dogs, or cats combined with the dialogue's rueful satire of human culture chides notions of human exceptionalism. Auden blends animal kinship and difference through a wide range of formal devices that continually resist any stable sense of power dynamics in knowledge, voice, or subjectivity. In this way, his work manifests more recent concerns articulated by posthumanist animal studies critics, such as Wolfe, Philip Armstrong, and Carrie Rohman, while also overlapping with ecophenomenological concepts of human and nonhuman interrelationship that were being articulated by Merleau-Ponty around the same time Auden was writing his later work. As theories in literary animal studies suggest, the link between engendering human empathy for the nonhuman environment and appreciating distinctive nonhuman value in nature and other animals may seem paradoxical. Yet the bond of empathy, or even anthro-pomorphism, cultivates a respect for commonalities shared between all living beings while formal properties of disruption forestall an objectifica-tion or idealization of the nonhuman other.

Auden's canonically popular early poems such as "The Watershed," "Musée des Beaux Arts," and "Lullabye" may not be fully ecocentric, but they do show the gestation of values that prove fundamental to the environmental themes of his later poems. "The Watershed" (1927) begins with an indeterminate, observing "who"[9] identified at the end of the poem as a nonhuman mammal "taller than the grass / ears poise before decision, scenting danger."[10] Employing an initially unidentified nonhuman animal as a framing device highlights the shared capacity for witnessing and experiencing as well as making decisions, perhaps even suggesting that the heightened awareness of the nonhuman might lead it to choose more wisely. In "The Watershed" human and natural elements are consistently shown as participating in a common fate of pain and anxiety in response to the straggling remnants of a once-thriving area. The inadvertent human visitor must "turn back again, frustrated and vexed"[11] as the wind is driven to "hurt itself on pane, on bark of elm."[12] Nonetheless "sap, unbaffled rises"[13] akin to the "industry already comatose, / Yet sparsely living."[14] The ebullience of churning water and human workers has been replaced by slow sap and a shadow of corporate presence eking out an existence. The natural elements and human beings who lived in this place are depicted as having a shared fate, underscoring the equivalency between human and nonhuman. In "Musée des Beaux Arts" (1938) humans are depicted as unconscious of or wilfully ignorant about significant traumatic events taking place in their midst. Inspired by paintings where individual humans are diminished in a large, active landscape, Auden notes how the "suffering"[15] of others often goes unnoticed "While someone else is eating or opening a window or just walking dully along";[16] – ideas reprised to a more environmental effect in Auden's later poems. Similarly, "Lullabye" (1937), Auden's famously human-centered poem about the nature of love and betrayal, focuses on the responsibility a conscious being owes to an unconscious, sleeping, other that will take on green registers when that other becomes nonhuman in subsequent poetry. "Lullabye" affirms the comforting presence of "involuntary powers"[17] of fleshly and ecological origin, hinting at later interests in the body and environment as funda-mental to knowledge and feeling. Additionally, "Lullabye"'s recognition that fault still admits deep love, is a revelation that Auden will declare about humanity's abiding affection for the places they inhabit and abandon in "Amor Loci" (1965). Thus, thematically, familiar concepts established by the canon of Auden's early poetry do not disappear in his later poetry; rather they become more prominently ecocentric, suggesting that elements constitutive of human relationships with industry, art, divinity, and a beloved are also present in human relationships with place and nonhuman animals.

Auden purchased the only home he ever owned, in Kirchstetten, Austria, during 1957,[18] and wrote a series of twelve poems between 1962 and 1964 that celebrate the intimacy of one's relationship within the rooms of a built, human dwelling, which he titles "Thanksgiving for A Habitat." As one would expect from such a title, nature isn't shooed out of the space of the house; it is allowed to move freely within as well as without, a hallmark of the speaker's personal relationship with it. Reminiscent of Forster's hesitancy about feelings of feudal power after purchasing Piney Copse, Auden's acquisition seems to have prompted an initial proprietary pride. The speaker of the opening poem proclaims he is "dominant over three acres and a blooming conurbation of country lives."[19] The next nine stanzas, close to half the poem, are dedicated to nonhuman occupants of the speaker's home. Even though spiders "give me the shudders"[20] the speaker refuses to exterminate them, suggesting a parallel to the Nazis: "fools / who deface the emblem of guilt / are germane to Hitler: the race of spiders / shall be allowed their webs."[21] Auden uses the resemblance between a swastika and the black legs protruding from a spider's body as a warning against mistreating any human or ecological other as a result of prejudice; both spiders and humans have a right to build homes in the same place, a maneuver that is tacitly linked to current theoretical recognitions by Cary Wolfe and others that "the discourse of animality has historically served as a crucial strategy in the oppression of humans by other humans."[22] Whether the subject is divisions between people or differences between species, what they have in common is more significant than any features that separate one from another.

Similarly, in this same poem, Auden notes the distance between human languages and bird songs while overlapping them in a common space and assuming shared responses to emotional stimuli:

> ... I should like
> to be to my water-brethren as a spell
> of fine weather: Many are stupid,
> and some, maybe, are heartless, but who is not
> vulnerable, easy to scare,

and jealous of his privacy? (I am glad
  the blackbird, for instance, cannot
tell if I'm talking English, German or
  just typewriting: that what he utters
I may enjoy as an alien rigmarole.)[23]

The speaker's contentment with indecipherability is based on what he
assumes to be a mutual desire for privacy – an empathy that denotes
sympathetic connection to the ways nonhuman animals may share
the same feelings that humans do – vulnerability, jealousy, protective
privacy – even as he relishes the difference between them. All of the lines
in this poem begin at alternating margins, suggesting a measured gap
between human and nonhuman that isn't too wide, but still allows for
an easy compromise and cooperation, a habitat "where I needn't, ever,
be at home *to* those I am not at home *with*"[24] and a "place I may go
both in and out of"[25] as humans and nonhumans move within permeable boundaries in shared place, and images of nature commingle with
emblems of culture in a relationship not always blissful, but consistently
comfortable.

Auden's more mature personal notations and correspondence indicate
how his own conscious patterns of daily habit often revolved around
plants, food, and nonhuman family members. Diary jottings record particular dates when morning glories or strawberries first bloom each year,
when corn seeds need to be planted, and many other such detailed
observations of domestic habitat.[26] Regarding the animals in his life,
Auden's diary notebooks consistently mark events in the lives of his cats,
Leonora and Lucinda, as well as the birthday of his kitten, Tamino.[27] He
wrote several letters about the capacity of his dog, Mosè, to get the better
of a neighbor's goat,[28] and in addition to the eulogies composed for such
luminaries as W.B. Yeats and Sigmund Freud, he also penned a memorial
to his beloved cat, Lucinda, "In Memoriam L.K.A, 1950–1952," presumably giving her Chester Kallman's and his own last name. Auden's letters
are replete with updates on his furred family members and he also asks
after the pets of others. In and of themselves, these events are merely
commonplace, and certainly Auden is not the first poet to commemorate a
beloved pet in verse, but when paired with his larger oeuvre, they attest to
a sustained contemplation of the exchanges between humans and nonhumans and the ethical relationships implicated by shared habitation.
Although Auden does not record any Derridian confrontation of a cat
viewing his naked body, his nonhuman figures do poetically "respond" to
the human subject in a myriad of ways.

Another marked change in Auden's later life is a more profound orientation toward the body – whether it be ordinary bodily functions such as those he irreverently versifies in "Thanksgiving for A Habitat"'s homage to the bathroom, "The Cave of Making," or an increased awareness of being an aging animal himself, and the ways in which embodied experiences actually trigger cerebral thought or creative reflection. Edward Mendelson traces these influences to Auden's first summer in Italy during 1948: "In place of the weightless archetypes and faculties that he had admired in Jung, in place of the daemon and the mysterious forces, he now wrote about an ordinary human shape";[29] "The poems he wrote in Italy were the first that noticed the daily ordinariness of a place where he actually lived."[30] Mendelson describes the significance of this new sense of scale and intimacy with daily habit:

> Auden's poems try to understand the human body as it is, not as a sign of something else, not as something to be transcended or escaped, and never as something to be valued or devalued for any reasons that the human mind projects on it. For Auden, the body, and the human scale of the body, was the measure of all things. Its rhythms provided him with the raw materials of his metres and cadences. It provided a vision of connectedness and relationship among persons who would otherwise be separate. . ... The body was at the heart of Auden's literary, ethical, and theological understanding of the world.[31]

While Mendelson doesn't explicitly make the connection between Auden's developing awareness of embodiment and how the perceiving body prioritizes the link between humans and other animals, or representing humans embedded in a more-than-human environment, these themes parallel Auden's growing interest in the body and are dramatically apparent throughout the corpus of his later work.

However, it is Auden's later prose essays that most explicitly announce his profound commitment to environmental ethics. Auden devotes several essays to working out his own vision of a more ethical relationship between the human species and nonhuman others broadly termed "Nature." The main tenets of Auden's own environmental philosophy tend to revolve around two recurring principles. The first is that humans must recognize – in both literary and scientific representations of nature and "progress" – that human advancement has changed the game of Man versus Nature; humans have mastered, trampled, and plundered so many other resources and life-forms as to now need to protect rather than battle or enslave Nature. Second, the foundation for the moral recognition of a new, more gracious and nurturing partnership with Nature should emanate from personal attachment to place and intimate encounters with the nonhuman other that foster the kind of ethical consciousness provoked by bonds of love.

In a 1953 essay titled "Transplanted Englishman Views U.S." Auden suggests that cultural environmental ethics and people's actions related to nature are, to some extent, a result of how literary texts encode those values. Specifically, he seems concerned that the reality of humanity's position of overreaching and the limited capacity of earth to sustain human greed were not yet reflected in most people's literary imagination. Moreover, such discord presented a dangerous impediment to cultural awareness of current environmental crises. He begins this section of the article by explaining how British and American stories about Nature have depicted different models of the human–nature relationship:

> The primitive religion of Europe, which neither Greek philosophers nor the church have ever succeeded in completely eradicating, was a polytheistic, magical worship of Nature. Nature was alive, immensely powerful, capricious. Man was at her mercy, and his fate depended upon securing her good favor; if she were against him, no practical activity of his could succeed. The bad side of this is obvious, an acceptance of disease, poverty, social injustice, etc. as the divine will, instead of a problem God requires man to solve. But it also had a good side; it inculcated a reverence for Nature, a sense that man has a duty towards things as well as towards his human neighbors. In the States, on the other hand, Nature is seen as the Other, the blind neuter savage realm of necessity against which man may pit his will and his wits; Nature, so to speak, is the dragon and Man St. George. To fight the dragon is the test of his manhood, but, when you have conquered a dragon, what can you do with it, except enslave it? The trouble about this is that, while you can respect an as yet unconquered enemy, a slave is a mere thing to exploit.[32]

Other writings tend to suggest that all nations, particularly industrialized ones, share this conceptual handicap to developing a more productive and respectful stance toward ecological issues. This is evident in a libretto Auden wrote with Benjamin Britten, titled *Paul Bunyan*, where the literary metaphor for America's consumptive and aggressive habits takes the form not of a heroic knight battling a dragon, but rather a supersized American woodsman saint, Paul Bunyan, and his larger-than-life blue oxen. In an introduction to the libretto Auden writes:

> At first sight it may seem presumptuous for a foreigner to take an American folk-tale as his subject, but in fact the implications of the Bunyan legend are not only American but universal. . ... All countries are now faced at the same and for the first time with the same problem; now that, in a material sense,

we can do anything almost we like, how are we to know the right thing to do, and what is the wrong thing to avoid, for Nature is no longer a nurse with her swift punishments and rewards. Of what happens when men refuse to accept this necessity of choosing, and are terrified or careless about their freedom, we have now only too clear a proof.[33]

It is noteworthy that for both cultural metaphors of environmental conquest – St. George fighting the dragon and the Bunyan tale – Auden chooses completely unrealistic animals, pointing up, perhaps, how utterly fantastical imaginary representations of nature can infiltrate the cultural imagination and impact very real cultural practices that result in harm to the actual animals we share our habitats with. Auden, himself, believed his family had Icelandic ancestry and was interested in Nordic folklore that also mixes mythology and stories of creation and destruction of the environment. Thus, by propounding these tales and using them as metaphors in his own work, Auden isn't necessarily signaling that we need to eradicate mythological beasts, but rather that the twentieth-century reader become more cognizant of his own contextualization in a historical period where the morals and ethics of those childhood tales taking anthropocentric conquest as their theme need to be examined, revised, and retold in new ways. This ethic of human limitation, the recognition that we must reimagine our relationship with nature so that art and literature can help to shape new ethical orientations to the nonhuman world, is replete in much of Auden's own work, which frequently reimagines the Christian creation story.

In another essay, written for a retrospective anthology published twenty years after bombs were dropped on Hiroshima and Nagasaki, Auden uses the impact of nuclear holocaust on the human imagination to argue for the adoption of more ecocentric practices. Depicting a common cultural sense of overwhelming destruction and individual disempowerment caused by the looming nuclear threat, he uses this awareness as a catalyst for igniting a more fervent belief in the necessity of restraining human power in favor of protecting the planet. An environmental manifesto reprising principles found in the other essays concludes Auden's chapter:

> The time has come when we must choose to treat nature not as a slave but as a partner, or, more accurately perhaps, as a loving father treats his children. We have first to admit that every created thing has as much right to its kind of existence as we have to ours, and then go on to ask what, with our help, it could become but cannot by its own unaided efforts. The model for our right relations to nature should be that of the good trainer of animals. It seems obvious to me, for instance, that a well-trained sheepdog

has more realized its 'dog nature' than a wild one, just as a spoiled lapdog or one terrified by ill usage has had its 'dogginess' debased. This means of course, reintroducing the notion of teleology, for a long time now a dirty word with scientists, but they will get over the shock. Our world will be a safer and healthier place when we can admit that to make an atomic bomb is morally to corrupt a host of innocent electrons below the age of consent.[34]

Anthropocentric thinking is deftly smashed by phrases such as "every created thing has as much right to its kind of existence as we have to ours." Once again pointing toward a more personal ethical model, such as the relationship of father and children or trainer and domestic animal, Auden uses the historic occasion of the nuclear anniversary to reorient his reader to ecocentric morality. Further, his trainer paradigm anticipates the human–animal ethical bonds described in detail by Vicki Hearne, who seems unaware of these essays, but uses Auden's notions of society and community in his "The Virgin and the Dynamo" to differentiate between authority based on necessity and authority based on a shared love for the acts that bond humans and domestic working animals in her book, *Adam's Task*. Yet, with this adult–child or trainer–pet analogy, Auden also falls into what Cary Wolfe critiques in Hearne's philosophy, an assumption of paternalism that risks speciesist assumptions of superiority. Thus, while Auden is certainly still writing within the cultural constructs of humanism, these essays pointedly demonstrate how environmentalism flourishes even within modernism (or in Auden's case, work that shuttles between modernism and postmodernism) and exemplifies how forcefully some writers pushed and pulled at the boundaries of humanist presumptions of anthropocentric progress. The goal of this critical inquiry is not to present Auden as a fully posthuman writer; to the contrary, as detailed poetic analysis will demonstrate, Auden's poetry offers a robust variety of nonhuman interactions that experiment with irony, voice, and embodiment in ways that sometimes comport with the environmental philosophies articulated in the essays above, but also express the imaginative challenges and complexities at stake in any human effort to engage the possibilities of nonhuman consciousness.

An inquiry into Auden's poetic representations of nonhumans and the ecocritical implications of his frequent use of place both break new trails into what many would otherwise consider to be fully excavated terrain. Many critics have used much of Auden's landscape imagery as religious symbolism or metaphors for social and romantic interactions between humans. Certainly, these elements are significant in Auden's poetry; yet, his invocations of places are often based on real, personal experiences with the environment and a growing sense of human responsibility for it. As a result, Auden's work is often more grounded in real places and environs than literary critics have recognized, but doesn't conform to more realistic genres of nature writing either, because it unapologetically employs the emotional and intellectual power of the imaginary to stimulate an awareness of one's personal and moral relationship with nature. One of the few critics to analyze Auden's use of the nonhuman, Rainer Emig, notes the limitations of early ecocritical analyses focusing on genres of wilderness writing, and helpfully reminds readers that "the very terms 'ecology' and 'ecocriticism' derive from the Greek root *oikos*, meaning household, the domestic sphere."[35] Although Emig does not connect this etymology with Auden's "Thanksgiving for a Habitat," the definition is an apt reflection of Auden's efforts in this poem and others to examine the parallels between built and natural environments, including both architectural forms and structures of language. Emig argues that Auden's poetry renders nature as always a part of culture, claiming that Auden's "images of nature are always manmade constructs";[36] I propose we should take this useful starting point one step farther. While Emig's analysis always circles back to the conclusion that Auden's poetry is "inevitably anthropocentric"[37] or continually "returns to a narcissistic anthropocentrism,"[38] this chapter will show that although Auden's *speakers* are often decidedly anthropocentric, his manipulation of imagery and poetics is meant to stimulate a contrasting awareness in the *reader*. Auden's poetics mince political and natural imagery together in ways that don't simply reconstitute human-centered values. Instead, these poems expose the human ingredient so that the cultural constructs can be recognized and judged. This practice doesn't insist on a purification of the natural from all human artifice, but offers modulation. It develops an awareness of the ecological components of human identity using social and political metaphors to create sympathetic identification with nature. In other words, Auden uses anthropocentric imagery to coax his reader toward more ecocentric values. J. Scott Bryson, who doesn't make any mention of Auden, reproachful or otherwise, synthesizes earlier theories advanced by Gifford, Scigaj, and Buell, defining ecopoetry using three main characteristics: "ecocentrism, a humble appreciation of wildness, and a skepticism toward hyperrationality and its resultant overreliance on technology."[39] While it would oversimplify the complexity and diversity of Auden's work to label all of it "ecopoetry," much of his later poetry amply demonstrates all of these qualities.

Indeed, poetry is a genre often dependent on sensory experience and shared emotion to convey meaning. Prolific gaps are inherent to poetic form; using Merleau-Ponty's terms, the chasm between metaphorical signifier and signified is analogous to that between the visible and the invisible. Latent or "invisible" association and emotion, created by our shared experience in the world, suffuses the symbolic word with meaning. In notes collected from some of his last lectures, Merleau-Ponty identifies poetry as a particularly apt form for environmental expression: "The philosophy of Nature needs a language that can take up Nature in its least human aspect, and which thereby would be close to poetry."[40] The interplay of aural rhythm, the reliance on multifarious associations that will produce layers of meaning beyond the literal words on the page, and the possibility of presenting a disruption between a human speaker's claims and a contrasting argument made by the formal texture of the poem are elements that create the kind of language that may best "take up Nature." What poetry can do to affirm the embodied principles of ecophenomenology is, as Todd Balazic phrases it, "reenact perception's immediate relation to meaning."[41] The prominent quality of this poetry is not the mere idea of nature as subject matter, but rather the operation of language as it stimulates the reader to a new awareness of the environment through metaphor, juxtaposition, intertextual references, and unreliable human speakers. Recent philosophers like Mark Johnson and George Lakoff have theorized that the human mind is biologically wired to comprehend knowledge largely through metaphor: "We have a system of primary metaphors simply because we have the bodies and brains we have and because the world we live in, where intimacy does tend to correlate significantly with proximity, affection with warmth, and achieving purposes with destinations."[42] Materialist ecocriticism identifies a similar correspondence, as represented here by Hubert Zapf: "As in biosemiotics, metaphor emerges as a mode of biological, mental, and textual-semiotic operation that translates these processes into language and cultural discourse … because metaphor is used in the most intense, complex, and self-reflexive ways in poetic language, the discourse of ecology and the discourse of poetry and literature are intrinsically related to each other through the shared relevance of metaphor."[43] Literary metaphors replicate human cerebral patterns of organizing one's experience in the world. Poems are thus well-suited to artistically expressing the embodied experience of human and nonhuman interaction. As Auden himself succinctly states, "Man is an analogy-drawing animal."[44]

Like the prose of Forster and Woolf, Auden's poetry questions nature's capacity to mirror human emotion and depicts the nonhuman as having its own unique value revealed through sensory interaction. Auden makes use of the devices singled out as modernist techniques by Paul Peppis in "Schools, movements, manifestos" to create a new representation of nature and the nonhuman, including "free verse, montage, juxtaposition, inter-textuality, linguistic abstraction,"[45] and poetic speakers that are discredited by the argument inherent in the form of the poem itself. Literary devices that enhance identification with the nonhuman complement other techniques that insert uncertainty or highlight the artifice of literary characterization.

Perhaps not coincidentally, both Forster and Woolf were influential to Auden's work. Auden's admiration for his friend Forster is expressed in a poem dedicated to the older writer, which includes several of Forster's fictional characters. In the last poem of his "Sonnets from China" (1938) sequence, Auden references Forster characters who want to do the right thing but often make a muddle of it: Lucy from *A Room With A View*, Turton, who sets up the failed "bridge" party in *A Passage to India*, and Philip from *Where Angels Fear to Tread*. The speaker identifies with these characters, depicted as mischievous children, or perhaps as humanists who haven't yet recognized the problems inherent in their naïve goals: "Yes, we are Lucy, Turton, Philip: we / Wish international evil, are delighted / To join the jolly ranks of the benighted / Where reason is denied and love ignored, / But, as we swear our lie, Miss Avery / Comes out into the garden with a sword."[46] Their imperialistic fervor, imagined here as being "knighted" or "nighted" and kept in the dark, recalls martial honor and conquest. They are rebuked for the "lie" of glorifying "international evil" by Miss Avery, the prophetic country housekeeper of *Howards End*, who waves a sword that recalls the human sacrifice of the soldier who once owned it and Leonard Bast, who died by its blade, reminding them of the higher calling of love and humility in a world of war and prejudice. Auden also invokes Forster himself: "still you speak to us, / Insisting that the inner life can pay. / As we dash down the slope of hate with gladness, / You trip us like an unnoticed stone,"[47] critiquing dangers of over-zealous national-ism. Just as the stones in *Passage to India* cry out, preventing the immature union of Fielding and Aziz, Forster is a stone that blocks misdirected enthusiasm. Forster serves as a reminder of the kind of moral responsibility that will become a hallmark of Auden's treatment of the nonhuman other.

Where Forster may have influenced Auden's themes, Woolf seems an inspiration for Auden's theories of form. Passages from *A Writer's Diary*, edited by Leonard Woolf, appear frequently in Auden's commonplace book, *A Certain World.* Several of these focus on Virginia Woolf's struggles with the craft of writing. Auden pays homage to her by quoting Woolf in titles to two essays written on the subject of poetic form, both referring to "Squares and Oblongs." The phrase comes from Woolf's novel *The Waves,* wherein Rhoda comments on a symphony:

> There is a square; there is an oblong. The players take the square and place it along the oblong. They place it very accurately; they make a perfect dwelling-place. Very little is left outside. The structure is now visible; what is inchoate is here stated; we are not so various or so mean; we have made oblongs and stood them upon squares. This is our triumph; this is our consolation.[48]

The paradoxical idea of finding meaning in the negative space that is made visible by surrounding forms, "the structure ... now visible; what is inchoate is here stated," rather than in the explicit forms themselves, could symbolize the union between visible and invisible in literature. Innate sensory awareness and connections of meanings latent between the words take precedence in deciding how to place each block or phrase. As Carrie Rohman notes of modernist writers generally, "In their famed discontinuous and irrational speech, modernists write their own animality, which cannot be represented by traditional literary forms."[49] Writers like Woolf and Auden notice negative spaces, and the animate possibilities of other lifeforms that many overlook. Likewise, they use discordant gaps and fissures to insert doubt about teleological rationality and to experiment with new ways of communicating embodied perception.

Auden's description of his own approach to analyzing poetry combines questions of language with ethics of place: "Speaking for myself, the questions which interest me most when reading a poem are two. The first is technical: 'Here is a verbal contraption. How does it work?' The second is, in the broadest sense, moral: 'What kind of guy inhabits this poem? What is his notion of the good life or the good place? His notion of the Evil One? What does he conceal from the reader? What does he conceal even from himself?'"[50] As Victoria Arana notes, "The critical stance is phenomenological."[51] Even the human aspects of Auden's questions – "What kind of guy *inhabits* this poem?" – are contextualized with ideas of what it means to live in a particular habitat and be in relationships reminiscent of hunter and hunted with others who share that literary space – "What does he conceal from the reader? What does he conceal even from himself?" Although Auden's pairing of mechanical concerns for the technicality of syntax with investigations of ethics and notions of "the good place" may seem initially quixotic, his early fascination with the landscapes of abandoned mines creates a more pragmatic connection between the two sets of inquiries about a poem.

In an essay ostensibly reviewing the autobiographies of Leonard Woolf and Evelyn Waugh, Auden stirs in generous helpings of his own remembrances as well: "Between the ages of six and twelve, I spent a great many of my waking hours in the construction and elaboration of a private sacred world, the basic elements of which were a landscape, northern and limestone, and industry, lead mining."[52] Auden's early interest in natural sciences and geology arose from his boyhood experience in northern England, in the Pennine region. When Auden playfully set about answering his own questionnaire titled "What is your dream of Eden?" he lists "Landscape: Limestone uplands like the Pennines plane, a small region of igneous rocks with at least one extinct volcano. A precipitous and indented sea-coast."[53] It is also noteworthy that Eden Valley is an actual place name of one of the regions bordering the Pennines, a fact that allows a productive slippage between symbolic cultural associations with a lost paradise and a very specific genius loci. Another biographer writes, "The terrain of limestone landscape and derelict lead-mines became, as Auden wrote of the old mine at Rookhope which he visited in 1922, 'my symbol of us all.'"[54] Ecocritical analysis of Auden's work suggests that these northern English boyhood landscapes, where water, rock, and humanity's tools are at work in hidden pockets of earthly flesh, symbolize a deeply intimate and embodied experience of all humanity's fraught, amorous relationship with the nonhuman world.

In 1965, Auden wrote a love poem for this landscape, titled "Amor Loci." Where some see "Any musical future most unlikely"[55] in a place of "dejected masonry, moss, decomposed machines,"[56] the speaker knows the terrain as a lover knows his beloved's body: "I could draw its map by heart, / showing its contours, / strata and vegetation, / name every height, / small burn and lonely sheiling."[57] His abiding affection for this place and the ability of the place to still reach out and touch the recesses of his own emotions teaches him there are loves that endure despite the deterioration of age and stretches of forlorn abandonment:

> How but with some real focus
> of desolation
> could I, by analogy,
> imagine a Love
> that, however often smeared,
> shrugged at, abandoned
> by a frivolous worldling,
> does not abandon?[58]

As Tony Sharpe has pointed out, the poem is "uncoercively asserting inwardness with place, rather than exclusion from it,"[59] a position as loving member of the environment, rather than an outside observer. For Auden, combinations of humanity embedded in larger environmental flesh and even traces of mechanization within rural place aren't incongruous or antagonistic. Thus, tinkering with "verbal contraptions" is already implicated in representations of the environment. Questions of human invention are "naturally" embedded in images of natural landscape. Yet Auden doesn't simply render deterioration into something aesthetic; there is an awareness of the cost and loss it represents: "When a mine is opened, everyone knows already, that however rich it may turn out to be, sooner or later it will become exhausted, and be abandoned" making mining, according to Auden, "the one human activity that is by nature mortal,"[60] a reminder that both individual humans and discreet places are fragile, mortal, and imperfect. In analyzing the natural descriptions of Derek Jarman and Jan Zita Grover in memoirs about AIDS, Mortimer-Sandilands calls such compassion for a wounded world "hard-won and profoundly ethical," reminding us that in relationships of love, whether for a mortal human animal or a place of comfort and identification, "their natures are not saved wildernesses; they are wrecks, barrens, cutovers, nuclear power plants: unlikely refuges and impossible gardens. But they are also sites for extraordinary reflection on life, beauty, and community"[61] because, like Auden, "rather than mourn the loss of the pristine" the attitude of writers Grover and Jarman is "grounded in a commitment to recognizing the simultaneity of death and life in these landscapes, the glut of aspen loving birds in the clear-cut, the swallows, turkey vultures, and bald eagles near the landfill."[62] In "Amor Loci" the fragmented mine works pocking the terrain are visual reminders that even humanity's measured and modest extractions should be regarded as acts of relationship meriting reciprocal care, and that the wounds of desolation can reveal our capacity for fidelity and love even in the landscapes of lost nostalgia. Artifice isn't divorced from natural representations in Auden's work; it is an ethical component of the discovery of place and human history within it.

Like Forster and Woolf, Auden seemed to believe that knowledge of natural science and daily encounters with the land and other species were necessary components of a writer's life. Auden's list of five requirements for a "college bards" curriculum includes: "Every student would have to select three courses out of courses in mathematics, natural history, geology, meteorology, archaeology, mythology, liturgics, cooking; Every student would be required to look after a domestic animal and cultivate a garden plot."[63] Auden's own training follows this formula. His scientific proclivities, his extensive knowledge of particular flora and fauna, as well as the time he spent getting to know local environs and observing creatures that shared his home, shape the ecocritical themes of his later poetry.

Subversive natural science and the human subject

W.H. Auden's lifelong friend and collaborator, Christopher Isherwood, declared that a reader of his poetry should know "First, that Auden is essentially a scientist."[64] Like many modern writers, Auden's perspectives on self-identity and the relationship between humans and the natural world were informed by advances in physics, biology, and psychoanalysis. Auden acknowledged that the life sciences profoundly affect his artistic vocation: "Physics, geology and biology have now replaced this everlasting universe with a picture of nature as a process in which nothing is now what it was or what it will be."[65] Auden's later poetry exacerbates the tension between science's claims to objective knowledge and its depiction of an inchoate world in perpetual flux. Several late poems that are rarely anthologized or critically analyzed, including "Bestiaries Are Out," "Et in Arcadia Ego," "After Reading a Child's Guide to Modern Physics," and "Ode to Terminus," disrupt any anthropomorphic certainty that science claims to reveal by employing scientific rhetoric for the purposes of undermining scientific presumptions of control. These poems create a lexicon of scientific systems but combat their own hermeneutics by slipping toward the opposite binary in any dialectic the poem presents, whether it be scientific order versus organic chaos, human observer versus nonhuman subject, or poetic imagination versus scientific fact.

In the poem "Bestiaries Are Out" (1964), which ostensibly examines the evolution of our knowledge about bees, Auden interrogates the practice of personification and its limits through scientific analogy: "We sought from study of their hives / To draw some moral for our lives."[66] The title refers to medieval works known as bestiaries, which allegorized the appearances or habits of animals. "Bestiaries Are Out" suggests such fables are outmoded and no longer suited to the more enlightened and objectively scientific modes of understanding the world. An ecocritical reading adds another gloss to the title – that what it means to be animal, or "beast," escapes the safe categorical boundary that has been presumed to separate humans from other nonhuman animals. Indeed, the formal aspects of the poem stridently resist the speaker's efforts to rationally distance humans from animals: "Now bestiaries are out, for now / Research has demonstrated how / They actually behave, they strike us / as being horridly unlike us."[67] The break in the enjambed line isolates "for now," inserts the idea of temporal uncertainty despite the speaker's strident tones of authority. The human-oriented words "behave" and "being" audibly play on the insect-oriented words "beehive" and "bee-ing." Further, the use of pairs of rhyming couplets throughout the stanzas and the exact word repetition in this couplet, "us" and "us," formally contradict the differences the speaker asserts.

Philosophy and literature articulate a struggle that has particular poignancy for the modernist era: the unsettling awareness that the very point where contrast is established through brushing against another entity is, at the same time, a point of connection through coming into shared experience with the other, whether it be through colonialism, a burgeoning global market, increased world tourism, or mass communication. Specifically, the moment of contact with the nonhuman other both marks a boundary of difference and creates a surface of exchange that blurs demarcations between separate entities. In *The Visible and the Invisible*, Merleau-Ponty writes: "The body stands before the world and the world upright before it, and between them there is a relation that is one of embrace. And between these two vertical beings, there is not a frontier, but a contact surface."[68] In the first half of the twentieth century new understandings of particle and wave theory, evolutionary biology, and the breakdown of traditional belief systems challenged fundamental assumptions about human control over nature. As we've seen with Forster and Woolf, modernist literary innovations also broke down customary symbolic uses of natural imagery that had heretofore affirmed pastoral ideology or established a mimetic subservience of nature to humans. In Auden's poetry, confronting a nonhuman environment no longer fettered by human desire or scientific control provokes disturbing revelations of both alienation and kinship.

Rather than reinforcing human superiority over nature, Auden's invocation of progress and science in "Bestiaries Are Out" becomes a tool for exposing human ignorance about how those same rules, when applied to the species Homo sapiens, uncover human failings. The conflation of human and nonhuman occurs both through the personification of the bees and the zoofication of humans, presented here as "Urban Man" becoming insect. While the speaker flatly denies that "Urban Man" might be made into an insect through consumerism and drugs, the regular four-foot iamb is haltingly disrupted by the speaker's "No."[69] As a result, the human speaker's continued claim to difference and superiority, not the idea of identification between human and insect, is what disrupts the poem's order.

In the poem's two concluding stanzas, the speaker attempts to strip away familiar devices of personification that compare humans to nonhumans:

> How, for us children of the word,
> Anthropomorphic and absurd
> To ask what code they satisfy
> When they swoop out to sting and die,
> Or what catharsis undergo
> When they put on their biggest show,
> A duel to the death between
> A tooting and a quacking Queen.[70]

Paradoxically, the effort to discard a search for "codes" that merely satisfy humans' own quest for logic and meaning persistently comes back to the very questions that humans ask themselves about the larger significance of life. To hypothesize what purpose bees fulfill when they "swoop out to sting and die" or interrogate the ultimate advancement of monarchies that are cyclically toppled and overthrown is to ask the fundamental question related to the significance of human existence, both individually and as a society. The analogy between humans and bees isn't quite the pathetic fallacy the speaker assumes; rather there is some verification of the human–apiary kinship in the very terms of its imagining. We know ourselves through the nonhuman other. The theatrical connotations of "catharsis" and "show" emphasize the act of assuming the role of another being. The desire to inscribe separation – to imagine any kinship as "absurd" – only heightens the fear of our own animal instincts and drives. Thus, the categories that humans create ultimately divulge more about human beings than about the "lesser" animals the speaker claims superiority over. Although this kind of poetical representation risks reinscribing the humanistic focus, and thus not fully participating in what current animal studies would term posthumanism, it poses significant challenges to schemas of knowledge that impose categorical divides between animals.

Thus, Auden elaborates an inextricable relationship between humans and nonhumans through his technique of undercutting the viability of imposed systems of control. In "Et in Arcadia Ego" (1964), humans have presumably tamed the wild into a cultivated garden state: "Her jungle growths / are abated, Her exorbitant / Monsters abashed."[71] But subsequent lines subvert the connotations of good and evil as well as the role of aggressor and victim: "I well might think myself / A humanist, / Could I manage not to see . . . The farmer's children / tiptoe past the shed / Where the gelding knife is kept."[72] Humans are the ones performing monstrous acts of castration. Moreover, castration aligns the abhorred sexuality with what is "natural" and insinuates that society's efforts to thwart that innate, embodied desire are actually what constitute the sinful behavior. Likewise, misguided sanctimonious assumptions about superiority filter through critiques of human violence toward the organic environment.

Like Forster's characters Maurice and Alec who seek refuge in the greenwood, in "Woods," part of Auden's pastoral series titled "Bucolics," the speaker imagines a forest retreat for lovers who would be scorned by a society that teaches "their silly flocks" to "abhor the licence of the grove."[73] There is a suggestion of indecorous bodily function in this poem: "And late man, listening through his latter grief, / Hears, close or far, the oldest of his joys, / Exactly as it was, the water noise. / A well-kempt forest begs Our Lady's grace; / Someone is not disgusted."[74] While this water echoes the aquatic images that flow through all the poems until they culminate in "Streams," the need to beg nature's pardon may also insinuate that someone has just peed in the forest. But the poem goes on to remind the reader that the occasional bladder incident is not the real source of the wood's defilement. Instead, what "The trees encountered on a country stroll / Reveal" about "a country's soul" is the "small grove massacred to the last ash" and "an oak with heart-rot" that "give away the show" portending "This great society is going smash."[75] Again, the processes of deforestation and artful pruning (as Simon Schama notes, the English were even known to cut road-sized arches into larger oaks),[76] put nature in the service of society and rob the trees of their own strength and vitality as natural beings, processes that ultimately show up the stunted ethical standards of a not-so "advanced" human culture. These same oblivious citizens also ineptly attempt to claim the mountains as a measure of their own solipsistic achievement in "Mountains":

> Clumping off at dawn in the gear of their mystery
> For points up, are a bit alarming;
> They have the balance, nerve,
> And habit of the Spiritual, but what God
> Does their Order serve?[77]

The speaker ruefully insinuates that these seeming devotees of nature seek their own glory rather than any holy or spiritual quest. As Auden proclaims in a 1948 letter to Elizabeth Mayer bemoaning human immodesty in politics and the will to overthrow, "What awful ideas have been suggested to the human mind by huge plains and gigantic mountains!"[78] By pointing out that humans are nearly always striving to construct and control the non-human, Auden accentuates the reader's awareness of how society divests nature of its own independent beauty or authority. Further, as in "Et in Arcadia Ego," Auden's work suggests that humans often exhibit the very traits of bestiality and violence they proclaim to have excised through "superior" social and scientific order. Auden subversively portrays the human animal as having more similarity with than difference from other nonhuman animals.

Auden's "Prologue at Sixty" (1967) consciously invokes personification and anthropomorphism to heighten the reader's awareness of how human perspectives impose themselves on natural subjects. An aging speaker contemplates forest landscapes tamed by warring factions, modern technology, and layers of European history that provide a background for New York City in 1967, while a canine cosmonaut "blinked at our sorry conceited O."[79] The "O" takes on the connotations of a microcosmic planetary globe as seen by the astronaut-dog; the solipsistic enclosed human mind that threatens the future of the planet; the mortal zero-value of every individual, including the speaker, that human conceit – "our sorry conceited O" – attempts to mask; and a blank face of human gullibility characterized by a slack "O"-shaped mouth and wide vacuous eyes – the titular political "Heads who are not all there."[80] This cluster of images pointing toward the cultural and political history of human arrogance, conquest, and destruction is directly juxtaposed with the refocusing acuity of the dog's blink. The dog's position of the surveying glance presents a similar reversal of traditional roles of the observer and the observed. In terms of animal studies, this maneuver represents an attempt to imaginatively construct nonhuman subjectivities that jostle us out of a humanistic frame of reference. Ecophenomenology contains a related precept, that an openness to being on the part of the perceiver is a precursor to truly understanding the perceived subject: "he who sees cannot possess the visible unless he is possessed by it, unless he is *of* it, unless . . . he is one of the visibles, capable, by a singular reversal, of seeing them – he who is one of them,"[81] writes Merleau-Ponty. Thus, animals gain potential for sentience as humans become animals to be examined. Poems such as these offer to teach something to the sciences, namely that no perspective is objective; all knowledge is situated and contextualized from one's subjective experience and desires. The scope of human history appears small and mean from a nonhuman, global vantage point.

The wisdom of humanity's insatiable desire to discover and master the nonhuman world, from the tiniest atomic particles to the farthest reaches of the cosmic continuum, is questioned in "After Reading a Child's Guide to Modern Physics" (1961). The first lines, "If all a top physicist knows / About the truth be true"[82] describe truth and knowledge as a circular, self-reflexive axiom at best, "If . . . truth be true." Merleau-Ponty explains how scientific knowledge often fails to account for the instability of systems by offering totalizing theories: "Physics should not be conceived as a search for the truth, it should give up determining a real physics . . . Formalist physics receives all freedom, but it loses its ontological content. It signifies no mode of being, no reality."[83] Similarly, the poem's vague reference to "all the so-and-so's" deflates knowledge to a forgettable, nonsensical absurdity. Humanity's childish desire to cling to a reality that can be mastered by scientific knowledge is disturbed by the division between learned explanation and personal experience. Or, as primatologist and ethologist Frans de Waal frames his research questions, "But what if morality is created in day-to-day social interaction, not at some abstract mental level? What if it is grounded in the emotions, which most of the time escape the neat categorizations that science is fond of? . . . This approach deserves attention at a time in which even avowed atheists are unable to wean themselves from a semireligious morality, thinking that the world would be a better place if only a white-coated priesthood could take over from the frocked one."[84] As Auden and de Waal notice, humans often choose to discard embodied knowledge in favor of sources that are presumed to be more authoritative. The rhyme scheme of "After Reading a Child's Guide to Modern Physics" itself resists the comfort of predictable patterns; each stanza contains eight lines, four of which rhyme with another four lines in the stanza, but the order of the rhyming lines is different in every stanza. The central argument of the poem in stanzas five and six interrogates whether factual knowledge of extremes serves any purpose in our daily lives or whether its pursuit is more harmful than edifying:

> The passion of our kind
> For the process of finding out
> Is a fact one can hardly doubt,
> But I would rejoice in it more
> If I knew more clearly what
> We wanted the knowledge for,
> Felt certain still that the mind
> Is free to know or not.
> It has chosen once, it seems,
> And whether our concern
> For magnitude's extremes

> Really become a creature
> Who comes in median size,
> Or politicizing Nature
> Be altogether wise,
> Is something we shall learn.[85]

The previous stanzas' references to mundane routines such as kissing, shaving, and an appreciation of habitable space suggest the farcical application of atomic knowledge and cosmic science to an embodied experience of daily life. In his *Secondary Worlds* lectures, Auden touches upon this theme more literally: "The only real world which is 'real' for us, as in the world in which all of us, including scientists, are born, work, love, hate, and die, is the primary phenomenal world as it is and always has been presented to us through our senses."[86] Yet, the refusal of science to value embodied perception creates a tension between the value of knowledge and the value of life.

The theme of this poem doesn't discredit science generally as much as it questions the hidden agendas science might obscure. "After Reading a Child's Guide to Modern Physics" strikes a tragic note by linking the application of atomic fission or cosmic expansion to a lexicon of violence; "pelt," "break," and "explode," as well as an image of the aftermath of violence, "indeterminate gruel."[87] All recall the destructive potential of knowledge to harm living bodies, particularly in times of war. Auden is concerned about "what / We want the knowledge for," suggesting that science can be misappropriated or divested of its ambiguity for political gain.

The trepidation contained in the final stanzas is produced by the uneasy mixture of theology and physics. Auden's speaker seems like Milton's Adam warning Eve against desiring knowledge that doesn't concern them and might disrupt their daily bliss. Earlier references to "Thank God" and "architects" who "enclose / a quite Euclidian space"[88] subtly allude to a garden state. The last stanza's claim that "it," the mind, "has chosen once"[89] before, recalls the choice that resulted in a fall from grace. As in Milton's *Paradise Lost*, the poem insinuates that humanity's insatiable lust for knowledge is inevitable. As the speaker asserts a desire to be assured "still that the mind / Is free to know or not,"[90] the very freedom of choice is rejected in the homophone "know" which becomes audibly indistinguishable from "no," making the seeming dialectical opposites collapse into a singular negation of choice – "no" and "not." The poem assumes that humans will learn from the ominous consequences of their overreaching, even as it argues for caution and limitation. Science, the poem warns, should not be pursued in a detached manner for its own sake, but rather constantly assessed in the context of moral and ethical consequences for the life of other humans and the larger "garden" of human stewardship. Forster and Auden's mutual concerns about moral responsibility and property rights form one of the important environmental links between them. Both were attentive to the ethical strictures inherent in caring for land that other animals also shared. Mendelson underscores the ethical bonds that linked Auden with the nonhuman inhabitants of his land: "Auden's responsibility for three acres put him, he believed, under the same obligations that scientists, and those who defer to their authority, prefer to ignore."[91] This admonition of kinship with all living beings eviscerates a solipsistic "objectivity" that only concerns itself with the existence of others as it can be exploited for human glory or power.

"Ode to Terminus" (1968) also counsels responsible restraint and compares the scientist with the poet. The first stanza of the poem – "The High Priests of telescopes and cyclotrons / keep making pronouncements about happenings / on scales too gigantic or dwarfish / to be noticed by our native senses"[92] – associates science with an aggressively dogmatic faith and reprises the discrepancy between scientific phenomena and the experience of everyday life. The poem asserts that the "elegant / euphemisms of algebra" are "too symbolic of the crimes and strikes and demonstrations / we are supposed to gloat on at breakfast,"[93] suggesting that scientific achievement incapable of verification by the common person is too often affiliated with nationalist causes, allowing science to become mere propaganda. For Auden, no perspective is objective; all knowledge is situated and contextualized by political discourse.

Thus, the poem exposes science as another kind of cultural construction. Science relies on images and languages through which we know and understand the world even when it goes against humans' daily sensory experience of the lived environment: "scales too gigantic or dwarfish / to be noticed by our native senses." The poem's concerns are necessarily based on an appreciation of the body's centrality to human knowledge: "The very notion of scale is an absolutely incomprehensible notion if we do not refer to perceptual experience."[94] What we deem credible is determined by our degree of faith in the authority of scientific claims. In this way, both poetry and science can be misquoted or misused for rhetorical effect. The seventh stanza juxtaposes the kinds of romanticized personifications used to explain the natural world with the data provided by physics, contrasting sunlight represented as a "Sun-Father" whose "light is felt as a friendly presence" with an understanding of the sun's rays as a type of "photonic bombardment."[95] Both are constructed models for reality – one a romantic simile that figuratively imagines the sun in terms of human relations, and the other a construct produced by science, which doesn't comport with humans' daily lived experience of sunlight. The poem goes so far as to claim that humanity's need to create meaning through language doesn't justify human superiority, but rather puts humans outside of the more natural harmony of the rest of the ecologic world: "where to all species *except the talkative* / have been allotted the niche and diet that / become them."[96] What redeems humanity then is an acknowledgment of boundaries, both linguistic and scientific, that allow us to discern truth and meaning. To discard "rhythm, punctuation, metaphor" leads to babble that "sinks into driveling monologue, / too literal to see a joke or / distinguish a penis from a pencil."[97] Or one might add, playing on the pun, to distinguish a phallus (biological) from a fallacy (the written interpretations of human power through science and art). The formal technique allows the astute reader to get the joke and apprehend its significance through conscious formal structures. Pauses of punctuation and the boundaries of rhythm and metaphor promote meaning through limitation. Read in a time of global warming, this poem raises questions about how we might recognize the significance and truth of global temperature change when we don't yet feel its impact on our bodies and daily lives, but its pronouncement against political uses of science is still apt.

The poem's final remonstration claims that science has been deployed to justify a self-serving, gluttonous exploitation that must be similarly checked:

> In this world our colossal immodesty
> has plundered and poisoned, it is possible /
>   You still might save us, who by now have
>   Learned this: that scientists, to be truthful,
> must remind us to take all they say as a
> tall story, that abhorred in the Heav'ns are all
>   self-proclaimed poets who, to wow an
>   audience, utter some resonant lie.[98]

These stanzas recreate the sensation of uncontrolled abandon: each line is enjambed and the auditory lack of rhyme as well as the visual placement of the lines on the page replicates a jarred sense of discordance and imbalance. The poetic powers of creation are akin to the scientific imagination; both must evidence some exercise of self-restraint in order to be effective. Either one can tell a "tall story" uttered with a rhetorical or political flourish, concealing truth rather than revealing it. In a review of the poetry of

Robert Graves, Auden rebukes his meteorological inaccuracy in "Turn of the Moon": "The lines are beautiful and, at first reading, I was carried away. But, then, a tiresome doubt inserted itself: 'Are drought and rainfall really caused by the moon? What would a meteorologist say?'"[99] Yet it isn't the details of individual metaphor and scientific inaccuracies that trouble Auden most in "Ode to Terminus." Larger ethical questions are at stake: the poet and the scientist are equally capable of poorly crafted lies if they do not remain attentive to whether the form adheres to the theme and whether the act or deed has a worthy purpose. Merleau-Ponty's philosophy locates the origins of scientific myth-making in a misplaced acceptance of Cartesian dualisms and undisclosed emotional motivations: "Science is not an unmotivated instance. We have to psychoanalyze science, purify it. . . . Moreover, science still lives in part on a Cartesian myth. . . . Its concept of Nature is often only an idol to which the scientist makes sacrifices, the reasons for which are due more to affective motivations than to scientific givens."[100] Auden's insistence on an awareness of embodied knowledge rejects the Cartesian divisions erected by science.[101] However, Auden also expresses latent distrust of any language that makes truth claims. He inserts a suspicion that science doesn't reflect the full, textured richness of human experience through its objective impersonality. Both science and literature are powerful and provocative translations of human experience while ultimately still merely interpretations of the embodied relationship between humans and the nonhuman world. In our own time, physics and science, even in its popular modes, such as Neil deGrasse Tyson's *Cosmos*, or the works referred to in this book by Karan Barad and others, seems more dexterous with acknowledging the unknown and offering us metaphors that describe a tentative complexity of alternate worlds, microscopic convergences, or multiplying subjectivities – representations of a circumscribed scientific knowledge that were not as prominent in Auden's era. But Auden's wariness might anticipate and advocate for the more interrogative and ethically oriented rhetorical approaches science seems to speak within today.

According to George Bahlke, Auden's contemporaries chastised him for "turn[ing] his back on the left-wing views they believed him to have espoused in the thirties" or implying that "civilization . . . requires well-educated, sophisticated, and witty human beings . . . who devote themselves . . . to an effete art in which form and verbal play outweigh content."[102] While Auden's "scientific" methodologies may create a sense of detachment in his speakers, it is equally important to be cognizant of the way his work critiques the supposed objectivity of the scientific gaze.

An ecocritical reading of Auden's poetic treatment of science reveals a profound involvement with the larger world, particularly the social and ethical ramifications of scientific knowledge. Thus, if we take seriously Isherwood's claim that Auden is "essentially a scientist" we should consider him as a highly skeptical practitioner whose artistic experiments often resist facile scientific facts and reveal humans as brute animals to be examined.

Talking animal

Auden's conviction that human knowledge must be tempered with ethical responsibility is also evident in his poems about nonhumans. In the essay "The Virgin and the Dynamo," Auden explains that a lack of personal accountability is created when nonhuman presences are given a god-like mask that absolves humans of responsibility for their actions. Auden further states that the inverse situation is also true; humans often efface unique aspects of the ecological other, particularly nonhuman animals, in an effort to evade moral obligations:

> By nature we tend to endow with a face any power which we imagine to be responsible for our lives and behavior; vice versa, we tend to deprive of their faces any persons whom we believe to be at the mercy of our will. In both cases we are trying to avoid responsibility. In the first case, we wish to say: 'I can't help doing what I do; someone else, stronger than I, is making me do it' – in the second: 'I can do what I like to N because N is a thing, an x with no will of its own.' ... It is permissible, and even right, to endow nature with a real face, e.g., the face of the Madonna, for by so doing we make nature remind us of our duty towards her, but we may only do this after we have removed the pagan mask from her, seen her as a world of masses and realized that she is not responsible for us.[103]

Here, Auden enjoins his readers to discard two common anthropocentric approaches to nature, that of deification and that of human exceptionalism. Instead, he argues the proper relationship with the nonhuman is one that sees a "real face" of familial, biological kinship. Several poems about the earth represent nature as a "Madonna," or an originating mother deserving of human respect yet no longer responsible for the actions of a mature human species. "Ode to Gaea" (1954) proclaims that "Earth, till the end, will be Herself" (556 l.93) and "Dame Kind" (1959) labels those who may be tempted to rage against her – "... ONE BOMB WOULD BE ENOUGH ... Now look / who's thinking gruesome" – as "worse than a lonesome Peeper / or a He-Virgin / Who nightly abhors the Primal Scene / in medical Latin," admonishing, "She mayn't be all She might be / but She *is* our Mum."[104] These lines are a tacit reminder that violence is linked to a rage for order, a perverse desire to abolish the mess of sex and the uncertainty of emotions that accompany embodied participation in life.

It is not surprising then that Auden takes on the fundamental problem of food, prey, and cultural ritual in several poems about hunting, including the early poem "Our Hunting Fathers" (1934), "The Sabbath" (1959), and perhaps most radical in its approach to this question, "Hunting Season" (1952). Auden maintained a wary attitude toward hunting and other pastimes usually associated with celebrating nature, indicting them as activities that more often reflect human desires for social conquest: "The ever growing popularity of hunting, fishing, and mountain climbing" has the tendency to "make the relation to Nature one of contest, the goal of which is human victory, and limit contacts with her to those of the greatest dramatic intensity," which may "exacerbate rather than cure that unnatural craving for excess and novel thrills which is the characteristic of urban disease."[105] Mortimer-Sandilands has described such wilderness conquest narratives as "a site for the enactment of a specific heteromasculinity."[106] From Auden's perspective, the appreciation for nature that hunting and other outdoor sports supposedly inspire is hypocritical because they still require a vanquishing of the very thing they are purportedly designed to exalt. Literary homages to nonhuman rivals are similarly fraught with hypocrisy. As early as 1934, Auden was aware that the device of personification allowed humans to assuage guilt for killing. He revealed that "the story" told by "Our hunting fathers" relied on seeing "In the lion's intolerant look, / Behind the quarry's dying glare, / Love raging for the personal glory / That reason's gift would add."[107] He goes on to condemn such mirroring as artifice, marveling that man could so change the lion's essential being: "His southern gestures modify / and make it his mature ambition / To think no thought but ours."[108] Thus, human efforts to revel in nature are tinged with egotistical impulses rather than respectful appreciation of an independent nonhuman subjectivity.

In "The Sabbath" Auden gives readers insight into the kind of tale the nonhuman animal might tell about the human hunter's superiority: "Waking on the Seventh Day of Creation" the nonhuman creatures, identified by their own relationship to food, warily look for the newest member of the garden: "Herbivore, parasite, predator scouted, / Migrants flew fast and far – / Not a trace of his presence: holes in the earth, Beaches covered with tar."[109] The human effect on the environment recalls the earth itself as another body, able to be shot up, foul fluid spilled like a noxious kind of blood. Yet the animals, emboldened by the temporary absence of man, reassure themselves: "Well, that fellow had never really smelled / like a creature who would survive: / No grace, address or faculty like those / Born on the First Five,"[110] specifically refuting the more refined qualities that humans might wish to claim set them apart from other beasts: "grace" or beauty, "address" or speech, and "faculty" or intelligence. "First Five," referring to animals created on the first five days God created the world, also draws attention to the superior sensory abilities, or "first" five senses (there may be even more), of nonhuman animals. Yet, the human does return: "A rifle's ringing crack / Split their Arcadia wide open, cut / Their Sabbath nonsense short. / For whom did they think they had been created? / That fellow was back, / More bloody-minded than they remembered, / More god-like than they thought."[111] It is the human who defiles what is "their Arcadia," "their Sabbath." Further, the other creatures' "nonsense" is made so only by sheer human force – a "bloody-mind," rather than any power of reasoning and argumentation. In this poem, Auden doesn't escape from anthropomorphism in his description of animals, but the poem's message still pointedly resists anthropocentrism. It is the imagined perspective of the nonhuman animal that is given the greater claim to intellect while "god-like" human hierarchy is revealed to rest merely on the physical, retributive might of gun power, more like the mythological gods' lightning bolt than God's laws, which the human is violating by hunting on the ordained day of rest. Auden's treatment of hunting in poems like this one offers a productive contrast between his satirical blow to human exceptionalism and Phillip Armstrong's assessment of Hemingway's modernist therio-primitivism, where "access to the revitalizing energy of the wild animal depends upon its harnessing and eventual conquest ... whereby the human captures and consumes the animal's vitality and purity."[112] Auden's treatment of what might be termed an "indulgence" of human violence inverts the modernist approach Armstrong astutely identifies in Hemingway, swapping the usual signifiers for civilized restraint and unthinking bestial violence, which, in Auden's work, drains rather than ignites human vitality.

Auden more subtly reverses these expectations in "Hunting Season," which intermingles its human and nonhuman subjects, offering an ars poetica for the poet who aims to capture animals in verse. It is written in the pattern of ABCBDD – the same verse form as W.B. Yeats' "Wild Swans at Coole," a poem about a flock of swans rising into the air after being suddenly startled and reminding the speaker of a past love, and the verse form in much of the poetry of Emily Dickenson. Although Dickinson's "My life stood – a loaded gun," a poem about the violent potential of the poet as well as the eternal life of poetry, only replicates the ABCB format in its first and last verses, the themes of "Wild Swans at Coole" and "My life stood – a loaded gun" might add to our understanding of the complex set of relationships elliptically revealed in "Hunting Season":

> A shot: from crag to crag
>   The tell-tale echoes trundle;
> Some feathered he-or-she
>   Is now a lifeless bundle
> And, proud into a kitchen, some
> Example of our tribe will come.
>
> Down in the startled valley
>   Two lovers break apart:
> He hears the roaring oven
>   Of a witch's heart;
> Behind his murmurs of her name
> She sees a marksman taking aim.
>
> Reminded of the hour
>   And that his chair is hard,
> A deathless verse half done,
>   One interrupted bard
> Postpones his dying with a dish
> Of several suffocated fish.[113]

Edward Mendelson's brief treatment of this poem elucidates one possible reading. His interpretation rests on a distinction between first person "I/Thou" and second person "he/she" and assumes the second stanza involves a pair of human lovers hearing the distant shot. He equates the crack of the gun with a ruptured demise of emotional intimacy at the very moment of coital penetration: "The startled valley is an anatomical as well as a geographical place, and the two lovers suddenly sense the impersonal sexual hungers that drive their personal love."[114] Mendelson also presumes that the rifle shot is what "remind[s]" the poet "of the hour," noting that "a 'deathless verse half done'" serves as a "reminder that persons, whether first, second, or third, are not all deathless."[115] Yet an ecocritical reading adds another interpretation by prioritizing the relationship between the prominent nonhuman animals and the character of the poet as well as the ambiguous antecedent of "two lovers."

Like the "tell-tale echoes" in line two, there are dual echoes in this literary tale. The earlier reference to "Some feathered he-or-she" offers a second possibility for the "two lovers" who "break apart." While the hunter is indifferent to the identity of the felled bird, the second stanza could be read as a recounting of two hunted birds in flight. Pursuant to that reading, the male bird, knowing the shot means that they may soon be cooked and eaten, "hears the roaring oven," and calls to his winged companion as she spots the hunter below "taking aim." Thus the second stanza can be read as either a dangerous realization occurring between two human characters at the moment their love is physically consummated or a veiled sympathetic rendering of two avian characters, one of whom is shot and consumed. A reader has to be willing to imagine that animals may share similar feelings of peril, love, and grief in order to apprehend the second reading. The form of the poem replicates the issue of difference and similarity between humans and nonhumans as well as the motif of coupling and couples, featuring two unrhymed lines, two rhymed lines, and a final couplet in each stanza. Accordingly, "Hunting Season" allows two divergent possibilities for the same "him" or "her" couple.

The figure of the poet in the final stanza prompts the reader to examine more than one type of hidden ambiguity. As the identity of the two lovers is uncertain, the position of the poet in the poem is also indeterminate. Is he simply another person who was startled by the sound of the hunter's rifle? Or is his writing of the first two stanzas of the poem interrupted by the chime of a clock, "Reminded of the hour," thus leaving the reader hanging at the climax of an unfinished plot in the second stanza, "She sees a marksman taking aim"? Is his "deathless verse half done" merely temporally coincidental to the other events, or does it refer to the death left unfinished in the second stanza? The poet has a dual role that the reader must assign. The only definite quality is the stark contrast between the dramatic emotion in the second stanza and the deflated ennui of the third. Juxtaposed with the heightened intensity of the imminent death or violent romantic loss of the previous stanza, the poet insipidly complains "that his chair is hard." His "deathless verse" gives him the power to immortalize other lives, even though the poet himself is still prey to the inevitable deterioration of all flesh and participates in killing and consuming himself by eating the meal. The word "suffocated" and the alliteration in "A dish of several suffocated fish" – the repeated "s" sound requiring the reader to force out air – implies a murderous responsibility. Pairing "suffocated" with "fish" which don't breathe air, links the hunter's avian prey with the aquatic animals the poet consumes. It also unexpectedly combines allusions to sex, fish being a common symbol for a penis, and the violent death of the bird prepared in the hunter's kitchen, thus once again confirming two alternate readings. Whether the victims in the second stanza are human mammals or birds, the poet is still guilty of participating in their loss and consummation, questioning whether the poet's power of immortality really sets him apart from hunters or whether the poet unconsciously shares in the tragedy of "several" deaths. Equating true suffering with a hard chair or analogizing the poet's dinner with saving a life in the phrase "postpones his dying" (it is still unclear whether the death that is postponed is the one occurring in the poet's verse or his own slow progress to the grave), makes the third stanza hyperbolic in comparison to the peril of the second verse. The poet-figure seems self-centered and ironically unaware. But the poem itself prompts the reader to be more acute than the persona of the poet. Victoria Arana explains a similar impulse in Auden's *Epistle to a Godson*: "Auden slyly alerts readers to 'the Managers' and their worldly maxims. He also wittily nudges the reader to question whether Auden, as the coiner of worldly maxims, is to be taken quite seriously as a pundit. Thus forewarned, the reader proceeds cautiously, reads alertly."[116] The reader is challenged to think beyond anthropocentric notions that only humans are capable of experiencing affection or fear and encouraged to recognize the multiple layers of culpability in any violent act. This maneuver is reminiscent of the reminder in "Museé des Beaux Arts" that suffering usually happens because others renounce the ability to intercede.

Auden's concern for the poet's treatment of animals in literary contexts extends well beyond "Hunting Season." "Two Bestiaries" (1948), an essay in which he analyzes the poetry of Marianne Moore and D.H. Lawrence, classifies five different ways animals have been anthropomorphized in poetry. The beast fable, the animal simile, the animal as allegorical emblem, and the romantic encounter of man and beast offer different strategies for using the animal as a mirror for human emotions. Such treatments present the animal without any kind of accuracy in the context of their own natural history. However, Auden identifies a fifth category, animals as objects of human interest and affection that avoids a human-centered approach. Using this kind of poetic treatment, the poet describes animals "in the same way that he would describe a friend, that is to say, every detail of the animal's appearance and behavior will interest him."[117] While Auden acknowledges that even this method participates in anthropomorphism, it is because "it is almost impossible to make such a description communicable to others except in anthropomorphic terms."[118] Understanding each animal as an individual being establishes a shared experience – a posture of response and respect that anticipates the "respecere" advanced by current animal advocate Donna Haraway.[119] The affectionate attention to "every detail of the animal's appearance and behavior" is unlike other literary formulations because, as Auden explains, "the Homeric simile is reversed"[120] so that the animal is the subject that is then compared to the human, and metaphors for an individual nonhuman animal may be drawn from other animals and plants, not just humans. This strategy may employ anthropomorphism, but unlike the other ways of using animals in literature, it does not participate in anthropocentrism.

In "Two Bestiaries," Auden singles out Marianne Moore as particularly adept at allowing the reader to experience a familiar and personal relationship with her nonhuman subjects, but Auden's own poetry also attempts to acknowledge animals as having distinct personalities and a particular relationship with the speaker. Indeed, personal human interactions with animals shape some of Auden's most prominent ideas about ethical dwelling in the world. In his essay "Justice of Dame Kind" (1973) Auden draws distinctions between "a naturalist" who "studies the ways of creatures in their natural habitat and, if he interferes at all, confines his interference to establishing a personal relation with them" and "Professors of animal psychology and behavioral scientists" who "subject animals to abnormal conditions of their own contriving ... those, in other words, who perform experiments on animals which they would never dream of performing on themselves or their children."[121] Endorsing the "naturalist approach," in another essay, "Concerning the Unpredictable" (1973), Auden quotes a long passage describing Dr. Eisley's response to a wild "fox inviting me to play": "Gravely I arranged my forepaws while the puppy whimpered with ill-concealed excitement. I drew the breath of a fox's den into my nostrils. On impulse, I picked up clumsily a whiter bone and shook it with teeth that had not entirely forgotten their purpose."[122] This playful freedom, the willingness to forget decorum and act from generous instinct of interspecies exchange, delights Auden, who aligns himself with Eisley: "Neither of us can enjoy crowds and loud noises. But even introverted intellectuals can share the Carnival experience if they are prepared to forget their dignity, as Dr. Eisely did."[123] This is the kind of inspired connectivity that Auden attempts through his poetic play of interspecies communication. Both humor and theatricality, the ability to take on and imagine ourselves in other roles, are recurrent motifs in Auden's animal poems. Yet many of these poems also critically examine the ways humans violently sever the bond between themselves and other animals, a theme that might have been influenced by the feelings of revulsion Auden experienced at witnessing the dissection of a whale carcass in Iceland. Michael Yates, Auden's companion that day, attributes the following statement to Auden: "It gives one an extraordinary vision of the cold, controlled ferocity of the human species."[124] Both of these poles of human response – interspecies exchange and violent attack – are depicted in Auden's animal poetry.

In "Talking to Dogs" (1970), "Talking to Mice" (1971), and "Talking to Myself" (1971), Auden explores a conversational relationship with the animals that share the space of his home. As Mendelson notes in a summary of Auden's canon, variations on the personal voice constitute a recognizable cornerstone of Auden's poetic career.[125] All three of the poems employ some form of free verse, enhancing their colloquial and conversational effect. The inclusion of "Talking to Myself" in this triad sets up an equivalency between the human and nonhuman while playfully accentuating the very artifice of the construct, suggesting that perhaps any effort to "talk to" another species is always filtered through the self who imagines their end of the dialogue.

Theatricality, a mode Auden knows well as a playwright, peeks out from each of these poems. In "Talking to Dogs" Auden references Goethe and Lear, ending with "Let difference / remain our bond, yes, and the one trait / both have in common, a sense of theatre."[126] The sense of dialogue is created by the inserted "yes," as if the dog was adding his assent to the speaker's claims. This is carried forth in "Talking to Mice," which begins with the lines commonly uttered by people when they encounter a mouse:

> Creepy! Get HER! Good Lord, what an oddity! One to steer clear of!
> Fun! Impossible! Nice but a bore! An adorable monster!"
> But those animates which we call in our arrogance *dumb* are
> judged as a species and classed by the melodramatic division,
> either *Goodies* or *Baddies*.[127]

This opening cacophony of jumbled responses, akin to "Hunting Season," begins to smudge the boundaries between human and nonhuman subjects. Phrases like "Nice but a bore!" are apt descriptions of human beings; consequently the surrounding lines take on multiple registers and the "adorable monster" could be either a furry little creature with pink ears or a beautiful but cloyingly "dumb" human peer. The divisions erected between humans and other species are only a matter of degree, like "melodramatic division[s]." Melodrama may even humorously indicate that the common attitude to the fact of genetic kinship is a fearful overreaction or melodramatic response, as the use of italics throughout the poem suggests a thickly spread emphatic tone.

Similarly, "Talking to Myself," in which the speaker's consciousness addresses the speaker's physicality, likens the mind/body relationship to a dramatic production where both the spoken lines and performed gestures create meaning:

> Our marriage is a drama, but no stage-play where
> what is not spoken is not thought: in our theatre
> all that I cannot syllable You will pronounce
> in acts whose *raison-d'etre* escapes me.[128]

The "animal" aspect of the human being isn't disavowed, but rather given a primary role in conveying meaning. Formally, this relationship is enacted by the conjoining "but" as well as the colon, which visually create division in the middle of the first two lines of the stanza, yet rhetorically join the adjacent phrases. The inclusion of the French phrase highlights the idea that the transfer between conscious thought and unconscious movement is a relationship of translation rather than incommunicability.

All three of these poems describe personal interactions with the animal being addressed. These direct and individual relationships evoke questions of ethical responsibility in the deaths that also transect each poem. "Talking to Dogs" is dedicated to a specific canine: "In memoriam Rolfi Stroble. Run over, June 9th, 1970."[129] Although the "you" of the poem is plural, the dedication lends a eulogistic particularity to the poem. When the speaker recounts, "Being quicker to sense unhappiness / without having to be told the dreary / details or who is to blame, in dark hours / your silence may be of more help than many / two-legged comforters" the absence of the named dog and the sentiment of grief is poignantly recalled. Although the human culprit is anonymous, the fact that Rolfi's death was caused by an automobile confirms human culpability. Indeed, the subject of the dog in the poem is frequently overshadowed or "run over" by metaphors that have more to say about humans than canines. The poem begins with an awareness of a dog's perception of the world:

> From us, of course, you want gristly bones
> and to be led through exciting odorscapes
> – their colors don't matter – with the chance
> of a rabbit to chase or of meeting

> a fellow arse-hole to snuzzle at,
> but your deepest fury is to be accepted
> as junior members of a Salon
> suaver in taste and manners than a pack[130]

The opening lines are still tinted with skeletal reminders of death, "gristly bones," but convey the sense of a canine's experience of "odorscapes," where "colors don't matter." Yet the lines quickly shift to metaphors that are more reminiscent of class differences between humans: "but your deepest fury is to be accepted / as junior members of a Salon." These quickly moving references, from images that display a biological knowledge of how actual dogs behave to images that focus on grossly obvious human fetishes, continue throughout the poem. Taken as a whole, they create a heightened contrast between representations of the dog that are truly canine and representations of a dog that are only a thin veil for a human subject. The repeated back-and-forth juxtaposition highlights the accuracy of some descriptions and the falsity of others, like the Salon. While the speaker may be unaware of the hairpin turns in these literary representations, they become markedly apparent to the attentive reader.

In "Talking to Mice" the speaker confesses himself to be the agent of the mice's death. Initially, the two mice are described as "the most comely of all the miniature mammals," and are compared to the dressed-up and personified illustrations of Beatrix Potter. The pair of mice live in placid cohabitation with the speaker and his other, unnamed, human companion. The pleasantry ends when the pair of mice exceed the human population by having a litter. The decision to kill them is figured as political genocide perpetrated on innocents:

> What occurred now confirmed that ancient political axiom:
> When Words fail to persuade, then Physical force gives the orders
> Knowing you trusted in us, and would never believe an unusual
> object pertaining to men would be there for a sinister purpose,
> traps were baited[131]

Of course, the fact that the humans couldn't have used "words" to persuade the mice superficially justifies the subsequent resort to violence. But the admitted trust of the mice and the description of the dead body – "one more broken cadaver, its black eyes beadily staring" – imputes blame. As the political analogy continues, it becomes clear that accepted nationalistic rationale doesn't absolve the human actors, but rather reveals the immorality of socially accepted "civil" forms of behavior: "As / householders we had behaved exactly as every State does, / when there is something It wants, and a minor one gets in the way."[132] A poem that begins as a farcical look at social interaction between different people and between humans and rodents becomes a darker exploration of the socially acceptable sacrifice of any being that disconcerts those in power.

The anxiety concerning human connections to "lesser" animals is reprised in "Talking to Myself" when the speaker, beginning the poem to the "self" with a stanza describing "all feeders, vegetate or bestial" and "the deathless minerals," recounts his beginning:

> Unpredictably, decades ago, You arrived
> among that unending cascade of creatures spewed
> from Nature's maw. A random event, says Science.
> Random my bottom! A true miracle, say I,
> for who is not certain that he was meant to be?[133]

Although the timeframe of "decades ago" signals the speaker's own birth, the progress of the poem and the references to "Nature" and "Science" suggest a larger Darwinist context as well; the speaker is determined to exert his own uniqueness and the "miracle" of the emergence of the human form generally. The two agents that "say" in this stanza are the speaker and science; the speaker protests science to assert his preeminence. Yet even when attempting to defy natural science's conclusions that humans are merely effluvia, spit or "spew," the human speaker's idiom for disagreement, "my bottom!," refers to animal functions and affirms a kind of random assignment of words and significance, just as the human form may not be "bottom" or top of any preordained chain of being. At the end of the poem, the speaker envisions his own physical decay and pleads for the body to ignore the requests of the mind:

> When Le Bon Dieu says to You Leave him!,
> please, please, for His sake and mine, pay no attention
> to my piteous *Don'ts*, but bugger off quickly.[134]

The body has more authority to decide than either of the "speakers" of this stanza: God and intellect. This suggests that the life of the mind is limited to what body and nature will allow – the capacity for speech doesn't always mean one will get the last word. As "bugger" implies, not only are humans insignificant and ephemeral, the human body may dictate sexuality in ways that reason or "talking cures" can't change or control.

In "A New Year Greeting" (1969) Auden considers the perspective of parasitic symbiots on a human host. The poem's epigraph gives credit to

Mary J. Marples' article in the January 1969 edition of *Scientific American* for inspiring Auden's address to bodily beasties. As Tony Sharpe has pointed out, "Late in his life, [Auden] declared that the only two magazines to which he regularly subscribed were *Nature* and *Scientific American*,"[135] attesting to interests evident in many poems. The human speaker in "A New Year Greeting," is cast as a hospitable ecological niche:

> my greetings to all of you, Yeasts,
> Bacteria, Viruses,
> Aerobics and Anaerobics:
> A Very Happy New Year
> To all for whom my ecotoderm
> is as Middle-Earth to me.
> For creatures your size I offer
> a free choice of habitat,
> so settle yourselves in the zone
> that suits you best, in the pools
> of my pores or the tropical
> forests of arm-pit and crotch,
> in the deserts of my fore-arms,
> or the cool woods of my scalp[136]

In poems like "A New Year Greeting" and "Address to the Beasts" (1973), the speaker's attitude is one of respect and admiration for the nonhuman other, even when one might expect a reaction of abhorrence. The speaker is willing to imagine his most private parts as "forests" for yeasts who have their own lives to enjoy. And even though the tone is wry, the poem wrestles with one's ethical positioning as a planet for other lives and, as Louise Westling keenly interprets the poem, has the effect of making the inquiry applicable to the reader too, who "'hears' that voice in his or her mind and experiences a witty understanding of our close kinship with other creatures that includes intricate dialogues and responses within our very bodies, of bewildering complexities of interrelationship."[137] In the poem's god-like, yet mortal, planetary body an "ethical space of transcorporeality" emerges, akin to what Stacy Alaimo describes: "demand[ing] that we inquire about all of the substances that surround us, those for which we may be somewhat responsible, those that may harm us, those that may harm others, and those that we suspect we do not know enough about."[138] As we saw with Woolf, Auden persistently includes more-than-human life in his work and in his dialogue, both as imagined address or embodied communication, with other beings. Further, as with the description of a dog's comforting presence in times of grief, in "Address to the

Beasts" Auden gives nonhuman animals credit for gifts that exceed human habits, including hunting: "Of course you have to take lives / to keep your own, but never / kill for applause"[139] and identifies their songs as the precursor to human lyrics:

> Exempt from taxation,
> you have never felt the need
> to become literate,
>
> but your oral cultures
> have inspired our poets to pen
> dulcet verses[140]

Although "oral cultures" may implicate bacterial sicknesses, the phrase also credits nonhumans with "cultures" and languages that may not be written, but have an oral art that humans attempt to emulate through poetry. Yet the lack of guile in nonhuman animals coincides with a lack of complex thought:

> But you exhibit no signs
> of knowing that you are sentenced.
> Now could that be why
>
> we upstarts are often
> jealous of your innocence,
> but never envious?[141]

"Sentenced" here refers to both an awareness of mortality and the skill of language and composition. The stanza suggests that humans wouldn't give up their claims to higher learning for a blissful animal ignorance of sin, guilt, shame, or death.

   Unlike the plethora of information we have now about non-human capacity for feeling and intricate means of verbal communication, the presumption of a lack of higher functioning intellect in other animals, including the capacity for emotion and language, was commonplace during the latter half of the twentieth century. Even Merleau-Ponty, who emphasized the shared aspects of human and nonhuman experience, muses: "Is there an animal consciousness, and if so, to what extent?"[142] Therefore, it is not surprising that Auden's celebration of the positive qualities of nonhumans retains a skepticism about nonhuman self-awareness. What *is* remarkable is the frequency with which Auden often worked against this premise, representing nature and the nonhuman as *capable* of speaking through meaningful, communicative codes. Even in an essay about the craft of writing, Auden can't resist an aside about nonhuman animals:

Many animals have a code of communication, auditory or visual or olfactory signals by which individual members of the species convey to each other information about food, sex, territory, the presence of enemies, etc, which is essential to their survival and in social animals like the bee, this code may become extremely complex, but no animal, so far as we know addresses another personally, though some domesticated animals like dogs can respond to their names when addressed by humans. All animal signals, one might say, are statements in the third person. . . . If we only used words as a communication code, then it seems probable that, as with animals, the human species would only have one language with, at most, dialect variations like the song of the chaffinch. . . . But as persons we are capable of speech proper. In speech one unique person addresses another unique person and does so voluntarily: he could keep silent if he chose. We speak as persons because we desire to disclose ourselves to each other and to share our experiences, not because we need to share them, but because we enjoy sharing them.[143]

Although Auden persists in distinguishing nonhuman parlance as inferior to the intricacies of human speech, it is revealing that animals play a prominent role in an essay about the ostensibly unrelated topic of human language. He is even compelled to acknowledge that animals have a gestural and sensory language that has a counterpart, albeit a simplistic one, in human speech. As this essay demonstrates, the question of the animal was often at the forefront of Auden's thoughts about creativity and the literary arts. Like the lingering doubt that creeps into this essay, his poetry also betrays an allegiance to the possibility that the communication of other species may be closer to human language than commonly thought.

Poems such as "Their Lonely Betters" (1950), "Symmetries and Asymmetries" (1961), and "Natural Linguistics" (1969) analogize human and nonhuman modes of communication. Early critics interpreting "Their Lonely Betters" presume the speaker transparently announces the poem's theme.[144] A closer reading reveals that the poem derides claims to superiority as spurious:

> As I listened from a beach-chair in the shade
> To all the noises that my garden made,
> It seemed to me only proper that words
> Should be withheld from vegetables and birds.
>
> A robin with no Christian name ran through
> The Robin-Anthem which was all it knew,
> And rustling flowers for some third party waited
> To say which pairs, if any, should get mated.
>
> Not one of them was capable of lying,

> There was not one which knew that it was dying
> Or could have with a rhythm or a rhyme
> Assumed responsibility for time.
>
> Let them leave language to their lonely betters
> Who count some days and long for certain letters;
> We, too, make noises when we laugh or weep:
> Words are for those with promises to keep.[145]

The privileged, leisure-class position of the speaker is foregrounded and a power dynamic is implied with the verb "withheld." The following stanzas reinforce an association between smug class-prejudice and the speaker's assumptions about the animals in "his" garden property. The robin's song becomes a nationalistic anthem and the flowers resemble gowned girls eager for marriage, invoking upper-class stereotypes of "commoners" naïve about their government and preoccupied with romantic fanfare. As a result, the phrase "lonely betters" is less applicable to the human species as a whole than it is to an elite class of educated writers who are capable of thoughts and feelings the lower-class masses don't have access to: "Let them leave language to their lonely betters." Phrases such as "We, too" underscore a tone of undeserved self-pity. The "loneliness" is related to the position of the chosen few who "long for certain letters," referring both to correspondence from an absent community and to the struggle of trying to compose great literature. "Those with promises to keep" are not just any people; they are poets like Robert Frost, whose poem "Stopping by Woods on a Snowy Evening," is echoed here.[146] Of course, this speaker, in ironic contrast to Frost's speaker in "Stopping by Woods on a Snowy Evening" is dozing in his beach chair on a warm summer afternoon rather than ending a long day of work in the biting cold, contemplating the "sleep" of mortality and death. One might argue that the fluid intermingling of natural imagery and social bias diminishes the ecocritical importance of the poem. However, the poem draws attention to the flimsy logic and latent bias that fuels distinctions between both human "others" and ecological "others." "Their Lonely Betters" shows how often these prejudices about nature reside in cultural, human constructions of value that ought to be scrutinized, exposed, and changed. The inability to accurately perceive nonhuman capabilities and perspectives is highlighted when the reader is challenged to see him or herself in a light that encourages criticism of narcissistic self-interest.

"Symmetries and Asymmetries," a long poem that recalls William Blake's *Songs of Innocence and Experience* in its form and content, begins by unearthing hidden symmetries in organic form and the human desire to possess natural riches: "Deep in earth's opaque mirror, / The old oak's roots / Reflected in its branches: / Astrologers in reverse, / Keen-eyed miners / Conned their scintillant gems."[147] Unlike astrologers who look for shining objects in the night sky, the miners who look for sparkles in the dark loam seek personal gain. Their "sin" is buried in the sounds of "scintillant." From there, the poem transitions to mythic and pastoral imagery, suggesting that one of the things humans have taken from the earth is a natural imagery put in the service of tales that cover up darker human motives. Seventeen stanzas later, the poem asks "Could any tiger / Drink martinis, smoke cigars, / And last as we do?"[148] The question toys with the problem of personification and the paradigm between the ominous luster of Blake's tiger eyes in "The Tyger"—"Tyger! Tyger! burning bright / In the forests of the night" – and monikers of a "brilliant" witty society that is actually going up in smoke. But, more importantly, these lines are part of several stanzas that mark a transition within the poem from the presumed "innocence" of pastoral imagery employed in earlier stanzas and the more mature or modern "experience" of nature, embodiment, and society:

> To himself the Brute Fact:
> To others (sometimes)
> A useful metaphor
>
> Because the level table
> Made him think of steppes,
> He knew it was there.
>
> Like the redstart,
> He recalls but a formless fragment
> Of his real tune.
>
> A sign-post points him out his road:
> But names no place,
> Numbers no distance.
>
> Not daring to saunter,
> He made forced marches,
> Uphill, against the wind.
>
> Hunting for some lost object
> He was meant to forget,
> He lost himself.[149]

The brute fact of our own self-knowledge is compared with the way we are perceived by others. As Blake uses the lamb and tiger for symbols of the light and dark sides of human nature, Auden recalls that we are all flattened into shadows of our embodied selves when we are employed as vehicles for some other person's chosen tenor. Just as a tiger can be employed for a poetic point, humans can be urged into "forced marches / Uphill, against wind" – an image that recalls the way men are used to serve nationalistic purposes. Unlike earlier poems that rely on place-names and maps as central imagery for nature and place, "Symmetries and Asymmetries" suggests that the embodied experience of being within a place should be predominant. The continual search for objects and mythological totems that give ultimate meaning or never-ending life are fruitless quests that only result in forgetting the more elemental experiences of a meaningful existence. No particular "there" is named. Instead, the relationship of metaphor insists on bringing together the individual and local with the global and geographic: "Because the level table / made him think of steppes / He knew it was there." The "level table" is both a homely kitchen table and the top of a plateau, just as "steppes" audibly conflates the steps of a staircase with vast stretches of grassy plain. The divergent scales are brought into balance. A tiger's territory and the boundaries of familiar human habitat become symmetrical. Further, these stanzas suggest that both tigers and humans are capable of being misled, used to fulfill another's purpose. Each must ask, as Blake's "The Tyger" does, "Did he who made the Lamb make thee?"; each must interrogate whether there is a dark side of any force that claims the power to construct the meaning of another's life. The literary devices of personification and metaphor are implicated in constructing those relationships.

Words in the flesh of the world

The enduring belief that only humans have language is persistently invoked to justify acts of human superiority over other animals. This attitude, which the speaker of the poem "Their Lonely Betters" assumes, is deconstructed in "Natural Linguistics" (1969). The poem begins by announcing, "Every created thing has ways of pronouncing its ownhood."[150] Using techniques reminiscent of Gerard Manley Hopkins, who offers nature's presumed flaws as signs of god's infinite variety in "Pied Beauty," Auden parallels grammar with other natural codes:

> basic and used by all, even the mineral tribes,
> is the hieroglyphical *koine* of visual appearance
>   which, though it lacks the verb, is, when compared with our own

> heaviest lexicons, so much richer and subtler in shape-nouns,
>   color-adjectives and apt prepositions of place.
> Verbs first appear with the flowers who utter imperative odors
>   Which, with their taste for sweets, insects are bound to obey
> motive, too, in the eyes of beasts is the language of gesture
>   (urban life has, alas, sadly impoverished ours),
> signals of interrogation, friendship, threat and appeasement,
>   instantly taken in, seldom, if ever, misread.[151]

Auden's colloquial free verse hides linguistic intricacy just as humans are used to overlooking the patterns in nonhuman signals. All organic forms are identified by visual markers, just as the Greek *koine* provided a common language uniting the Alexandrine empire. Merleau-Ponty explains the natural world as a primordial structure from which language arises: "The origin of language is mythic; that is, there is always a language before language, which is perception. Architectonic of language. . ... Language as a resumption of the logos of the sensible world in another architectonic."[152] Auden acknowledges that the visual plane introduces us to signs and symbols that can be "read" to coalesce into a specific meaning or a particular element. As Serpil Oppermann reminds us, "Every organism, every geological formation, every object carries 'evolutionary stories of co-existence, inter-dependence, adaptation and hybridization, extinctions and survivals.'"[153] Even crystalline patterns of growth present a language of signs that pronounce their identity. The theme of the poem overlaps with Hopkins' notion of "inscape," or the bringing forth of the individual essence of each thing. The Hopkins-esque conjoined adjectives "shape-nouns" and "color-adjectives" rub together to reveal a unique sheen of meaning. These combinations not only recall combinations like "couple-colour" and "chestnut-falls" from Hopkins' "Pied Beauty," but also set up an equation, the hyphen serving as an "=" sign between forms accessed through embodied perception, "shape" and "color," and their grammatical counterparts, "nouns" and "adjectives." Conversely, natural forms also resemble written punctuation: The flowers "utter imperative odors" and the symbol for the grammatical imperative "!" has the form of a petal attached to a flower's round center, the source of orders and odors. For animals, the "eyes" reveal their "I." The range and subtlety of what their gestural communication conveys surpasses human ability and, since it is rarely "misread," seems to get closer to accuracy and truth than human language will allow. The poem proceeds to recognize even the spray of urine as "messages" of "an indicative AM."[154] As Wendy Wheeler, whose book opens with Auden's "Horae Canonicae" without referring to him explicitly in her text, states about biosemiotics, "What all this means is that the semiological (Saussurean) escape from nature, in which human meaning is believed to be restricted to articulate language alone, must give way to a wider semiotic (Peircian) understanding, in which embodied acts and deeds are more clearly understood as meaningful signs also."[155] Auden concludes: "'Dumb' we may call them but, surely, our poets are right in assuming / all would prefer that they were rhetorized *at* than *about*."[156] As in "Hunting Season," Auden makes use of an unclear antecedent to provide an example of the potential misreadings of human language. "All would prefer that they were rhetorized *at* than *about*" does not specify whether "they" refers just to the non-humans – "them in the previous line" – or whether "they" refers back to an "all" that encompasses both humans and nonhumans. In one sense, humans might agree that everyone would prefer to be spoken to directly or talked "at" (as Auden does in "Talking to Dogs," and "Talking to Mice") rather than spoken "about" as gossip to others. But the word "rhetorized" also invites one to consider the grammatical functions of words like "at" and "about" – prepositions that specify relationships between two nouns, as the poem seeks to define a closer relation between human and nonhuman communication. It seems noteworthy that the words "at" and "about," both begin and end with the same letters, just as the nature of human and nonhuman language may have more in common than initially presumed.

The extent to which the environment is a constant companion in Auden's poetry, a voice to be listened to, and a presence that provokes and nourishes the human speakers, is epitomized in "First Things First" (1956). The poem begins with a solitary sleeper awakened by the sound of night rain:

> Woken, I lay in the arms of my own warmth and listened
> To a storm enjoying its storminess in the winter dark
> Till my ear, as it can when half-asleep or half-sober,
> Set to work to unscramble that interjectory uproar,
> Construing its airy vowels and watery consonants
> Into a love-speech indicative of a Proper Name.[157]

Both the speaker and the storm are content with themselves, the human "in the arms of my own warmth" and the "storm enjoying its storminess." This conflation doesn't erase the ecocritical significance, but heightens the ways in which, as Hubert Zapf phrases it "The characteristic environments of human beings are not just external but internal environments, the inner worlds and landscapes of the mind, the psyche, and the cultural imagination that make up the habitats of humans as much as their external natures and material environments."[158] The stanza is flush with physical sensation – the recognition of the self-generating heat of one's own flesh, the almost involuntary process of making meaning from the "airy vowels" and "watery consonants" of the symphony of plinks and plonks wetly making contact with the exterior surfaces of the home, are all sensory elements. As Westling explains, in terms of ecophenomenology, "For Merleau-Ponty, the human body is a nexus in a web of significations woven throughout a world full of immanent meaning."[159] Auden twines matter as text and human as reader, making the heavy raindrops, metallic roof, and speaker's sleepy warmth into what Serenella Iovino and Serpil Opperman cite as a "corporeal palimpsest in which stories are inscribed."[160] The drive to divine language from sound is an innate part of a human response to the promptings of the nonhuman environment. Merleau-Ponty explains that the connection between natural patterns of meaning and human efforts to communicate through particular combinations of sounds that make up words and sentences have a common origin: "The Nature in us must have some relation to the Nature outside of us; moreover, Nature outside of us must be unveiled to us by the Nature that we are."[161] The urge to order is also attributed to the finely coordinated relationships abundant in the natural world: "There is a Logos of the natural esthetic world, on which the Logos of language relies."[162] Human language is only one form Logos takes. Akin to the presence of pigments in plants and animals that create a perfect camouflage for their environments, or the physical attributes of some species that are uniquely necessary for life in their particular geographic region, human manifestations, including language, are embedded within the larger structures of the natural world. This embodiment does not separate flesh from mind; rather neurological function emanates from an anatomically embodied brain and signals of sensory experience. Auden's poem evinces this understanding when the voice of the rain begins to sound to him like a "Proper Name" of a lover he once knew. This unnamed lover is described in terms of landscape, and the colors of a moist, verdant climate, inverting literary personification: "Likening your poise of being to an upland country, / Here green on purpose, / there pure blue for luck."[163] Yet the comparison to the storm itself seems to end here.

In the third stanza, the story the storm tells to the fitful sleeper is a memory of love in an entirely different weather:

> Loud though it was, alone as it certainly found me,
> It reconstructed a day of peculiar silence
> When a sneeze could be heard a mile off, and had me walking

> On a headland of lava beside you, the occasion as ageless
> As the stare of any rose, your presence exactly
> So once, so valuable, so there, so now.[164]

The physicality of the day, the landscape, and the beloved is what is recalled, rather than any particular conversation between them. A decidedly unromantic bodily function, the sneeze, is heard, and the "silence" is filled with palpable meaning. Walking together, the "presence" of the person is recalled so vividly that it is "exactly / so." Yet the inability for any living thing to be captured in still-frame, preserved against time, is also denied by the poem. The speaker may wish the "stare of any rose" to be "ageless," but for a living plant, or the unblinking eye of a corpse, deterioration is inevitable. Just as the bedrock is forever altered by eruptions of viscous flows of molten lava, what seems solid is subject to metamorphosis. Water or rain also changes from one state to another, and this remembered human relationship, once apparently strong, has at some point dissolved.[165] Even the repetition of "so" showcases the shifting meanings of this simple two-letter word: "exactly / so" as to fix a thing precisely, "so valuable" as in very or much, "so there" meaning as it was, and "so now" meaning the same as. Indeed the ability of the memory to recall through time and through place suggests the vast mutability of existence itself.

The poem's speaker pauses to reflect that this unexpected recollection of love offered by the storm directly contrasts with the fears that normally wake him in the night "when only too often / A smirking devil annoys me in beautiful English, / Predicting a world where every sacred location / Is a sand-buried site all cultured Texans do."[166] The speaker dreads an apocalyptic landscape where genuine discovery is replaced by a greed for oil (an un-natural fluid eruption in comparison to lava and snot) or consumer tourism – a vision of a more horrific kind of transformation that is specifically human-created, "in beautiful English." In juxtaposition, the memory the storm creates for the speaker is affectionate and kind.

The problem of who is actually "speaking" this verse – the conflation of stormy voice and human translation – is recognized in the poem's final stanza:

> Grateful, I slept till a morning that would not say
> How much it believed of what I said the storm had said
> But quietly drew my attention to what had been done
> – So many cubic metres the more in my cistern
> Against a leonine summer – , putting first things first:
> Thousands have lived without love, not one without water.[167]

The source becomes syntactically intermingled in the twists of "not say," "I said," "had said," suggesting that the product is both human and environmental in origin. The product, " – So many cubic metres the more in my cistern," is both the measure of accumulated rain and the manifold lines of the metered poem. Yet, nature's yield is deemed the more significant of the two as the poet concedes, "Thousands have lived without love, not one without water." The storm has given the human speaker sensations of love that endure though interactions of place and memory, as well as actual water, but the body's needs must be met before such art is possible. Further, the water sustains not only humans, but also "thousands" of nonhuman beings that coexist, leading divergent and overlapping lives.

However, the poem's title "First Things First," with its exact word repetition at the beginning and end of the phrase, reminds the reader that final products are often inseparable from the inspirations that generate them. Thus fostering love (as Auden might put it), or emotional connection with nature and the nonhuman, is just as vital to the success of the environmental movement as the objective measurements of scientific data. Unless moved to act, people will not respond to that data. Consequently, literature serves a function toward global change. As Auden reminds readers in differentiating how British and American stories have shaped distinctive cultural attitudes toward nature in his 1953 essay, "Transplanted Englishman Views U.S.," literature shapes and reflects cultural attitudes. It also allows us to reimagine our relationship with the environment by critiquing anthropocentrism, representing nature as autonomous and humans as dependent, as well as depicting other creatures as having their own consciousness and value. This does not mean it will always be a major catalyst for change. Rather, as Hubert Zapf states, literature does "provid [e] a discursive space for articulating those dimensions of human life that [are] marginalized, neglected, or repressed in dominant discourses and forms of civilization" including "emotions, eros, the body, non-human nature."[168] Literature records the voices that are often lost in mainstream stories. It witnesses our ongoing struggle to let Nature speak for itself in its cacophony of voices, and ruminates on ethical values that might yet compete with industry, economy, and greed. As a result, the kinds of reevaluations that literature can provoke are fundamental to persuading readers to feel themselves as embedded within a thriving net of interacting, pulsating, worldly flesh. Ultimately, the measure of our literary words may be the first impetus for putting the natural world first.

Epilogue

He disappeared in the dead of winter:
The brooks were frozen, the airports almost deserted,
And snow disfigured the public statues;
The mercury sank in the mouth of the dying day.
What instruments we have agree
The day of his death was a dark cold day.

* * *

Now he is scattered among a hundred cities
And wholly given over to unfamiliar affections,
To find his happiness in another kind of wood
And be punished under a foreign code of conscience.
The words of a dead man
Are modified in the guts of the living.

* * *

Now Ireland has her madness and her weather still,
For poetry makes nothing happen: it survives
In the valley of its making where executives
Would never want to tamper, flows on south
From ranches of isolation and the busy griefs,
Raw towns that we believe and die in; it survives,
A way of happening, a mouth.

* * *

With the farming of a verse
Make a vineyard of the curse,
Sing of human unsuccess
In a rapture of distress;
In the deserts of the heart
Let the healing fountain start,
In the prison of his days
Teach the free man how to praise.
– excerpts from W.H. Auden's "In Memory of W.B. Yeats"

Modernists resist endings. The ambiguous phrase and interrogative leap is meant to prod a reader to self-awareness. It is tempting to do that with this book as well and leave off any attempt at conclusion. Many ecocritical conclusions seem to claim too great a role for literature in rescuing the planet, enacting a kind of false pastoral note that twangs into a postpastoral mockery, reminiscent of how E.M. Forster subverts the happy ending of many of his novels. Instead, I find myself repeating the phrase of W.H. Auden's that has been so battered and twisted: "Poetry makes nothing happen," but tempering its seeming pessimism with the reminder "It survives, / A way of happening, a mouth." Indeed, as industry, persistent human violence, and climate change remind us, the "happiness in another kind of wood" can easily metamorphose from beloved tree-filled copse to coffined corpse, and the movement of poetic lips or pen, even the "guts" of readers that embody those words anew, may seem quite indirect in comparison with more forceful material human actions. But Auden's elegy for the great pastoral poet of Ireland doesn't foreclose a role for poetry in the world; it still likens poetry to the flow of rivers that carry us onwards, "a way of happening, a mouth," which as Aiden Wasley has also noted, provides "a living emblem for how his [Auden's] own poetry – and art generally – can change, survive and, in the face of war and despair, still be a way of happening."[1] The role of literature is slow-moving. Like the paragraphs of Virginia Woolf's stream of consciousness writing that must be read through whole to see the patterns and pricks of their points. As I have argued in this book, a literary imagination can alter cultural perceptions, which then might transform ideas and action. That is no small thing, even though the currents of its influence run slow, so slow that it might seem nothing at all is actively happening as a result of any one poem, novel, or writer. But perhaps it is the very promise of slow scholarship that might help to reveal what our digital prose and click-bait narratives do not: what Rob Nixon so aptly names "slow violence."

Although Nixon and I differ on our interpretations of the critique of empire in E.M. Forster's work and the value of formalist close-reading, Nixon's recognition of the phenomena of slow violence – large-scale devastation ignored because it does not conform to the speed of a stock-market exchange or a tweet – is of crucial importance to us both:

> One of the most pressing challenges of our age is how to adjust our rapidly eroding attention spans to the slow erosions of environmental justice. If, under neoliberalism, the gulf between enclaved rich and outcast poor has become ever more pronounced, ours is also an era of enclaved time wherein for many speed has become a self-justifying, propulsive ethic that renders

'uneventful' violence (to those who live remote from its attritional lethality) a weak claimant on our time.[2]

Further, as a collectively authored 2014 treatise on the Environmental Humanities suggests, literary scholarship can contribute to altering the course of that violence through making it eminently visible and pointing us toward better ethical models:

> Such crucial ideas as "climate change," "bioengineering," and even "the environment" refer to distinct material entities and phenomena, and to social practices, too; but they also help shape our sense of what it means for humans to live on Earth. It takes "slow scholarship" to bring this human dimension into view. . ... "Slow scholarship" is not mere dalliance, bourgeois self-indulgence, or belletrism. It opposes the "attention regime" of the news media, particularly in their current digital incarnation."[3]

The reorientation toward embodied knowledge, shifting scales of time, and an awareness of how human agency depends on and is part of a larger animate world of agencies that must also be heard and recognized (despite the years of cultural assumptions that have rendered them invisible and mute) – these are the ethical recognitions that literary art, particularly green modernism, provides and academic work can forefront. In part because these flows, as Auden reminds us "are where executives / would never want to tamper." Loss must be reclaimed and understood for any meaningful healing action to result. As Auden might be read to insinuate, we must struggle out of the self-centeredness of our "ranches of isolation" and "busy griefs" to participate "with the farming of a verse" and yield up a song "of human *un*success" (my emphasis added). It is up to each individual reader then to make something new happen, or as Auden ends, to find the "healing fountain" and learn how to "praise" even in the "desert" or "prison of his days." This choice of individuals acting in concert is the step that any one artist can only hope to inspire, but can't enact without the human reader. As Timothy Clark admonishes, "The evasion of the question of human nature makes many ecocritical exhortations to some vast revolution in cultural attitudes seem on a par with fantasies that pigs might fly."[4] Thus, changing the way we see ourselves by stripping away our illusions of anthropocentrism and fostering empathy for a community of nonhuman life is crucial to environmental action. In our new centennial of environmental catastrophe, Clark states, "human beings will, as they always have, continue to act on a stage dominated by unpredictable nonhuman agency, but this time increasingly divested of illusions of sovereignty."[5]

Instead, as we face the manifestations of the long-term impact of the Anthropocene during the centenary of the First World War, I am reminded of Wilfred Owen's exhortation: "All a poet can do today is warn. That is why the true poet must be truthful."[6] Or what Pablo Picasso once said about his desire "to show what I have found and not what I am looking for" so that "Art is a lie that makes us realize the truth."[7] It is the tension between poetry and violence, as well as the rub of ethical truths and imagination, which might reveal the causes and harms of slow processes that are difficult for any one human to perceptively grasp alone. I believe literary narrative and metaphor can help us glimpse these larger natural processes, and our own failures to live responsibly within them. In order to further that effort, the modernist ecocritic must be attuned to the variety of tensions within a work – the fissures and fault lines of our struggle to engage with the nonhuman and participate as members of a shared community – doubts and fears that still trouble our environmental imagination today, exposing our ethical conflicts with prioritizing nonhuman life.

And so I read again Woolf's reminder in *Mrs. Dalloway* that there are fibers of connection that bind us to each other, other generations, the nonhuman world, and perhaps even a network of planetary consciousness:

> Somehow in the streets of London, on the ebb and flow of things, here, there, she survived, Peter survived, lived in each other, she being part, she was positive, of the trees at home; of the house there, ugly, rambling all to bits and pieces as it was; part of the people she had never met; being laid out like a mist between the people she knew best, who lifted her on their branches as she had seen the trees lift the mist, but it spread ever so far, her life, herself.[8]

Indeed, as a common reader, this passage personally reminds me that the cry of "Black Lives Matter" is twined to Neil De Grasse Tyson's *Cosmos* and discoveries about planetary "mists of matter" that were often the result of funding meted out to particular scientists who were able to claim positions of privilege, which in turn is linked to the human desire to build the pipelines that will enable other positions of privilege as we forgo morning walks to speed away in our cars to our own individual destinations without noticing much along the way. Or the waves of immigrants leaving their own familiar trees and landscapes so that they can survive; how will those branches connect throughout the globe as the ebb and flow of human life, slow violence, and environmental impact continues to evolve? As Forster admonishes in his epigraph to *Howards End*, "... only connect."

Similarly, Forster's acknowledgement of how disappearing and evolving language reflects what we no longer notice in *The Longest Journey* is relevant to contemporary environmental humanities too:

> "Those verlands – " said Stephen, scarcely above his breath.
> "What are verlands?"
> He pointed at the dusk and said, "Our name for a kind of field."
> > Then he drove his whip into its socket, and seemed to swallow something. Rickie, straining his eyes for verlands, could only see a tumbling wilderness of brown.
> "Are there many local words?"
> "There have been."
> "I suppose they die out."[9]

Likewise, Robert MacFarlane records the way our natural sensibilities have changed by comparing the words found in the *Peat Dictionary* to the new edition of the *Oxford Junior Dictionary*, where "bluebell" is deleted to make room for "broadband," and words that Yeats might have recognized, such as feadan, "a small stream running from a moorland loch," have no place in our consciousness and don't need naming.[10] Without the human vocabulary that makes such things visible to us, we are like Rickie in the passage above, who "straining his eyes for verlands, could only see a tumbling wilderness of brown." Wild processes run the risk of melting out of human environmental perception.

But changing practices of green knowledge can be traced and recalled through slow scholarship and the memory of story. Here I am prompted to repeat Simon Schama's remarks about the power of such retelling and reminding:

> Instead of being yet another explanation of what we have lost, it is an exploration of what we may yet find. In offering this alternative way of looking, I am aware that more is at stake than an academic quibble. . ... by revealing the richness, antiquity, and complexity of our landscape tradition, to show just how much we stand to lose. Instead of assuming the mutually exclusive character of Western culture and nature, I want to suggest the strength of the links that have bound them together.[11]

Our challenge is to keep telling these stories, making the poems "survive" by taking shape in our mouths, and to recognize that we "[live] in each other, she being part, she was positive, of the trees at home; of the house there, ugly, rambling all to bits and pieces as it was." And sharing new ones, creating room for other perspectives that shed the fetters of ego and material ease for a more profound respect for the well-being of all life, human and nonhuman. The struggle for better ways to live and create has never been the product of one movement or generation. We unfurl our leaves and pages, in concert with the logos of a larger creative and living world, to do our best to fight against the slow forces of human solipsism and greed. Moreover, we must continually retouch, reencounter, and reimagine our embodied relationship with the environment as all the individual lifeforms and manifestations within it – organic and cultural – grow and change through time. Even as readers and scholars, we participate in making the folds of the page, the form of the manuscript, the choice of our own words, and the actions that inspire them, more visible. Thus reawakening our academic consciousness to the meaning immanent in the blank spaces between the inky type where we must gesture toward interpretation through our own embodied relationships to art and planet.

Notes

Introduction

1 Joseph Conrad, *Heart of Darkness*, 3rd edn. (New York: Norton, 1988), 9.
2 Henry D. Thoreau, "Walking," *Wild Apples and Other Natural History Essays* (Athens: University of Georgia Press, 2002), 59. Emphasis added.
3 Thomas Nagel, "What Is it Like to Be a Bat?" *The Philosophical Review* 83.4 (October 1974), 439, 440–1.
4 Ursula K. Heise and Allison Carruth, eds. "Introduction to Focus: Environmental Humanities," *The American Book Review* 32.1 (2011), 3.
5 Donna J. Haraway, *When Species Meet*, (Minneapolis: University of Minnesota Press, 2008), 10.
6 Judith Paltin, "'An Infected Carrier of the Past': Modernist Nature as the Ground for Anti-Realism," *Interdisciplinary Studies in Literature and the Environment* 20.4 (Autumn 2013), 779.
7 Timothy Clark, *The Cambridge Introduction to Literature and the Environment* (New York: Cambridge University Press, 2011), 78.
8 *Ibid.*, 80–1.
9 *Ibid.*, 80.
10 Stacey Alaimo, *Bodily Natures: Science, Environment, and the Material Self* (Bloomington: Indiana University Press, 2010), 21.
11 Serpil Oppermann, "From Ecological Postmodernism to Material Ecocriticism: Creative Materiality and Narrative Agency," in *Material Ecocriticism*, ed. Serenella Iovino and Serpil Oppermann (Bloomington: Indiana University Press, 2014), 29.
12 Clark, *Cambridge Introduction*, 86.
13 Hannes Bergthaller, "Limits of Agency: Notes on the Material Turn from a Systems-Theoretical Perspective," in *Material Ecocriticism*, ed. Serenella Iovino and Serpil Oppermann (Bloomington: Indiana University Press, 2014), 38.
14 Louise Westling, *The Logos of the Living World: Merleau-Ponty, Animals, and Language* (New York: Fordham University Press, 2014), 34.
15 Haraway, *When Species Meet*, 15.
16 Lawrence Buell, *The Future of Environmental Criticism: Environmental Crisis and Literary Imagination* (Malden, MA: Blackwell, 2005), 44.

17 Ezra Pound, *Make It New: Essays By Ezra Pound* (New Haven: Yale University Press, 1935).

18 Ezra Pound, "Canto LXXXI," in *Cantos of Ezra Pound* (New York: New Directions, 1993), 518, l.53.

19 E.M. Forster, *Aspects of the Novel* (New York: Harcourt, 1964), 149.

20 Virginia Woolf, "Modern Fiction," in *The Common Reader* (New York: Harcourt, 1984), 150.

21 W.H. Auden, "Today's Poet," *The Complete Works of W.H. Auden: Prose 1956–1962*, ed. Edward Mendelson, vol. IV, (Woodstock: Princeton University Press, 2010), 405.

22 John Marx, *The Modernist Novel and the Decline of Empire.* (New York: Cambridge University Press, 2005), 2.

23 Malcolm Bradbury, "The Cities of Modernism," *Modernism 1890–1930* (London: Penguin, 1991), 96.

24 Douglas Mao, *Solid Objects: Modernism and the Test of Production* (Princeton, New Jersey: Princeton University Press, 1998), 16.

25 Bonnie Kime Scott, *In the Hollow of the Wave: Virginia Woolf and the Modernist Uses of Nature* (Charlottesville: University of Virginia Press, 2012), 14.

26 Catriona Mortimer-Sandilands and Bruce Erickson, "Introduction: A Genealogy of Queer Ecologies," *Queer Ecologies: Sex, Nature, Politics, Desire* (Bloomington: Indiana University Press, 2010), 23.

27 Paul Peppis, *Sciences of Modernism: Ethnography, Sexology, and Psychology* (New York: Cambridge University Press, 2014), 138.

28 *Ibid.*, 102.

29 Mortimer-Sandilands and Bruce Erickson, *Queer Ecologies*, 342.

30 Edward Said, *Culture and Imperialism* (New York: Knopf, 1993), xi.

31 *Ibid.*, xii.

32 Jed Esty, *A Shrinking Island: Modernism and National Culture in England* (Princeton: Princeton University Press, 2004), 7.

33 Alexandra Harris, *Romantic Moderns: English Writers, Artists and the Imagination from Virginia Woolf to John Piper* (New York: Thames & Hudson, 2010), 10.

34 E.M. Forster, *England's Pleasant Land* (London: Hogarth Press, 1940), 8.

35 Louise Westling, "Virginia Woolf and the Flesh of the World," *New Literary History* 30.4 (Autumn 1999), 866.

36 Maurice Merleau-Ponty, "Metaphysics and the Novel," in *Sense and Nonsense* trans. Hubert L. Dreyfus and Patricia Allen Dreyfus (Evanston: Northwestern University Press, 1991), 28.

37 W.H. Auden, "Paul Bunyan," in *The Complete Works of W.H. Auden: Libretti 1939–1973*, ed. Edward Mendelson (Woodstock: Princeton University Press, 1993), 6–7.

38 Carrie Rohman. *Stalking the Subject: Modernism and the Animal* (New York: Columbia University Press, 2009), 48.

39 Louise Westling, "Literature and Ecology," in *Teaching Ecocriticism and Green Cultural Studies*, ed. Greg Garrard (London: Palgrave Macmillan, 2012), 76.

40 *Ibid.*, 81–2.

41 *Ibid.*, 76.

42 Peder Anker, *Imperial Ecology: Environmental Ecology in the British Empire 1895–1945.* (Cambridge, MA: Harvard University Press, 2001), 3.

43 *Ibid.*, 36.

44 Anker, *Imperial Ecology*, 116.

45 *Ibid.*, 75.

46 P.N. Furbank, *E.M. Forster: A Life*, vol. II (London: Secker and Warburg, 1978), 29.

47 Virginia Woolf, *The Diary of Virginia Woolf*, ed. Anne Olivier Bell, vol. V (New York: Harcourt, 1982), 99. Entry for June 25, 1937.

48 Harris, *Romantic Moderns*, 25.

49 *Ibid.*, 29.

50 Virginia Woolf, "The Novels of E.M. Forster," in *The Death of the Moth and Other Essays* (San Diego: Harcourt, 1970), 174.

51 E.M. Forster, "Virginia Woolf," in *Two Cheers for Democracy* (New York: Harcourt, 1951), 242.

52 *Ibid.*, 253.

53 E.M. Forster, "The Ascent of F6," *Two Cheers for Democracy* (New York: Harcourt, 1951), 264.

54 Virginia Woolf, *Diary of Virginia Woolf*, 98–9. Entry for June 25, 1937.

55 *Ibid.*, 99.

56 *Ibid.*, 107–8.

57 W.H. Auden, "Squares and Oblongs," *Poets at Work* (New York: Harcourt, 1948), 173.

58 W.H. Auden, "Squares and Oblongs," *Language: An Enquiry into Its Meaning and Function*, ed. Ruth Nanda Anshen, (New York: Harper, 1957), 176.

59 E.M. Forster, *A Passage to India* (New York: Harcourt, 1999), 163. Emphasis added.

60 John Parham, *Green Man Hopkins: Poetry and the Victorian Ecological Imagination* (New York: Rodopi, 2010), 43.

61 Serpil Oppermann, "Ecological Imperialism in British Colonial Fiction," *Edebiyat Fakültesi Dergisi / Journal of Faculty of Letters* 24.1 (Haziran/June 2007), 30.

Chapter 1

1 Although critics have different takes on Forster's humanism, disagreeing about whether it was subversive, what kind of humanist philosophy it draws upon, or whether Forster's work represents a growing rejection of it, most critics don't doubt that his values of "progress, collectivism, and humanitarianism" operate solely for human empathy and human advancement. For more on Forster and humanism, see Lionel Trilling, *E.M. Forster* (New York: New Directions, 1943), Frederick Crews' *E.M. Forster: The Perils of Humanism* (Princeton: Princeton University Press, 1962), Wilfred Stone's "E.M. Forster's Subversive

Individualism" in *E.M. Forster: Centenary Revaluations*, ed. Judith Scherer Herz and Robert K. Martin (Toronto: University of Toronto Press, 1982), 15–29, Michael Levenson's "Liberalism and Symbolism in *Howards End*" from his book *Modernism and the Fate of Individuality: Character and Novelistic Form from Conrad to Woolf* (Cambridge: Cambridge University Press, 1990), 78–93, and David Medalie's *E.M. Forster's Modernism* (New York: Palgrave, 2002).

2　Timothy Clark, "Nature, Post Nature" in *The Cambridge Companion to Literature and the Environment*, ed. Louise Westling (New York: Cambridge University Press, 2014), 78.

3　Terry Gifford, *Pastoral* (New York: Routledge, 1999), 11.

4　*Ibid.*, 10.

5　Randall Stevenson, "Forster and Modernism" in *The Cambridge Companion to E.M. Forster*, ed. David Bradshaw (New York: Cambridge University Press, 2007), 209.

6　Paul Peppis, *Sciences of Modernism: Ethnography, Sexology, and Psychology* (New York: Cambridge University Press, 2014), 138.

7　P.N. Furbank, *E.M. Forster: A Life*, vol. 2 (London: Secker and Warburg, 1978), 177.

8　W.H. Auden, "E.M. Forster," in *The Complete Works of W.H. Auden: Prose 1949–1955*, ed. Edward Mendelson, vol. 3 (Princeton: Princeton University Press, 2008), 613–14.

9　Daniel Shwarz, *Reading the Modern British and Irish Novel: 1890–1930* (Malden, MA: Blackwell, 2005), 244.

10　For a more detailed treatment of how Forster's themes justify categorizing him as a modernist writer see Medalie, *E.M. Forster's Modernism* (New York: Palgrave, 2002).

11　Catriona Mortimer-Sandilands and Bruce Erickson, "Introduction" in *Queer Ecologies: Sex, Nature, Politics, Desire* (Bloomington: Indiana University Press, 2010), 23.

12　E.M. Forster, *Commonplace Book* (Stanford: Stanford University Press, 1985), 242.

13　*Ibid.*, 204.

14　*Ibid.*, 214.

15　E.M. Forster, epigraph to *Howard's End* (New York: Vintage, 1989)

16　Terry Gifford, "Pastoral, Anti-Pastoral, and Post-Pastoral," in *The Cambridge Companion to Literature and the Environment*, ed. Louise Westling (New York: Cambridge University Press, 2014), 8.

17　Raymond Williams, *The Country and the City* (New York: Oxford University Press, 1973), 255–6.

18　J.H. Stape, *An E.M. Forster Chronology* (London: MacMillan, 1993), 6.

19　Particularly, the treatment of Forster's pastoral assumes a stereotypical reference to leisure and ease more associated with later versions of the pastoral in Dominic Head's "Forster and the Short Story" from *The Cambridge Companion to E.M. Forster*, ed. David Bradshaw (New York: Cambridge University Press, 2007), 77–91, John Colmer's chapter "Short Stories" in

E.M. Forster: The Personal Voice (Boston: Routledge, 1975), 25–41, and Denis Godfey's "The Short Stories" in *E.M. Forster's Other Kingdom* (London: Oliver and Boyd, 1968), 9–19.

20 Virgil, *The Eclogues of Virgil*, trans. David Ferry (New York: Farrar, 1999), 9.

21 *Ibid.*, 71.

22 Foster, Clark, and York, *Ecological Rift*, 29.

23 E.M. Forster, "The Story of a Panic," in *Collected Short Stories* (New York: Penguin, 1977), 12–13.

24 *Ibid.*, 15.

25 *Ibid.*

26 *Ibid.*, 17.

27 *Ibid.*

28 *Ibid.*, 18.

29 *Ibid.*, 17.

30 *Ibid.*, 18.

31 Mortimer-Sandilands and Erickson, *Queer Ecologies*, 11.

32 Virgil, *Eclogues*, 11.

33 *Ibid.*, 13. It is also interesting to note the similarity between the names of the shepherd boy in this Idyll, "Alexis" and Maurice's rustic lover, "Alec." The two boys are similar in that they are both under the control of another master and the beloved is urging them to come and live in the country, surviving together by farming, hunting, and herding.

34 Forster, "Story of a Panic," 26.

35 *Ibid.*, 33.

36 Forster, Introduction to *Collected Short Stories*, (New York: Penguin, 1977), 5.

37 Williams, *Country and City*, 281.

38 E.M. Forster, "The Other Kingdom," in *Collected Short Stories*, (New York: Penguin, 1977), 67.

39 *Ibid.*, 80.

40 *Ibid.*, 74.

41 *Ibid.*

42 Mortimer-Sandilands and Erickson, *Queer*, 9.

43 Forster, "The Other Kingdom," 62.

44 *Ibid.*, 85.

45 *Ibid.*, 71.

46 *Ibid.*, 63.

47 Furbank, *E.M. Forster*, 199.

48 *Ibid.*

49 E.M. Forster, "My Wood," *Abinger Harvest* (New York: Harcourt, 1964), 23–24.

50 *Ibid.*, 25.

51 Furbank, *E.M. Forster*, 202–3.

52 Williams, *Country and City*, 216.

53 *Ibid.*, 217.

54 Leo Marx. *The Machine in the Garden: Technology and the Pastoral Ideal in America* (New York: Oxford University Press), 32.

55 *Ibid.*, 16.
56 M.H. Abrams, *A Glossary of Literary Terms*. 8th ed. (Boston: Thomson, 2005), 211.
57 Gifford, *Pastoral*, 128.
58 E.M. Forster, "London is a Muddle," in *Two Cheers for Democracy* (New York: Harcourt, 1951), 353–4.
59 E.M. Forster, "The Machine Stops," in *Collected Short Stories* (New York: Penguin, 1977), 109.
60 *Ibid.*, 113.
61 *Ibid.*, 110, 114.
62 *Ibid.*, 117.
63 *Ibid.*
64 *Ibid.*, 121.
65 *Ibid.*, 117.
66 *Ibid.*, 146.
67 *Ibid.*, 135.
68 *Ibid.*, 139.
69 In a letter Forster published in the May 30, 1919 issue of *The Daily Herald*, he expresses his frustration with society's failure to "wake up" and take notice of world events; he pinpoints this passivity as the tool governments exploit to speed the unquestioned centralization of world power. Specifically, he was appalled that the public was engrossed by the details of the first (unsuccessful) attempt of a flyer (Harry Hawker) to cross the Atlantic rather than the major political events that were occurring, including the Amritsar massacre in India, the full horrors of which had not yet been widely reported:
This planet is passing through the supreme crisis of its history. It is being decided whether we shall be governed openly, like a free people, or secretly as in the past. And how the cynics who govern us secretly must have gloated over the hysterics of last Tuesday! 'There goes the mob!' they must have thought; 'just the same as ever after four years of suffering— indifferent to truth, incapable of thought, and keen only on trifles. As long as we arrange for an occasional Hawker to be shouted at and boomed in the newspapers we can manage them as easily as ever.' (Forster, *Daily Herald* May 30, 1919)
70 Forster, "Machine Stops," 146.
71 *Ibid.*, 145.
72 Forster, *Commonplace*, 156.
73 E.M. Forster, *Howards End*, (New York: Vintage, 1989),120.
74 *Ibid.*
75 *Ibid.*, 51.
76 *Ibid.*
77 *Ibid.*, 56.
78 Stacy Alaimo, *Bodily Natures: Science, Environment, and the Material Self* (Bloomington: Indiana University Press, 2010), 30.
79 Forster, *Howards End*, 47.

80 William Empson, *Some Versions of Pastoral* (London: Chatto and Windus, 1950), 11–12.
81 David Bradshaw, "Howards End," in *The Cambridge Companion to E.M. Forster*, ed. David Bradshaw (New York: Cambridge University Press, 2007), 157.
82 Empson, *Some Versions*, 29.
83 Forster, *Howards End*, 4.
84 *Ibid.*, 328.
85 John Hegglund, "Defending the Realm: Domestic Space and Mass Cultural Contamination in *Howard's End* and *An Englishman's Home*," *English Literature in Translation* 40.4 (1997), 399.
86 Forster, *Howards End*, 269.
87 *Ibid.*, 210.
88 *Ibid.*, 51.
89 *Ibid.*, 335.
90 Rob Nixon, *Slow Violence and the Environmentalism of the Poor* (Cambridge, MA: Harvard University Press, 2011), 330 fn 53.
91 *Ibid.*, 331 fn 53.
92 Henry S. Turner, "Empires of Objects: Accumulation and Entropy in E.M. Forster's *Howards End*," *Twentieth Century Literature* 46.3 (Fall 2000), 330.
93 Foster, *Ecological Rift*, 35.
94 Alexandra Harris, *Romantic Moderns*, 56.
95 Forster, *Howards End*, 355.
96 Virgil, *Eclogues*, 90.
97 *Ibid.*, 94. The presence of thorns also links these stories with sex and the classic pastoral. In Theocritus' fifth Idyll the wound of a thorn in the hero's (Battus') foot suggests a crude reference to females as well as the wounding effects of multiple forms of passionate encounter: "Such a little wound, and it masters a man of my size!" Crydon: "You shouldn't go barefoot when you're out on the hillside, Battus; this whole hillside's covered with thorns and brambles, you know" (59). The image of the thorns reoccurs suggestively in "Albergo Empedocle" when Harold is describing his dream to Mildred: "He was holding back the brambles to prevent them from tearing her dress as he spoke. One of the thorns scratched him on the hand. 'Yes, I loved better too,' he continued, watching the little drops of blood swell out" (25). Adela's more famous encounter with thorns as she flees from imagined rape in the Marabar caves similarly references thorns during an implied sexual encounter.
98 Forster, *Howards End*, 355.
99 Daniel Born, "Private Gardens, Public Swamps: *Howard's End* and the Revaluation of Liberal Guilt," *Novel: A Forum on Fiction* 25.2 (1992), 157.
100 Forster, *Howards End*, 359.
101 Gifford, *Pastoral*, 134.
102 Forster, "Machine Stops," 115.
103 *Ibid.*, 124.
104 *Ibid.*, 125.
105 E.M. Forster, *Maurice* (New York: Norton, 1993), 323.

106 Nicola Beauman notes that the trials happened when Forster was sixteen years of age and coincided with a trip to Italy. Beauman surmises that Morgan's mother, Lily, decided to take this single vacation in the space of twenty-two years in order to avoid exposing her son to any prominent discussion of homosexuality, for fear that he would share his father's homosexuality. Nicola Beaman, *Morgan: A Biography of E.M. Forster* (London: Hodder and Stoughton, 1993), 120–1.

107 Furbank, *E.M. Forster*, 83.

108 Mortimer-Sandilands and Erickson, *Queer*, 7.

109 *Ibid.*, 11.

110 *Ibid.*, 13.

111 Furbank, *E.M. Forster*, 111.

112 Mortimer-Sandilands and Erickson, *Queer*, 27–8.

113 Claude Summers, "The Flesh Educating the Spirit: Maurice," in *Critical Essays on E.M. Forster*, ed. Alan Wilde (Boston: G.K. Hall, 1985), 97.

114 Forster, *Maurice*, 93.

115 *Ibid.*

116 *Ibid.*, 184.

117 *Ibid.*, 221.

118 *Ibid.*, 179.

119 *Ibid.*, 191.

120 E.M. Forster, "Arthur Snatchfold," *The Life to Come and Other Stories* (New York: Penguin, 1989), 130.

121 *Ibid.*, 128.

122 *Ibid.*, 129.

123 *Ibid.*, 135.

124 Empson, *Some Versions*, 17.

125 Forster, *Maurice*, 214.

126 Mortimer-Sandilands and Erickson, *Queer*, 18.

127 Forster, "Snatchfold," 133.

128 *Ibid.*, 132.

129 *Ibid.*, 133.

130 *Ibid.*, 141.

131 Forster, *Maurice*, 250.

132 *Ibid.*, 254.

133 Gifford, *Pastoral*, 150.

134 Stuart Christie, *Worlding Forster: The Passage from Pastoral* (New York: Routledge, 2005), 31.

135 Peppis, *Sciences*, 139.

136 Forster, *Howards End*, 63.

137 Foster, *Ecological Rift*, 29.

138 Furbank, *E.M. Forster* vol. II, 29.

139 *Ibid.*, 41.

140 Furbank, *E.M. Forster* vol. I, 173–4.

141 Furbank, *E.M. Forster* vol. II, 40.

142 *Ibid.*, 183.
143 Forster, "Challenge of Our Time," *Three Cheers for Democracy*. (New York: Harvest, 1951), 59.
144 Wilfred H. Stone, "Forster: The Environmentalist," in *Seeing Double: Revisioning Edwardian and Modernist Literature*, ed. Carola M. Kaplan and Anne B. Simpson (New York: St. Martin's, 1996), 175–9.
145 Similarly, Woolf betrays her own class prejudices when it comes to building houses that would obstruct her view at Monk's House. Bonnie Kime Scott writes: "The Woolfs acquired additional land, which they called the 'terrace' to the north of the original parcel in 1928, hoping to ensure that they would retain a cherished view of the water meadows of the Ouse River. At about that time they became distressed about developers coming into the area. . . . Woolf rants (in a letter to Ottoline Morrel to the name of the man 'connected with preserving the downs'): 'If I write my fingers off, I want to stop it. . . . It is one of the loveliest places in the world, and then they want to have a coast road and omnibuses—oh the damnable stupidity of the English middle class!' Woolf's ideas of conservation betray class bias. But they do focus upon enduring environmental problems of suburban scrawl, tourism, and highway construction to meet the growing demands of the internal combustion engine." Bonnie Kime Scott, *In the Hollow of the Wave: Virginia Woolf and the Modernist Uses of Nature* (Charlottesville: University of Virginia Press, 2012), 97. Scott quotes *The Letters of Virginia Woolf*, vol. 4, 139.
146 This kind of NIMBY ("Not In My Backyard") attitude is known as environmental racism, against which some environmental theorists and activists have written and mobilized. See Robert D. Bullard's *Dumping in Dixie: Race, Class, and Environmental Quality* (Boulder: Westview Press, 2000), and Luke W. Cole and Sheil Foster's *From the Ground Up: Environmental Racism and the Rise of the Environmental Justice Movement* (New York: New York University Press, 2001).
147 Several international environmental theorists have catapulted this issue to prominence, including Vandana Shiva in *Biopiracy: The Plunder of Nature and Knowledge* (Boston: South End Press), 1997, and Candace Slater in *Entangled Edens: Visions of the Amazon* (Berkeley: University California Press), 2002.
148 Foster, *Ecological Rift*, 267.
149 Forster, *Howards End*, 281.
150 Paul Peppis, "Forster and England," in *The Cambridge Companion to E.M. Forster*, ed. David Bradshaw (New York: Cambridge University Press, 2007), 47.
151 *Ibid.*, 51.
152 Forster, *Howards End*, 113.
153 In "Novels of E.M. Forster," 174, Virginia Woolf's brief analysis of *A Passage to India* recognizes the significance of the novel's nonhuman presence:
We notice things, about the country especially, spontaneously, accidentally almost, as if we were actually there; and now it was the sparrows flying about

the pictures that caught our eye, now the elephant with painted forehead, now the enormous but badly designed range of hills. The people too, particularly the Indians, have something of the same casual, inevitable quality. They are not perhaps quite so important as the land, but they are alive; they are sensitive.

Despite her seeming indifference to the formal purpose underlying Forster's nonhuman elements by describing them as "random," Woolf astutely identifies how the pervasive animal presences create verisimilitude and compel the reader's attention. Although she compares the Indians to the land in a manner that prejudicially exoticizes them, Woolf points out that the "people" are "not perhaps quite so important as the land."

154 Frederick Crews argues that both *A Passage to India* and *Howard's End* are "consistent with [Forster's] version of liberalism, which we can identify as a narrow but by no means private current within the wider liberal tradition." Frederick Crews, "Forster and the Liberal Tradition," in *Howards End*, ed. Paul B. Armstrong (New York: Norton, 1998), 332. Edward Said conflates Forster's own perspective with the "liberal, humane espousal of Fielding's views" and thus aligns what he perceives as the novel's "loss" with Fielding's humanism: "he would have been a perfect hero in Forster's earlier fictions, but here he is defeated." Edward Said, *Culture and Imperialism* (New York: Knopf, 1993), 201–2. Lidan Lin grounds her entire premise that Forster's ultimate endeavor is to justify English rule over India on the assumption that "liberal humanism" is "Forster's informing ideology." Lidan Lin, "The Irony of Colonial Humanism: 'A Passage to India' and the Politics of Posthumanism," *ARIEL: A Review of International English Literature* 28.4 (1997), 133. Lidan Lin contrasts what she perceives to be Forster's validation of liberal humanism with the values of posthumanism; however, she defines the posthuman "other" that must be integrated into the formation of the "self" as the colonized native Indians as opposed to the nonhuman "other" of India itself.

155 E.M. Forster, *A Passage to India* (New York: Harcourt, 1999), 362.

156 Said, *Culture and Imperialism*, 201.

157 Serpil Oppermann, "Ecological Imperialism in British Colonial Fiction," *Journal of Faculty of Letters* 24.1 (June 2007), 190–1.

158 Yomna Al-Abdulkareem, "*A Passage to India*: An Ecocritical Reading," in *Words for a Small Planet: Ecocritical Views*, ed. Nanette Norris (Landham, MD: Lexington, 2013), 93.

159 *Ibid.*, 97.

160 Gifford, *Pastoral*, 152.

161 *Ibid.*, 153.

162 *Ibid.*, 156.

163 *Ibid.*, 162.

164 *Ibid.*, 163.

165 *Ibid.*, 165.

166 Gifford, "Pastoral," 26.

167 It is surprising that even Benita Parry, one of Forster's most perceptive critics, denies the novel's modernist traits: "Neither stylistically nor syntactically does *A Passage to India* display that 'constitutive sense of creation through rupture and crisis' which has been described as the vocation of an aesthetic modernism (176, quoting Calinescu 92). Instead, Parry aligns Forster with earlier realist writers: "*A Passage to India* uses the language of realism to chronicle a tragic-comedy of culture discord and political conflict" (178). Benita Parry, "Materiality and Mystification in *A Passage to India*," *Novel: A Forum on Fiction* 31.2 (1998), 174–94. The first quotation is on 175, quoting Calinescu, 92. The second quotation is on 178.

168 Forster, "Three Countries," In *A Routledge Literary Sourcebook on E.M. Forster's A Passage to India*. ed. Peter Childs. (London: Routledge, 2002), 298.

169 Lidan Lin does not address any of the textual examples put forth in this essay, yet claims: "Forster fails to interrogate the rationalism that, as the cornerstone of English character, has served to germinate and nourish imperialism in the course of history." Lin, "Irony of Colonial," 140. Although Sara Suleri's critical approach to Forster's rationality is not as blunt as Lin's she also identifies Forster with a "Western project which represents India as an empty site that is bounded only by an aura of irrationality" (246) and locates what she argues is the novel's negative critique of India in terms of Forster's valorization of rationality: "India is ultimately reprehensible because it denies the fixity of an object that the narrative subject can pursue and penetrate." Sara Suleri, "The Geography of *A Passage to India*," in *Literature in the Modern World Critical Essays and Documents*, ed. Dennis Walder (New York City: Oxford University Press, 1990), 246 and 248.

170 Elizabeth DeLoughrey and George B. Handley, eds. *Postcolonial Ecologies: Literatures of the Environment* (New York: Oxford University Press, 2011), 4.

171 Forster, *Passage*, 5–6.

172 Jo Ann Hoeppner Moran, "E.M. Forster's *A Passage to India*: What Really Happened in the Caves," *MFS: Modern Fiction Studies* 34.4 (Winter 1988), 602.

173 *Ibid.*, 600.

174 Bonnie Roos and Alex Hunt, "Systems and Secrecy: Postcolonial Ecocriticism and Ghosh's The Calcutta Chromosome," in *The Cambridge Companion to Literature and the Environment*, ed. Louise Westling (Cambridge University Press: New York, 2014), 187.

175 DeLoughrey and Handley, *Postcolonial*, 8.

176 Forster, *Passage*, 214.

177 Iovina Serenella, "Theorizing Material Ecocriticism: A Diptych," *ISLE: Interdisciplinary Studies in Literature and Environment* 19.3 (Summer 2012), 457.

178 Maurice Merleau-Ponty, *The Visible and the Invisible*, trans. Alphonso Lingis, ed. Claude Lefort (Evanston: Northwestern University Press, 1968), 144.

179 Forster, *Passage*, 123.

180 *Ibid.*, 136.

181 *Ibid.*, 152.

182 *Ibid.*, 275.

183 David Abram, *The Spell of the Sensuous: Perception and Language in the More-Than-Human World* (New York: Vintage, 1997), 152.

184 Forster, *Commonplace*, 51.

185 Forster, *Passage*, 362.

186 *Ibid.*, 123.

187 *Ibid.*

188 *Ibid.*, 34.

189 *Ibid.*

190 *Ibid.*, 61.

191 *Ibid.*, 136.

192 *Ibid.*, 77.

193 Godbole's name "Itself suggests the omnipresence of divinity in the pantheism of God joined with nature (bole/tree)." See Peter Childs, ed. *A Routledge Literary Sourcebook on E.M. Forster's A Passage to India* (New York : Routledge, 2002), 194.

194 Forster, *Passage*, 80.

195 Medalie, *E.M. Forster's Modernism*, 134. The Marabar caves and their echo are generally described in terms of their negativity. For Suleri the caves are "areas of empty experience" and an "obliterating presence" giving off an "obscene echo." Suleri, "Geography," 249. Parry expounds on how the caves have been interpreted by other critics: "a hollow site which the narrative, parodying an act of rape, violently penetrates." Parry, "Materiality and Mystification," 185.

196 Roos and Hunt, "Systems and Secrecy," 196.

197 Parry, "Materiality and Mystification," 198.

198 Forster, *Passage*, 197.

199 *Ibid.*, 163, emphasis added. While Forster's novel is from the perspective of an English writer during the colonial period, some postcolonial authors seem to be adapting similar techniques for representing the nonhuman world in relation to colonial politics and memory, as explained in DeLoughrey and Handley's ecocritical reading of Guyanese author Martin Carter's 1951 poem "Listening to the Land": "The narrator repeatedly describes how he 'bent' and 'kneeled' down, in anticipation of listening, but confesses that 'all (he) heard was tongueless whispering / as if some buried slave wanted to speak again'. Written in an era of decolonization and postcolonial nationalism, Carter's poem suggests both the *recuperative* role of place, defining land via relations of property rather than as 'earth' or 'landscape,' while also demonstrating the impossibility of fully *translating* place because of the historical violence that produces 'tongueless whispering.'" Elizabeth DeLoughrey and George B. Handley, *Postcolonial Ecologies: Literatures of the Environment* (New York: Oxford University Press, 2011), 5.

200 Serenella Iovino and Serpil Oppermann, "Theorizing Material Ecocriticism: A Diptych," *ISLE: Interdisciplinary Studies in Literature and Environment* 19.3 (Summer 2012), 467.

201 Forster, *Passage*, 165.
202 *Ibid.*, 226–7.
203 Merleau-Ponty, *Visible*, 101–2.
204 Forster, *Passage*, 323.
205 *Ibid.*, 253.
206 *Ibid.*, 31.
207 *Ibid.*, 108.
208 *Ibid.*, 195.
209 *Ibid.*, 228.
210 *Ibid.*, 317.
211 *Ibid.*, 254.
212 *Ibid.*, 28.
213 *Ibid.*, 350.
214 *Ibid.*, 234.
215 Ibid., 344.
216 Gifford, *Pastoral*, 153.
217 Forster, *Passage*, 327–8, emphasis added.
218 *Ibid.*, 114.
219 *Ibid.*, 313.
220 E.M. Forster, *The Hill of Devi.* (Middlesex: Penguin, 1965), 47–8.
221 *Ibid.*, 117.
222 John Marx, *The Modernist Novel and the Decline of Empire* (New York: Cambridge University Press, 2005), 113.
223 Christie, *Worlding*, 173.
224 Forster, *Passage*, 277.
225 *Ibid.*, 233.
226 *Ibid.*, 326.
227 *Ibid.*
228 *Ibid.*, 362.
229 *Ibid.*, 349–50.
230 *Ibid.*, 343.
231 Mortimer-Sandilands, *Queer*, 30.
232 Forster, *Passage*, 354.
233 *Ibid.*, 352.
234 *Ibid.*, 353.
235 *Ibid.*
236 *Ibid.*, 362.
237 *Ibid.*, 353.
238 Forster, *Aspects of the Novel.* 1927. (New York: Harcourt, 1964), 96–7.
239 Forster, *Passage*, 169.

Chapter 2

1 E.M. Forster, "Virginia Woolf," in *Two Cheers for Democracy* (New York: Harcourt, 1951), 252.

2 *Ibid.*

3 Derek Ryan, *Virginia Woolf and the Materiality of Theory: Sex, Animal, Life* (Edinburgh: Edinburgh University Press, 2013), 3.

4 Alexandra Harris, *Romantic Moderns: English Writers, Artists and the Imagination from Virginia Woolf to John Piper* (New York: Thames & Hudson, 2010), 113.

5 *Ibid.*, 118.

6 Mark Hussey, *The Singing of the Real World* (Columbus, OH: Ohio State University Press, 1986), xx.

7 *Ibid.*, 29.

8 *Ibid.*, 142.

9 *Ibid.*, 115.

10 Mark Hussey, "Woolf: After Lives," in *Virginia Woolf in Context*, ed. Bryony Randall and Jane Goldman (New York: Cambridge University Press, 2012), 23.

11 Westling, *Logos*, 118–19, quoting Merleau-Ponty *Visible and Invisible*, 253

12 Beer, Gillian, *Virginia Woolf: The Common Ground* (Ann Arbor, MI: University of Michigan Press, 1997), 17.

13 Virginia Woolf, *The Diary of Virginia Woolf*. vols. I–V, ed. Anne Olivier Bell (New York: Harcourt, 1982), 21.

14 *Ibid.* vol. II., 304.

15 Virginia Woolf, "Modern Fiction," in *The Common Reader*, ed. Andrew McNeillie (New York: Harcourt, 1984), 147.

16 Virginia Woolf, "A Sketch of the Past," in *Moments of Being: Unpublished Autobiographical Writings*, ed. Jeanne Schulkind (New York: Harcourt, 1976), 114–15.

17 Maurice Merleau-Ponty, *The Visible and the Invisible*, trans. Alphonso Lingis, ed. Claude Lefort, ed. (Evanston: Northwestern University Press, 1968), 101.

18 *Ibid.*, 102.

19 Serpil Oppermann, "From Ecological Postmodernism to Material Ecocriticism: Creative Materiality and Narrative Agency," in *Material Ecocriticism*, ed. Iovino, Serenella and Serpil Oppermann (Bloomington: Indiana University Press, 2014), 34 quoting Karen Barad.

20 Donna J. Haraway, *When Species Meet* (Minneapolis: University of Minnesota Press, 2008), 27.

21 Merleau-Ponty, *Visible*, 102.

22 Virginia Woolf, *A Passionate Apprentice*, ed. Michael E. Leaska (London: Pimlico, 2004), 393.

23 Carole Bourne-Taylor and Ariane Mildenberg, "Introduction: Phenomenology, Modernism and Beyond" in *Phenomenology, Modernism, and Beyond* (Bern, Switzerland: Peter Lang, 2010), 23.

24 Jed Esty notes the tension between individualism and patriotism in *Between the Acts*: "Woolf uses the pageant to deflate nationalism and deflect political commitment.... And yet there are moments of communal longing and national sentiment that run against that grain." Jed Esty, *A Shrinking*

Island: Modernism and National Culture in England (Princeton: Princeton University Press, 2004), 92. What my analysis adds to Esty's observation is that the positive potential of a larger community in Woolf's work is often represented by inclusion of the nonhuman, rather than a merely cultural cohesion. For example, when Miss La Trobe is confronted with an audience that "sat staring ... whose mouths opened, but no sound came" the cows "took up the burden. . .. The cows annihilated the gap; bridged the distance; filled the emptiness and continued the emotion" *Ibid.*, 140–1. The force that creates continuation and meaning is the nonhuman presence inserting itself into the human story, the shared emotion that creates community transcends nationalism, or even humanism.

25 Virginia Woolf, "Outlines," *The Common Reader*, 184–5.
26 Virginia Woolf, "The Pastons and Chaucer," *The Common Reader*, 13.
27 Virginia Woolf, "The Russian Viewpoint," *The Common Reader*, 180.
28 *Ibid.*,181.
29 Harris, *Romantic Moderns*, 156.
30 Woolf, "The Russian Viewpoint," 181.
31 Virginia Woolf, "The Novels of Thomas Hardy," in *The Second Common Reader* (New York: Harcourt, 1986), 223.
32 *Ibid.*, 223–4.
33 *Ibid.*, 224.
34 *Ibid.*
35 *Ibid.*, 225.
36 Merleau-Ponty, *Visible*, 11, emphasis added.
37 Woolf, "The Novels of Hardy," 225, emphasis added.
38 Virginia Woolf, "Modern Fiction," *The Common Reader*, Andrew McNeillie, ed. (New York: Harcourt, 1984),150.
39 Westling, *Logos*, 34, quoting from Merleau-Ponty, *Visible*, 147–8.
40 Serpil Oppermann, "Material Ecocriticism and the Creativity of Storied Matter," *Frame* 26.2 (2013), 60.
41 John Oakland, "Virginia Woolf's 'Kew Gardens'," *English Studies* 68.3 (1987), 268.
42 *Ibid.*
43 Edward L. Bishop, "Pursuing 'It' through 'Kew Gardens'," *Studies in Short Fiction* 19.3 (1982), 271.
44 Elizabeth DeLoughrey and George B. Handley, eds., *Postcolonial Ecologies: Literatures of the Environment* (New York: Oxford University Press, 2011), 11–12.
45 Bonnie Kime Scott, *In the Hollow of the Wave: Virginia Woolf and the Modernist Uses of Nature* (Charlottesville: University of Virginia Press, 2012), 75.
46 Virginia Woolf, "Kew Gardens," in *The Complete Shorter Fiction of Virginia Woolf*, 2nd edn., ed. Susan Dick, (New York: Harcourt, 1989), 90.
47 *Ibid.*
48 *Ibid.*

49 Christina Alt, *Virginia Woolf and the Study of Nature* (New York: Cambridge University Press, 2010), 147–8.

50 Maurice Merleau-Ponty, *Phenomenology of Perception,* trans. Colin Smith (London: Routledge, 2002), 177.

51 Serenella Iovino and Serpil Oppermann, "After Green Ecologies: Prismatic Visions," in *Prismatic Ecology: Ecotheory beyond Green*, ed. Jeffrey Jerome Cohen (Minneapolis: University of Minnesota Press, 2013), 329.

52 Woolf, "Modern Fiction," 90.

53 Serenella Iovino and Serpil Oppermann, "Theorizing Material Ecocriticism: A Diptych," *ISLE: Interdisciplinary Studies in Literature and Environment* 19.3 (2012), 451.

54 Merleau-Ponty, *Phenomenology,* 342.

55 Woolf, "Kew Gardens," 90.

56 *Ibid.*, 91.

57 *Ibid.*

58 *Ibid.*

59 *Ibid.*, 90.

60 *Ibid.*

61 *Ibid.*, 91.

62 *Ibid.*, 91–2.

63 Frederick William Gamble, *The Animal World* (London: Williams and Norgate, 1911), 143.

64 Woolf, "Kew Gardens," 92.

65 *Ibid.*

66 *Ibid.*

67 *Ibid.*

68 *Ibid.*, 93.

69 *Ibid.*, 91.

70 Westling, *Logos*, 117.

71 *Ibid.*, 125.

72 Oppermann, "Ecological Postmodernism," 29.

73 Woolf, "Kew Gardens," 94.

74 *Ibid.*

75 *Ibid.*, 95.

76 Bishop, "Pursuing 'It'," 275.

77 Woolf, "Kew Gardens," 94.

78 *Ibid.*

79 *Ibid.*

80 Virginia Woolf, "Craftsmanship," *The Death of the Moth and Other Essays* (New York: Harcourt, 1974), 204.

81 *Ibid.* 205.

82 Woolf, *Diary.* vol. 3 (March 17, 1930), 297–8.

83 Serenella Iovino, "Theorizing Material Ecocriticism: A Diptych," *ISLE: Interdisciplinary Studies in Literature and Environment* 19.3 (2012), 454.

84 *Ibid.*, 455.

85 M.H. Abrams, *A Glossary of Literary Terms*, 8th edn. (Boston: Thomson, 2005), 211, emphasis added.

86 Lorraine Daston and Gregg Mitman, eds., *Thinking with Animals: New Perspectives on Anthropomorphism* (New York: Columbia University Press, 2005), 2.

87 Lawrence Buell, *The Future of Environmental Criticism: Environmental Crisis and Literary Imagination* (Malden, MA: Blackwell, 2005), 134.

88 Donna J. Haraway, *When Species Meet* (Minneapolis: University of Minnesota Press, 2008), 20.

89 Daston and Mitman, *Thinking with Animals*, 9–10.

90 *Ibid.*,10.

91 Caroline Hovanec, "Philosophical Barnacles and Empiricist Dogs: Knowing Animals in Modernist Literature and Science," *Configurations* 21.3 (Fall 2013), 255.

92 *Ibid.*, 253.

93 Eileen Crist, *Images of Animals: Anthropomorphism and the Animal Mind* (Philadelphia: Temple University Press, 1999), 11.

94 *Ibid.*, 17.

95 *Ibid.*, 15.

96 Charles Darwin, *The Expression of Emotions in Man and Animals* (Charleston, SC: Bibliobazaar, 2007), 50.

97 Mark Hussey, *Virginia Woolf A to Z: A Comprehensive Reference for Students, Teachers, and Common Readers to her Life, Work, and Critical Reception* (New York: Facts on File, 1995), 89.

98 *Flush* sold 14,390 copies in the first six months of its release, Hussey, *A to Z*, 89.

99 One reviewer satirically lamented "the passing of a potentially great writer who perished for lack of an intelligent audience," Hussey, *A to Z*, 89. Which was just the kind of attitude Woolf feared in a prepublication diary entry: "I must not let myself believe that I'm simply a ladylike prattler: for one thing it's not true. But they'll all say so. And I shall very much dislike the popular success of Flush," Woolf, *Diary* vol. IV, 181, 2 October 1933.

100 Snaith, 615.

101 For perspectives on *Flush* that analyze the work predominately as a political allegory see Anna Snaith's "Of Fanciers, Footnotes, and Fascism: Virginia Woolf's *Flush*," *Modern Fiction Studies* 48.3 (2002), 614–36; Philip Armstrong's *What Animals Mean in the Fiction of Modernity* (London: Routledge, 2008); Pamela Caughie's *Virginia Woolf and Postmodernism* (Champagne-Urbana: University of Illinois Press, 1991); and Susan Squire's *Virginia Woolf and London* (University of North Carolina Press, 1985).

102 Dan Wylie, "The Anthropomorphic Ethic: Fiction and the Animal Mind in Virginia Woolf's *Flush* and Barbara Gowdy's *The White Bone*," *ISLE: Inter-disciplinary Studies in Literature and Environment* 9.2 (2002), 117. For readings of *Flush* that emphasize Woolf's depiction of animal consciousness see Craig Smith's "Across the Widest Gulf: Nonhuman Subjectivity in Virginia

Woolf's *Flush,*" *Twentieth Century Literature* 48.3 (2002), 348–61; Wylie "Anthropomorphic Ethic"; and Anna Feuerstein's "What Does Power Smell Like?: Canine Epistemology and the Politics of the Pet in Virginia Woolf's *Flush*" and Jamie Johnson's "Virginia Woolf's Flush: Decentering Human Subjectivity through the Nonhuman Animal Character," both in *Virginia Woolf Miscellany*, Issue 84 (Fall 2013).

103 Virginia Woolf, *Flush* (London: Hogarth P, 1933), pp. 30–1.

104 Merleau-Ponty, *Visible,* 133.

105 Haraway, *When Species Meet,* my emphasis.

106 Derek Ryan, *Virginia Woolf and the Materiality of Theory: Sex, Animal, Life* (Edinburgh: Edinburgh University Press, 2013), 145.

107 Scott, *In the Hollow,* 173.

108 Ryan, *Virginia Woolf,* 138, quoting Woolf, Flush, 89.

109 Alison Light, *Mrs. Woolf and the Servants: An Intimate History of Domestic Life in Bloomsbury* (New York: Bloomsbury Press, 2008), 220.

110 Pamela Caughie, "Dogs and Servants," *The Virginia Woolf Miscellany* 84 (Fall 2013), 38.

111 Woolf, *Flush,* 80–1.

112 *Ibid.,* 137–8.

113 *Ibid.,* 140.

114 *Ibid.,* 128.

115 *Ibid.,* 129.

116 Wylie, "Anthropomorphic Ethic," 119.

117 Woolf, *Flush,* 140.

118 Woolf, "Kew Gardens," 94.

119 Woolf, *Flush,* 156.

120 Ryan, *Virginia Woolf,* 147.

121 Daston and Mitman, *Thinking with Animals,* 8.

122 Quentin Bell, *Virginia Woolf: A Biography* (New York: Harcourt, 1972), 410.

123 David Herman, "Modernist Life Writing and Nonhuman Lives: Ecologies of Experience in Virginia Woolf's Flush," *MFS: Modern Fiction Studies* 59.3 (Fall, 2013), 562.

124 *Ibid.,* 561.

125 Woolf, *Flush,* 19–20.

126 Ryan, *Virginia Woolf,* 157.

127 Woolf, *Flush,* 93.

128 *Ibid.*

129 *Ibid.,* 109.

130 Craig Smith, "Across the Widest Gulf: Nonhuman Subjectivity in Virginia Woolf's *Flush,*" *Twentieth Century Literature: A Scholarly and Critical Journal* 48.3 (September, 2002), 356.

131 Although Woolf critiques Barrett-Browning as a "bad poet" in her essay "Poets' Letters," she also accuses her circumstance as contributing to the alleged deficiencies in her work: "But it is not possible to consider what she might have done had her life been propitious – had not one half of it

dwindled in a London sick-room – had not the other been exposed suddenly to the fierce Italian sun and Robert Browning." See Woolf, "Poets' Letters," in *The Essays of Virginia Woolf* vol. 1, ed. Andrew McNeillie (New York: Harcourt, 1986), 101 and 103.

132 Woolf, *Flush*, 39.

133 Anna Snaith, "Of Fanciers, Footnotes, and Fascism: Virginia Woolf's *Flush*," *Modern Fiction Studies* 48.3 (2002), 623.

134 Woolf, *Flush*, 39.

135 Jutta Ittner, "Part Spaniel, Part Canine Puzzle: Anthropomorphism in Woolf's *Flush* and Auster's *Timbuktu*," *Mosaic: A Journal for the Comparative Study of Literature* 39.4 (2006), 189.

136 *Ibid.*, 188.

137 Feuerstein, "Power," 32.

138 Woolf, *Flush*, 43.

139 *Ibid.*, 86.

140 David Abram, *The Spell of the Sensuous: Perception and Language in the More-Than-Human World* (New York: Vintage, 1997), 48.

141 Woolf, *Flush*, 170.

142 Snaith, "Of Fanciers," 620.

143 Woolf, *Flush*, 176.

144 *Ibid.*, 125.

145 Haraway, *When Species Meet*, 53.

146 Woolf, *Flush*, 125.

147 Haraway, *When Species Meet*, 74.

148 DeLoughrey and Handley, *Postcolonial Ecologies*, 25.

149 Scott, *In the Hollow*, 156.

150 DeLoughrey and Handley, *Postcolonial Ecologies*, 25.

151 Scott Cohen, "The Empire from the Street: Virginia Woolf, Wembley, and Imperial Monuments," *Modern Fiction Studies* 50.1 (2004), 87.

152 Virginia Woolf, "Thunder at Wembley," *The Essays of Virginia Woolf*, vol. 3, ed. Andrew McNeillie (New York: Harcourt, 1986), 410.

153 *Ibid.*, 411.

154 DeLoughrey and Handley, *Postcolonial Ecologies*, 11.

155 Abram, *Spell of the Sensuous*, 153.

156 Oppermann, "Ecological Postmodernism," 35.

157 Woolf, "Thunder at Wembley," 412.

158 *Ibid.*

159 William Henry Hudson, *Birds In London* (London: J. M. Dent and Sons, Ltd., 1924), 115–8.

160 Alt, *Virginia Woolf*, p. 154.

161 Cohen, "The Empire from the Street," 93.

162 Abram, *Spell of the Sensuous*, 47.

163 Christine Froula, *Virginia Woolf and the Bloomsbury Avant-Garde* (New York: Columbia University Press, 2005), 153–4.

164 *Ibid.*, 157.

165 *Ibid.*, 147.

166 Julia Briggs, *Virginia Woolf: An Inner Life* (New York: Harcourt, 2005), 175.

167 Louise Westling, "Virginia Woolf and the Flesh of the World," *New Literary History* 30.4 (Autumn 1999), 860.

168 Laura Doyle, "'These Emotions of the Body': Intercorporeal Narrative in *To the Lighthouse*," *Twentieth Century Literature* 40.1 (Spring 1994), 43, 50.

169 On what would have been Leslie Stephen's 96th birthday, Virginia Woolf writes: "I used to think of him and mother daily; but writing The Lighthouse, laid them in my mind. And now he comes back sometimes, but differently. (I believe this to be true – that I was obsessed by them both, unhealthily; and writing of them was a necessary act)" (*Diary* III:208, 11/28/28).

170 Vita Sackville-West, *Country Notes* (London: M. Joseph, 1939), 11–12.

171 Virginia Woolf, *Diary* vol. II, 301.

172 Merleau-Ponty, *Visible*, 102.

173 Virginia Woolf, *To the Lighthouse*, ed. Mark Hussey, (New York: Harcourt, 2005), 21.

174 *Ibid.*, 25.

175 Merleau-Ponty, *Phenomenology*, 409, emphasis added.

176 Karen Barad, *Meeting the Universe Halfway* (Durham: Duke University Press, 2007), 185.

177 Woolf, *Lighthouse*, 24.

178 David Abram, "The Commonwealth of Breath," in *Material Ecocriticism*, ed. Serenella Iovino and Serpil Oppermann, (Bloomington: Indiana University Press, 2014), 302.

179 Merleau-Ponty, *Phenomenology*, 249.

180 Iovino Serenella and Serpil Oppermann, "After Green Ecologies: Prismatic Visions," in *Prismatic Ecology: Ecotheory beyond Green*, ed. Jeffrey Jerome Cohen (Minneapolis: University of Minnesota Press, 2013), 329.

181 Wendy Wheeler, *The Whole Creature: Complexity, Biosemiotics and the Evolution of Culture* (London: Lawrence & Wishart, 2006), 34.

182 Woolf, *Between the Acts*, 120.

183 Virginia Woolf, "The Death of the Moth," *The Death of the Moth and Other Essays* (New York: Harcourt, 1970), 4.

184 Woolf, *Lighthouse*, 67–8.

185 Doyle, "'These Emotions of the Body'," 53.

186 Catriona Mortimer-Sandilands and Bruce Erickson, "Introduction: A Genealogy of Queer Ecologies," in *Queer Ecologies: Sex, Nature, Politics, Desire*, ed. Catriona Mortimer-Sandilands and Bruce Erickson (Bloomington: Indiana University Press, 2010), 37.

187 Patricia Morgne Cramer, "Woolf and Theories of Sexuality," in *Virginia Woolf in Context*, ed. Bryony Randall and Jane Goldman (New York: Cambridge Press, 2012), 140.

188 Ryan, *Virginia Woolf*, 78.

189 Woolf, *Lighthouse*, 26.

190 Woolf, *Lighthouse*, 27.
191 Westling, "Virginia Woolf," 860.
192 Oppermann, "Ecological Postmodernism," 27.
193 Michael Lackey claims that Woolf rejected philosophical perspectives: "The philosopher sees a stable ontological structure behind the contingent and deceptive world of appearances, and that ontological structure is supposedly more real and more legitimate than the secondary-quality observations of non-philosophers." See Michael Lackey, "Modernist Anti-Philosophicalism and Virginia Woolf's Critique of Philosophy," *Journal of Modern Literature* 29.4 (2006), 88. While that may be true regarding philosophies that rely on a separation between mind and common, embodied knowledge, Lackey over-states his position by collapsing all philosophies into a single model. As this dissertation shows, both Merleau-Ponty and Woolf break down the opposition between consciousness and body that other philosophies take as their starting point.
194 Abram, *Spell of the Sensuous*, 47.
195 Woolf, *Lighthouse*, 86.
196 *Ibid.*, 96.
197 *Ibid.*, 86.
198 *Ibid.*, 99–100.
199 *Ibid.*, 99.
200 *Ibid.*
201 Merleau-Ponty, *Visible*, 11.
202 *Ibid.*, 13.
203 Woolf, *Lighthouse*, 20.
204 *Ibid.*, 137.
205 Merleau-Ponty, *Phenomenology*, 250–1.
206 Woolf, *Lighthouse*, 132.
207 Westling, "Virginia Woolf," 867.
208 Woolf, *Lighthouse*, 141.
209 Doyle, "'These Emotions of the Body'," 48.
210 Woolf, *Lighthouse*, 142.
211 Briggs, *Virginia Woolf: An Inner Life*, 176.
212 Adrienne Bartlett, "The Forces of Nature in *To the Lighthouse*: Friend or Foe?" *Virginia Woolf Miscellany* 78 (Fall/Winter 2010), 30.
213 Woolf, *Lighthouse*, 183.
214 Merleau-Ponty, *Visible*, 84.
215 *Ibid.*, 84.
216 Woolf, *Lighthouse*, 12.
217 *Ibid.*, 66.
218 *Ibid.*, 117.
219 *Ibid.*, 138.
220 *Ibid.*, 134.
221 *Ibid.*, 135.
222 *Ibid.*, 145.

223 *Ibid.*, 87.

224 Merleau-Ponty, *Phenomenology*, xxiii.

225 Merleau-Ponty, *Visible*, 133.

226 Mildenberg, Ariane, "Openings: Epoché as Aesthetic Tool in Modernist Texts," in *Phenomenology, Modernism, and Beyond* (Bern, Switzerland: Peter Lang, 2010), 50.

227 Woolf, *Lighthouse*, 149.

228 Bourne-Taylor and Mildenberg "Introduction: Phenomenology," 23.

229 Woolf, *Lighthouse*, 161–2.

230 *Ibid.*, 163.

231 Doyle, "'These Emotions of the Body',," 65.

232 Wendy Wheeler, *The Whole Creature*, 156.

233 Merleau-Ponty, *Visible*, 150.

234 *Ibid.*, 150–1.

235 *Ibid.*, 151.

236 Oppermann, "Ecological Postmodernism," 34.

237 Woolf, *Lighthouse*, 181–2.

238 Merleau-Ponty, *Visible*, 150.

239 Woolf, *Lighthouse*, 165.

240 Oppermann, "Ecological Postmodernism," 34.

241 Woolf, *Lighthouse*, 211.

242 *Ibid.*, 175.

243 Hubert Zapf, "Creative Matter and Creative Mind," in *Material Ecocriticism*, ed. Serenella Iovino and Serpil Oppermann (Bloomington: Indiana University Press, 2014), 54.

244 Merleau-Ponty, *Phenomenology*, 373.

245 Woolf, *Lighthouse*, 175.

246 *Ibid.*, 174–5.

247 *Ibid.*, 189.

248 Merleau-Ponty, *Visible*, 89.

249 Woolf, *Lighthouse*, 198.

250 Woolf, *Lighthouse*, 202.

251 *Ibid.*, 56, emphasis added.

252 Briggs, *Virginia Woolf*, 174.

253 Woolf, *Lighthouse*, 211.

254 Vanessa Bell's cover art for *To the Lighthouse* provocatively hints that Lily's line through the center of the painting might represent the lighthouse itself. Vanessa Bell's design has the lighthouse in the middle of the cover, represented by three thick vertical lines with small spaces in between, suggesting a fluted, columnar appearance (distinct from the black and white stripes mentioned on page 189 of the novel and that wrap around the St. Ives' Godrevy lighthouse that was the novel's inspiration). Further, the top of the lighthouse does not appear on the cover; instead, radiating dots stretch to the edges of both sides of just the top fifth of the visible field, representing the beams that radiate from the light without showing the square top that holds

the lamp. Rows of cresting waves comprise the bottom border. Thus, the three vertical lines of the tower part of the lighthouse are left to represent the entire structure.

Chapter 3

1 W.H. Auden, "Woods," *Collected Poems*, ed. Edward Mendelson (New York: Vintage, 1991), 560, line 54.

2 This particular line from Auden's "In Memory of W.B. Yeats," *Ibid.* 248, 36, is frequently quoted out of context. Standing alone, it seems to claim there is no social role for poetry, but this reading does not do justice to the poem's conclusion, nor the subtler textures of these words when put back in their proper context. Mendelson resuscitates the complexity of the aphorism explaining, "Poetry '*makes* nothing happen' – it *forces* nothing to occur – but it can teach the free to make their own triumphant choices." "W.H. Auden," *The Cambridge Companion to English Poets*, Claude Rawson, ed. (Cambridge: Cambridge University Press, 2011), 517.

3 Robert S. Morrison, "Environmental Concerns: Ecocritical landmarks, text-marks, benchmarks," *University of Toronto Quarterly*, 71.3 (2002), 811.

4 Jed Rasula, *This Compost: Ecological Imperatives in American Poetry*, (Athens: University Georgia Press, 2003), 6, quoting Whitman.

5 William Cronon was one of the first to insist that our understanding of nature is always bound up with layers of cultural assumptions: "Far from being the one place on earth that stands apart from humanity, [wilderness] is quite profoundly a human creation – indeed the creation of very particular human cultures at very particular moments in human history." *Uncommon Ground: Rethinking the Human Place in Nature* (New York: Norton, 1996). Now, ecocritics examine all kinds of environments, including suburban and urban landscapes as well.

6 Auden's later work was neglected even during his own lifetime. In a 1960 title of a *Spectator* review, Philip Larkin bemoaned "What's Become of Wystan?" See Edward Mendelson, *Later Auden*, (New York: Farrar, 1999), 423. In a 1967 postscript to his friend Naomi Mitchison, who disparaged recent revisions of some of his poems and expressed a concern that he needed to "make another jump into memorability," Auden remonstrates, "P.S. Believe it or not, I have got better. Please *try* 'Thanksgiving for a Habitat.'" *Ibid.*, 478. Although Edward Mendelson's book on Auden's later poetry may begin to reverse this trend, Auden's legacy remains primarily confined to his early work. Reviewer Michael Hennessey notes, "There is still a widely held perception that Auden's powers as a poet declined after he left England for America in 1939 – and that the decline accelerated rapidly during the final years of his life." Michael Hennessey, "Review: 'Believe It or Not, I Have Got Better': Auden after 1940," *Contemporary Literature*, 41.3 (2000), 564. Both the 1974 *Norton Anthology of English Literature* and the more recent 2000 edition include only three poems written after 1939, "none

of them written after 1952, leaving nearly twenty years of Auden's career unrepresented." *Ibid.*, 565.

7 Cary Wolfe, *Animal Rites: American Culture, the Discourse of Species, and Posthumanist Theory* (Chicago: University of Chicago Press, 2003), 4.

8 Cary Wolfe, ed., *Zoontologies: The Question of the Animal* (Minneapolis: University of Minnesota Press, 2003), xviii.

9 Auden, *Collected Poems*, 32.

10 *Ibid.*, 33, 29–30.

11 *Ibid.*, line 20.

12 *Ibid.*, line 27.

13 *Ibid.*, line 28.

14 *Ibid.*, 32, 5–6.

15 *Ibid.*, 179, 1.

16 *Ibid.*, line 4.

17 *Ibid.*, 58, 38.

18 Richard Davenport-Hines, *Auden* (New York: Pantheon, 1995), 297.

19 Auden, *Collected Poems*, 689, line 37–9.

20 *Ibid.*, line 43.

21 *Ibid.*, lines 43–6.

22 Wolfe, *Zoontologies*, xx.

23 Auden, *Collected Poems*, 690, line 46–55.

24 *Ibid.*, lines 76–7.

25 *Ibid.*, 691, lines 79–80.

26 New York Public Library, Berg Collection, W.H. Auden Diaries, 1963, 1964, 1965, 1967, 1969, 1973. Hereafter cited as 'Berg.'

27 *Ibid.*, 1964 and 1965.

28 Berg, letter from W.H. Auden to E. Mayer 8 November 1953.

29 Mendelson, *Later Auden*, 277.

30 *Ibid.*, 291.

31 Edward Mendelson, "The Body," in *W.H. Auden in Context*, ed. Tony Sharpe (New York: Cambridge University Press, 2013), 195.

32 W.H. Auden, "Transplanted Englishman Views US," *The Complete Works of W.H. Auden: Prose, 1956–1962* ed. Edward Mendson, vol. IV (Woodstock: Princeton University Press, 2010), 373–4.

33 W.H. Auden, "Paul Bunyan," *The Complete Works of W.H. Auden: Libretti*, ed. Edward Mendelson (Princeton: Princeton University Press, 1988), 572.

34 W.H. Auden, "The Bomb and Man's Consciousness," *Hiroshima Plus 20* (New York: Delacourt Press, 1965), 135.

35 Ranier Emig, "Auden and Ecology," in *The Cambridge Companion to W.H. Auden*, ed. Stan Smith (New York: Cambridge University Press, 2004), 222.

36 *Ibid.*, 212.

37 *Ibid.*, 215.

38 *Ibid.*, 218.

39 Scott J. Bryson, "Introduction," *Ecopoetry: A Critical Introduction* (Salt Lake City: University of Utah Press, 2002), 7.

40 Maurice Merleau-Ponty, *Nature Course Notes from the College de France*, comp. Dominique Segland, trans. Robert Vallier (Evanston: Northwestern University Press, 2003), 45.

41 Todd Balazic, "Embodied Consciousness and the Poetic Sense of the World," *SubStance* 32.1 (2003), 120.

42 George Lakoff and Mark Johnson, *Philosophy in the Flesh: The Embodied Mind and Its Challenge to Western Thought* (New York: Perseus, 1999), 59.

43 Hubert Zapf, "Creative Matter and Creative Mind," in *Material Ecocriticism*, ed. Serenella Iovino and Serpil Oppermann (Bloomington: Indiana University Press, 2014), 54.

44 W.H. Auden, "Making, Knowing and Judging," *The Dyer's Hand* (New York: Vintage, 1989), pp. 51–2.

45 Paul Peppis, "Schools, Movements, Manifestos," in *The Cambridge Companion to Modernist Poetry*, ed. Alex Davis and Lee M. Jenkins (New York: Cambridge University Press, 2007), 29.

46 W.H. Auden, "Sonnet XXI," *Collected Poems*, 195, lines 9–14.

47 *Ibid.*, 195, lines 3–6.

48 Virginia Woolf, *The Waves* (New York: Harcourt, 1978), 163.

49 Carrie Rohman, *Stalking the Subject: Modernism and the Animal* (New York: Columbia University Press, 2009), 39.

50 W.H. Auden, "Making, Knowing and Judging," 51.

51 R. Victoria Arana, *W.H. Auden's Poetry: Mythos, Theory, and Practice* (New York: Cambria Press, 2009), 265.

52 W.H. Auden, "As It Seemed to Us," *Forewords and Afterwords*, ed. Edward Mendelson (New York: Random House, 1973), 502.

53 Berg, enclosure in letter from W.H. Auden to Monroe Spears 19 February 1962.

54 Davenport-Hines, *Auden*, 21.

55 Auden, *Collected Poems*, 779, lines 26–7.

56 *Ibid.*, lines 18–20.

57 *Ibid.*, lines 1–5.

58 *Ibid.*, 780, lines 42–9.

59 Tony Sharpe, *W.H. Auden* (New York: Routledge, 2007), 101.

60 Katherine Bucknell, ed. *In Solitude, for Company: W.H. Auden after 1940: Unpublished Prose and Recent Criticism* (Oxford: Oxford University Press, 1996), 187.

61 Catriona Mortimer-Sandilands, "Melancholy Natures, Queer Ecologies," in *Queer Ecologies: Sex, Nature, Politics, Desire*, ed. Catriona Mortimer-Sandilands and Bruce Erickson (Bloomington: Indiana University Press, 2010), 343–4.

62 *Ibid.*, 348.

63 W.H. Auden, "The Poet and The City," *The Complete Works of W.H. Auden: Prose*, vol. IV, 77.

64 Christopher Isherwood, "Some Notes on Auden's Early Poetry," in *Auden: A Collection of Critical Essays*, ed. Monroe K. Spears (Englewood Cliffs, NJ: Prentice-Hall, 1964), 10.

65 Auden, "The Poet and The City," *The Dyer's Hand*, 78.

66 Auden, *Collected Poems*, 739, line 12.

67 *Ibid.*, lines 17–20.

68 Maurice Merleau-Ponty, *The Visible and the Invisible*, trans. Alphonso Lingis, ed. Claude Lefort (Evanston: Northwestern University Press, 1968), 271.

69 Auden, *Collected Poems*, 739, lines 22–5.

70 *Ibid.*, 740, lines 29–36.

71 *Ibid.*, 724, lines 7–9.

72 *Ibid.*, 725, lines 28–30, 34–6.

73 *Ibid.*, 558, lines 10–12.

74 *Ibid.*, 559, lines 40–4.

75 *Ibid.*, 559–60, lines 47–51.

76 Simon Schama describes the historical link between oak trees and nationalism in the eighteenth century, which coincides with the time when the oaks were being heavily deforested:
Repeated analogies were made between the character of the timber and the character of the nation. The "heart" of oak, the core of the tree, was its hardest and stoutest wood.
The association with this timber and English strength was literal as well as literary since the success of the British sailing fleet benefited from the oak's property of being particularly resistant to rot. Simon Schama, *Landscape and Memory* (New York: Vintage, 1995), 164.

77 *Ibid.*, 560, lines 18–22.

78 Berg, letter from W.H. Auden to Elizabeth Mayer 8 May 1948.

79 *Ibid.*, 831, line 92.

80 *Ibid.*, line 100.

81 Merleau-Ponty, *Visible*, 134–5.

82 Auden, *Collected Poems*, 740, lines 1–2.

83 Merleau-Ponty, *Nature*, 95–6.

84 Frans De Waal, *The Bonobo and the Atheist: In Search of Humanism Among the Primates*, (New York: Norton, 2013), 23.

85 Auden, *Collected Poems*, 741, lines 33–48.

86 Auden, "Words and the Word," *Secondary Worlds* (New York: Random, 1968), 144.

87 Auden, *Collected Poems*, 740–1, lines 11, 16, 30, 23, respectively.

88 *Ibid.*, lines 21, 28–9.

89 *Ibid.*, line 42.

90 *Ibid.*, lines 39–40.

91 Mendelson, *Later Auden*, 445.

92 Auden, *Collected Poems*, 809, lines 1–4.

93 *Ibid.*, lines 14–16.

94 Merleau-Ponty, *Nature*, 99.

95 Auden, *Collected Poems*, 810, lines 25–8.

96 *Ibid.*, 810, lines 33–5, emphasis added.

97 *Ibid.*, lines 41–4.

98 *Ibid.*, 811, lines 57–64.

99 W.H. Auden, "A Poet of Honor," *Complete Works*, 346.
100 Merleau-Ponty, *Nature*, 85.
101 In his 1973 poem "No, Plato, No" Auden also questions the persistence of a mind–body dualism: "I can't imagine anything / that I would less like to be / than a disincarnate Spirit, / unable to chew or sip / or make contact with surfaces." Auden, *Collected Poems*, 888, lines 1–5.
102 George W. Bahlke, "From *The Later Auden* ('Horae Canonicae')," in *Critical Essays on W.H. Auden* (New York: G.K. Hall, 1991), 14.
103 Auden, "The Virgin and The Dynamo," *The Dyer's Hand*, 63.
104 Auden, *Collected Poems*, 667, lines 29–36.
105 Mendelson, *Later Auden*, 381, quoting Auden's "Introduction" to *Yale Series of Younger Poets*.
106 Catriona Mortimer-Sandilands and Bruce Erickson, eds. "Introduction: A Genealogy of Queer Ecologies," *Queer Ecologies: Sex, Nature, Politics, Desire* (Bloomington: Indiana University Press, 2010), 3.
107 Auden, *Collected Poems*, 122, lines 1–8.
108 *Ibid.*, lines 13–18.
109 *Ibid.*, 672, lines 1, 5–8, respectively.
110 *Ibid.*, lines 13–16.
111 *Ibid.*, lines 21–8.
112 Philip Armstrong, *What Animals Mean in the Fiction of Modernity* (New York: Routledge, 2008), 153.
113 Auden, *Collected Poems*, 548.
114 Mendelson, *Later Auden*, 365.
115 *Ibid.*
116 Arana, *W.H. Auden's Poetry*, 277.
117 Auden, "Two Bestiaries," *The Dyer's Hand*, 302.
118 *Ibid.*
119 Donna J. Haraway, *When Species Meet* (Minneapolis: University of Minnesota Press, 2008), 27.
120 Auden, "Two Bestiaries," *The Dyer's Hand*, 302.
121 Auden, "The Justice of Dame Kind," *Forewords and Afterwords*, 459.
122 Auden, "Concerning the Unpredictable," *Forewords and Afterwords*, 473.
123 *Ibid.*
124 Davenport-Hines, *Auden*, 152.
125 Mendelson, "W.H. Auden," 508.
126 Auden, *Collected Poems*, 868, lines 50–3.
127 *Ibid.*, lines 1–5.
128 *Ibid.*, 871, lines 46–9.
129 *Ibid.*, 867.
130 *Ibid.*, lines 1–8.
131 *Ibid.*, 869, lines 31–5.
132 *Ibid.*, 870, lines 42–4.
133 *Ibid.*, 870–1, lines 21–5.
134 *Ibid.*, 872, lines 73–75.

135 Sharpe, *W.H. Auden*, 115.
136 Auden, *Collected Poems*, 838, lines 13–16.
137 Louise Westling, *The Logos of the Living World: Merleau-Ponty, Animals, and Language* (Fordham University Press: New York, 2014), 42–3.
138 Stacy Alaimo, *Bodily Natures: Science, Environment, and the Material Self* (Bloomington: Indiana University Press, 2010), 18.
139 Auden, *Collected Poems*, 890, lines 30–3.
140 *Ibid.*, 890, lines 37–42.
141 *Ibid.*, 891, lines 64–9.
142 Merleau-Ponty, *Nature*, 199.
143 Auden, "Words and the Word," 120–2.
144 Richard Bloom, "W.H. Auden's Bestiary of the Human." *The Virginia Quarterly Review*, 42.2 (1966), 218–19.
145 Auden, *Collected Poems*, 583.
146 Bloom, "Auden's Bestiary," 219.
147 Auden, *Collected Poems,* 731, lines 4–6.
148 *Ibid.*, 733, lines 55–7.
149 *Ibid.*, 734, lines 67–84.
150 *Ibid.*, 848, line 1.
151 *Ibid.*, lines 2–12.
152 Merleau-Ponty, *Nature*, 219.
153 Serpil Oppermann, "Material Ecocriticism and the Creativity of Storied Matter," *Frame* 26.2 (2013), 66.
154 Auden, *Collected Poems*, 14–15.
155 Wendy Wheeler, *The Whole Creature: Complexity, Biosemiotics and the Evolution of Culture*, (London: Lawrence & Wishart, 2006), 157.
156 Auden, *Collected Poems*, 849, lines 37–8.
157 *Ibid.*, 583, lines 1–6.
158 Zapf, "Creative Matter," 56.
159 Westling, *Logos*, 117.
160 Serenella Iovino and Serpil Oppermann, "Theorizing Material Ecocriticism: A Diptych," *ISLE: Interdisciplinary Studies in Literature and Environment* 19.3 (2012), 451.
161 Merleau-Ponty, *Nature*, 206.
162 *Ibid.*, 212.
163 Auden, *Collected Poems*, 584, lines 11–12.
164 *Ibid.*, lines 13–18.
165 "First Things First" loosely echoes Auden's earlier and more famous poem about two human lovers in bed, one asleep, and one awake with his lover's head laying "on my faithless arm," wishing that coming "Noons of dryness find you fed / By the involuntary powers, / Nights of insult let you pass / Watched by every human love." *Ibid.*, 157–8, lines 1, 37–40. In "First Things First" the storm is the companion and "involuntary power" that watches over the lover now alone, reminding him of past human love as well as the continuing gifts of sustenance offered by the non-human presences.

166 *Ibid.*, 584, lines 19–22.
167 *Ibid.*, lines 25–30.
168 Zapf, "Creative Matter," 57.

Epilogue

1 Aidan Wasley, "Ideas of America," in *W.H. Auden in Context*, ed. Tony Sharpe (New York: Cambridge University Press, 2013), 48.
2 Rob Nixon, *Slow Violence and the Environmentalism of the Poor* (Cambridge, MA: Harvard University Press, 2011), 8.
3 Rob Emmett Bergthaller, Adeline Johns-Putra, Agnes Kneitz, Susanna Lidström, Shane McCorristine, Isabel Pérez Ramos, Dana Phillips, Kate Rigby, and Libby Robin, "Mapping Common Ground: Ecocriticism, Environmental History, and the Environmental Humanities," *Environmental Humanities*, vol. 5 (2014), 266.
4 Timothy Clark, "Nature, Post Nature," in *The Cambridge Companion to Literature and the Environment*, ed. Louise Westling (Cambridge University Press: New York, 2014), 85.
5 *Ibid.*, 87.
6 Jon Stallworthy, *Wilfred Owen* (Oxford: Oxford University Press, 1998), 266.
7 Pablo Picasso, "Picasso Speaks," *The Arts,* New York, May 1923. Available at www.learn.columbia.edu/monographs/picmon/pdf/art_hum_reading_49.pdf (accessed October 14, 2015).
8 Virginia Woolf, Mrs. Dalloway (New York: Harcourt, 2005), 9.
9 E.M. Forster, *The Longest Journey* (New York: Penguin, 1989), 271.
10 Robert MacFarlane, "The word-hoard: Robert MacFarlane on rewilding our language and our landscape," *The Guardian*, February 27, 2015. Available at www.theguardian.com/books/2015/feb/27/robert-macfarlane-word-hoard-rewilding-landscape (accessed October 14, 2015).
11 Simon Schama, *Landscape and Memory* (New York: Vintage, 1996), 14.

Bibliography

Abram, David. *The Spell of the Sensuous: Perception and Language in the More-Than-Human World*. New York: Vintage, 1997.

"The Commonwealth of Breath." In *Material Ecocriticism*. Eds. Serenella Iovino and Serpil Oppermann. Bloomington: Indiana University Press, 2014. 301–14.

Abrams, M.H. *A Glossary of Literary Terms*. Boston: Thomson, 2005.

Al-Abdulkareem, Yomna. "A Passage to India: An Ecocritical Reading." In *Words for a Small Planet: Ecocritical Views*. Ed. Nanette Norris. Landham, MD: Lexington, 2013. 93–100.

Alaimo, Stacy. *Bodily Natures: Science, Environment, and the Material Self*. Bloomington: Indiana University Press, 2010.

Alt, Christina. *Virginia Woolf and the Study of Nature*. New York: Cambridge University Press, 2010.

Anker, Peder. *Imperial Ecology: Environmental Ecology in the British Empire 1895–1945*. Cambridge, MA: Harvard University Press, 2001.

Arana, R. Victoria. *W.H. Auden's Poetry: Mythos, Theory, and Practice*. New York: Cambria Press, 2009.

Armstrong, Philip. *What Animals Mean in the Fiction of Modernity*. New York: Routledge, 2008.

Auden, W.H. "As It Seemed to Us." In *Forewords and Afterwords*. Edward Mendelson, selected. New York: Random House, 1973. 492–524.

"The Bomb and Man's Consciousness." In *Hiroshima Plus 20*. New York: Delacourt Press, 1965. 126–32.

A Certain World: A Commonplace Book. New York: Viking Press, 1970.

Collected Poems. Ed. Edward Mendelson. New York: Vintage, 1991.

"Concerning the Unpredictable." In *Forewords and Afterwords*. Edward Mendelson, selected. New York: Random House, 1973. 464–73.

Diaries. 1963, 1964, 1965, 1967, 1969, 1973. *Berg Collection of English and American Literature*. New York Public Library.

"E.M. Forster." Written for but not published in *We Moderns: Gotham Book Mart 1920–1940*. *The Complete Works of W.H. Auden*. Prose. Vol. III, 1949–1955, Ed. Edward Mendelson. Princeton University Press, 2008. 613–14.

"Introduction to Paul Bunyan." In *The Complete Works of W.H. Auden*. Prose. Vol. IV, 1956–1962. Ed. Edward Mendelson. Woodstock: Princeton University Press, 2010.

"The Justice of Dame Kind." In *Forewords and Afterwords*. Edward Mendelson, selected. New York: Random House, 1973. 459–63.

"Making Knowing Judging." In *The Dyer's Hand*. New York: Vintage, 1989. 31–60.

"Paul Bunyan." In *The Complete Works of W.H. Auden*. Libretti. 1939–1973. Ed. Edward Mendelson. Princeton, NJ: Princeton University Press, 1993. 3–46.

"The Poet and The City." In *The Dyer's Hand*. New York: Vintage, 1989. 72–89.

"Squares and Oblongs." In *Language: An Enquiry Into Its Meaning and Function. Science of Culture Series*. Vol. VIII. Ed. Ruth Nanda Anshen. New York: Harper, 1957. 174–8.

"Squares and Oblongs." In *Poets at Work*. New York: Harcourt, 1948. 163–81.

"Today's Poet." 1962. In *The Complete Works of W.H. Auden*. Prose. Vol. IV, 1956–1962. Ed. Edward Mendelson. Woodstock: Princeton University Press, 2010.

"Transplanted Englishman Views US" In *The Complete Works of W.H. Auden*. Prose. Vol. IV, 1956–1962. Ed. Edward Mendelson. Woodstock: Princeton University Press, 2010.

"Two Bestiaries." In *The Dyer's Hand*. New York: Vintage, 1989. 277–305.

"The Virgin and The Dynamo." In *The Dyer's Hand*. New York: Vintage, 1989. 61–71.

"Words and the Word." In *Secondary Worlds*. New York: Random, 1968. 117–144.

Bahlke, George W. "From The Later Auden ('Horae Canonicae')." In *Critical Essays on W.H. Auden*. Ed. George W. Bahlke. New York: G.K. Hall, 1991. 14651.

Balazic, Todd. "Embodied Consciousness and the Poetic Sense of the World." *SubStance*. 32.1 (2003): 110–27.

Barad, Karen. *Meeting the Universe Halfway: Quantam Physics and the Entanglement of Matter and Meaning*. Durham, SC: Duke University Press, 2007.

Bate, Jonathan. *Romantic Ecology: Wordsworth and the Environmental Tradition*. London: Routledge, 1991.

Beauman, Nicola. *Morgan: A Biography of E.M. Forster*. London: Hodder and Stoughton, 1993.

Beer, Gillian. *Virginia Woolf: The Common Ground*. Ann Arbor, MI: University of Michigan Press, 1997.

Bell, Quentin. *Virginia Woolf: A Biography*. New York: Harcourt, 1972.

Bergthaller, Hannes. "Limits of Agency: Notes on the Material Turn from a Systems-Theoretical Perspective." Eds. Serenella Iovino and Serpil Oppermann. *Material Ecocriticism*. Bloomington: Indiana University Press, 2014. 37–50.

Bergthaller, Rob Emmett, Adeline Johns-Putra, Agnes Kneitz, Susanna Lidström, Shane McCorristine, Isabel Pérez Ramos, Dana Phillips, Kate Rigby, and Libby Robin. "Mapping Common Ground: Ecocriticism, Environmental History, and the Environmental Humanities." *Environmental Humanities.* Vol. 5 (2014): 261–76.

Bishop, Edward L. "Pursuing 'It' Through 'Kew Gardens'." *Studies in Short Fiction.* 19.3 (Summer 1982): 269–75.

Blake, William. "The Tyger." 1794. *Norton Anthology of English Literature: The Romantic Period.* Vol. 2A. New York: Norton, 2000. 54.

Booth, Howard J. "Maurice." In *The Cambridge Companion to E.M. Forster.* Ed. David Bradshaw. New York: Cambridge University Press, 2007. 173–87.

Born, Daniel. "Private Gardens, Public Swamps: Howard's End and the Revaluation of Liberal Guilt." *Novel: A Forum on Fiction.* 25.2 (1992): 141–59.

Bourne-Taylor, Carole and Ariane Mildenberg. "Introduction: Phenomenology, Modernism and Beyond." In *Phenomenology, Modernism, and Beyond* Bern, Switzerland: Peter Lang, 2010. 1–38.

Bradbury, Malcolm. "The Cities of Modernism." In *Modernism 1890–1930.* Eds. Malcolm Bradbury and James McFarlane. London: Penguin, 1991. 96–104.

Bradshaw, David. "Howards End." In *The Cambridge Companion to E.M. Forster.* Ed. David Bradshaw. New York: Cambridge University Press, 2007. 151–72.

Briggs, Julia. *Virginia Woolf: An Inner Life.* New York: Harcourt, 2005.

Bryson, Scott J. "Introduction." In *Ecopoetry: A Critical Introduction.* Ed. J. Scott Bryson. Salt Lake City: University of Utah Press, 2002. 1–13.

Bucknell, Katherine (ed.). *In Solitude, for Company: W.H. Auden After 1940:* Unpublished Prose and Recent Criticism (Auden Studies III), Oxford: Oxford University Press, 1996.

Buell, Lawrence. *The Future of Environmental Criticism: Environmental Crisis and Literary Imagination.* Malden, MA: Blackwell, 2005.

Caughie, Pamela. "Dogs and Servants." *Virginia Woolf Miscellany* 84 (Fall 2014): 37–9.

Childs, Peter (ed.). *A Routledge Literary Sourcebook on E.M. Forster's A Passage to India.* New York : Routledge, 2002.

Christie, Stuart. *Worlding Forster: The Passage from Pastoral.* New York: Routledge, 2005.

Clark, Timothy. *The Cambridge Introduction to Literature and the Environment.* New York: Cambridge University Press, 2011.

"Nature, Post Nature." In *The Cambridge Companion to Literature and the Environment.* Ed. Louise Westling. Cambridge University Press: New York, 2014. 75–89.

Cohen, Scott. "The Empire from the Street: Virginia Woolf, Wembley, and Imperial Monuments." *Modern Fiction Studies.* 50.1 (2004): 85–109.

Colmer, John. *E.M. Forster: The Personal Voice.* Boston: Routledge, 1975.

Conrad, Joseph. *The Heart of Darkness.* 1902. *Ed. Robert Kimbrough.* New York: Norton, 1988.

Cramer, Patricia Morgne. "Woolf and Theories of Sexuality." In *Virginia Woolf in Context*. Eds. Bryony Randall and Jane Goldman. New York: Cambridge Press, 2012. 129–46.

Crews, Frederick. "Forster and the Liberal Tradition." In *Howards End*. Ed. Paul B. Armstrong. New York: Norton, 1998. 331–40.

Crist, Eileen. *Images of Animals: Anthropomorphism and the Animal Mind*. Philadelphia: Temple University Press, 1999.

Cuddy-Keane, Melba. "Virginia Woolf, Sound Technologies, and the New Aurality." In *Virginia Woolf in the Age of Mechanical Reproduction*. Ed. Pamela L. Caughie. New York: Garland, 2000. 69–96.

Darwin, Charles. *The Expression of Emotions in Man and Animals. 1872*. Charleston, SC: Bibliobazaar, 2007.

Daston, Lorraine and Gregg Mitman (eds.). *Thinking with Animals: New Perspectives on Anthropomorphism*. New York: Columbia University Press, 2005.

Davenport-Hines, Richard. *Auden*. New York: Pantheon, 1995.

DeLoughrey, Elizabeth and George B. Handley (eds.). *Postcolonial Ecologies: Literatures of the Environment*. New York: Oxford University Press, 2011.

De Waal, Frans. *The Bonobo and the Atheist: In Search of Humanism among the Primates*. New York: Norton, 2013.

Doniger, Wendy. "Zoomorphism in Ancient India: Humans More Bestial Than the Beasts." In *Thinking with Animals: New Perspectives on Anthropomorphism*. New York: Columbia University Press, 2005. 17–36.

Doyle, Laura. "'These Emotions of the Body': Intercorporeal Narrative in To the Lighthouse." *Twentieth Century Literature*. 40.1 (Spring 1994): 42–71.

Ellem, Elizabeth Wood. "E.M. Forster's Greenwood." *Journal of Modern Literature*. 5.1 (1976): 89–98.

Emig, Ranier. "Auden and Ecology." In *The Cambridge Companion to W.H. Auden*. Ed. Stan Smith. New York: Cambridge University Press, 2004. 212–25.

Empson, William. *1935. Some Versions of Pastoral*. London: Chatto and Windus, 1950.

Esty, Jed. *A Shrinking Island: Modernism and National Culture in England*. Princeton: Princeton University Press, 2004.

Felder, Helena. *The Greening of Literary Scholarship: Literature, Theory, and the Environment*. Ed. Steven Rosendale. Iowa City: University of Iowa Press, 2002.

Feuerstein, Anna. "What Does Power Smell Like? Canine Epistemology and the Politics of the Pet in Virginia Woolf's *Flush*." *Virginia Woolf Miscellany*. 84 (Fall 2014): 32–3.

Forster, E.M. 1904. "Albergo Empedocle." *The Life to Come and Other Stories*. London: Edward Arnold, 1972. 10–35.

"Arthur Snatchfold." 1928. *The Life to Come and Other Stories*. New York: Penguin, 1989. 128–44.

"The Ascent of F6." In *Two Cheers for Democracy*. New York: Harcourt, 1951.

Aspects of the Novel. 1927. New York: Harcourt, 1964.

Commonplace Book. 1978. Stanford: Stanford University Press, 1985.

England's Pleasant Land. London: Hogarth Press, 1940.

The Hill of Devi. 1953. Middlesex: Penguin, 1965.

Howards End. 1910. New York: Vintage, 1989.

"The Last of Abinger." In *Two Cheers for Democracy*. New York: Harcourt, 1951. 358–63.

"London is a Muddle." In *Two Cheers for Democracy*. New York: Harcourt, 1951. 353–7.

The Longest Journey. New York: Penguin, 1989.

"The Machine Stops." In *Collected Short Stories*. New York: Penguin, 1977. 109–46.

Maurice. 1971. New York: Norton, 1993.

"My Wood." In *Abinger Harvest*. 1936. New York: Harcourt, 1964. 22–6.

"Other Kingdom." 1909. In *Collected Short Stories*. New York: Penguin, 1977. 59–85.

A Passage to India. 1924. New York: Harcourt, 1999.

"The Story of a Panic." 1904. In *Collected Short Stories*. New York: Penguin, 1977. 9–33.

"Three Countries." In *A Routledge Literary Sourcebook on E.M. Forster's A Passage to India*. Ed. Peter Childs. London: Routledge, 2002.

"Virginia Woolf." 1942. In *Two Cheers for Democracy*. New York: Harcourt, 1951. 242–58.

Foster, John Bellamy, Brett Clark, and Richard York. *The Ecological Rift: Capitalism's War on the Earth*. New York: Monthly Review Press, 2010.

Froula, Christine. *Virginia Woolf and the Bloomsbury Avant-Garde*. New York: Columbia University Press, 2005.

Furbank, P.N. *E.M. Forster: A Life*. Vols. 1 and 2. London: Secker and Warburg, 1978.

Gamble, Frederick William. *The Animal World*. London: Williams and Norgate, 1911.

Garrard, Greg. *Ecocriticsm. The New Critical Idiom*. New York: Routledge, 2012.

Gifford, Terry. *Pastoral*. Ed. John Drakakis. *New Critical Idiom*. New York: Routledge, 1999.

"Pastoral, Anti-Pastoral, and Post-Pastoral." In *Cambridge Companion to Literature and the Environment*. Ed. Louise Westling. New York: Cambridge University Press, 2014. 17–30.

Godfrey, Denis. *E.M. Forster's Other Kingdom*. London: Oliver and Boyd, 1968.

Haraway, Donna J. *When Species Meet*. Ed. Cary Wolfe. Minneapolis: University of Minnesota Press, 2008.

Harris, Alexandra. *Romantic Moderns: English Writers, Artists and the Imagination from Virginia Woolf to John Piper*. New York: Thames & Hudson, 2010.

Head, Dominic. "Forster and the Short Story." In *The Cambridge Companion to E.M. Forster*. Ed. David Bradshaw. New York: Cambridge University Press, 2007. 77–91.

Hearne, Vicki. *Adam's Task: Calling Animals by Name*. London: Heinemann, 1987.

Hegglund, Jon. "Defending the Realm: Domestic Space and Mass Cultural Contamination in Howard's End and an Englishman's Home." *English Literature in Translation*. 40.4 (1997): 398–423.

Heise, Ursula K. and Allison Carruth (eds.). "Introduction to Focus: Environmental Humanities." *The American Book Review* 32:1 (2011): 3.

Hennessey, Michael. "Review: 'Believe It or Not, I Have Got Better': Auden after 1940." *Contemporary Literature*, 41.3 (2000): 564–86.

Herman, David. "Modernist Life Writing and Nonhuman Lives: Ecologies of Experience in Virginia Woolf's *Flush*." *MFS: Modern Fiction Studies*. 59.3 (Fall, 2013): 547–68.

Hiltner, Ken. *Renaissance Ecology: Imagining Eden in Milton's England*. Pittsburgh: Duquesne University Press, 2008.

What Else is Pastoral?: Renaissance Literature and the Environment. Ithaca: Cornell University Press, 2011.

Hovanec, Caroline. "Philosophical Barnacles and Empiricist Dogs: Knowing Animals in Modernist Literature and Science." *Configurations*. 21.3 (Fall, 2013): 245–69.

Hudson, William Henry. *Birds In London*. London: J. M. Dent and Sons, Ltd., 1924.

Hutchings, Kevin. *Romantic Ecologies and Colonial Cultures in the British Atlantic World 1770–1850*. Montreal: McGill-Queens University Press, 2009.

Hussey, Mark. *The Singing of the Real World*. Columbus, OH: Ohio State University Press, 1986.

Virginia Woolf A to Z: A Comprehensive Reference for Students, Teachers, and Common Readers to her Life, Work, and Critical Reception. New York: Facts on File, 1995.

"Woolf: After Lives." *Virginia Woolf in Context*. Eds. Bryony Randall and Jane Goldman. New York: Cambridge University Press, 2012. 13–27.

Iovino, Serenella and Serpil Oppermann. "After Green Ecologies: Prismatic Visions." In *Prismatic Ecology: Ecotheory beyond Green*. Ed. Jeffrey Jerome Cohen. Minneapolis: University of Minnesota Press, 2013. 328–36.

"Theorizing Material Ecocriticism: A Diptych." *ISLE: Interdisciplinary Studies in Literature and Environment*. 19.3 (Summer 2012): 448–73.

Isherwood, Christopher. "Some Notes on Auden's Early Poetry." 1937. *Auden: A Collection of Critical Essays*. Ed. Monroe K. Spears. Englewood Cliffs, NJ: Prentice-Hall, 1964. 10–14.

Ittner, Jutta. "Part Spaniel, Part Canine Puzzle: Anthropomorphism in Woolf's Flush and Auster's Timbuktu," *Mosaic: A Journal for the Comparative Study of Literature*. 39.4 (2006): 181–96.

Lackey, Michael "Modernist Anti-Philosophicalism and Virginia Woolf's Critique of Philosophy." *Journal of Modern Literature*. 29.4 (2006): 76–98.

Lakoff, George and Mark Johnson. *Philosophy in the Flesh: The Embodied Mind and Its Challenge to Western Thought*. New York: Perseus, 1999.

Lee, Hermione. *Virginia Woolf.* London: Chatto and Windus, 1996.

"Virginia Woolf's Essays." In *The Cambridge Companion to Virginia Woolf.* Eds. Sue Roe and Susan Sellers. Cambridge: Cambridge University Press, 2000.

Levenson, Michael. *Modernism and the Fate of Individuality: Character and Novelistic Form from Conrad to Woolf.* Cambridge: Cambridge University Press, 1990.

Liberman, Kenneth. "An Inquiry into the Incorporeal Relations between Humans and the Earth." In *Merleau-Ponty and Environmental Philosophy.* Eds. Suzanne L. Cataldi and William S. Hamrick. Albany: State University of New York Press, 2007. 37–49.

Light, Alison. *Mrs. Woolf and the Servants : An Intimate History of Domestic Life in Bloomsbury.* New York: Bloomsbury Press, 2008.

Lin, Lidan. "The Irony of Colonial Humanism: 'A Passage to India' and the Politics of Posthumanism." *ARIEL: A Review of International English Literature.* 28.4 (1997): 133–53.

MacFarlane, Robert. "The Word-Hoard: Robert MacFarlane on Rewilding our Language and our Landscape." *The Guardian, February* 27, 2015. Available at www.theguardian.com/books/2015/feb/27/robert-macfarlane-word-hoard-rewilding-landscape (accessed October 14, 2015).

Mao, Douglas. *Solid Objects: Modernism and the Test of Production.* Princeton, New Jersey: Princeton University Press, 1998.

Marx, John. *The Modernist Novel and the Decline of Empire.* New York: Cambridge University Press, 2005.

Marx, Leo. *The Machine in the Garden: Technology and the Pastoral Ideal in America.* New York: Oxford University Press, 2000.

May, Brian. "Romancing the Stump: Modernism and Colonialism in Forster's A Passage to India." In *Modernism and Colonialism: British and Irish Literature, 1899–1939.* Durham: Duke University Press, 2007. 136–61.

Medalie, David. *E.M. Forster's Modernism.* New York: Palgrave, 2002.

Meeker, Joseph W. *The Comedy of Survival: Literary Ecology and a Play Ethic.* Tucson: University of Arizona Press, 1997.

Mendelson, Edward. "The Body." *W.H. Auden in Context.* Ed. Tony Sharpe. New York: Cambridge University Press, 2013. 195–204.

Later Auden. New York: Farrar, 1999.

"W.H. Auden." In *The Cambridge Companion to English Poets.* Ed. Calude Rawson. Cambridge: Cambridge University Press, 2011. 508–24.

Merleau-Ponty, Maurice. "Metaphysics and the Novel." *Sense and Nonsense.* Trans. Hubert L. Dreyfus and Patricia Allen Dreyfus. Evanston: Northwestern University Press, 1991. 26–40.

Nature: Course Notes from the College de France. Comp. Dominique Segland. Trans. Robert Vallier. Evanston: Northwestern University Press, 2003.

Phenomenology of Perception. Trans. Colin Smith. London: Routledge, 2002.

The Visible and the Invisible. Trans. Alphonso Lingis. Ed. Claude Lefort. Evanston: Northwestern University Press, 1968.

Mildenberg, Ariane. "Openings: Epoché as Aesthetic Tool in Modernist Texts." In *Phenomenology, Modernism, and Beyond* (Bern, Switzerland: Peter Lang, 2010). 41–73.

Moran, Jo Ann Hoeppner. "E.M. Forster's A Passage to India: What Really Happened in the Caves." *MFS: Modern Fiction Studies*. 34.4 (Winter 1988): 596–604.

Morrison, Robert S. "Environmental Concerns: Ecocritical Landmarks, Textmarks, Benchmarks" (book review). *University of Toronto Quarterly*. 71.3 (2002): 811–17.

Mortimer-Sandilands, Catriona and Bruce Erickson. "Introduction: A Genealogy of Queer Ecologies." In *Queer Ecologies: Sex, Nature, Politics, Desire*. Eds. Catriona Mortimer-Sandilands and Bruce Erickson. Bloomington: Indiana University Press, 2010. 1–47.

"Melancholy Natures, Queer Ecologies." In *Queer Ecologies: Sex, Nature, Politics, Desire*. Eds. Catriona Mortimer-Sandilands and Bruce Erickson. Bloomington: Indiana University Press, 2010. 331–58.

Nagel, Thomas. "What is it like to be a bat?" *The Philosophical Review*. 83.4 (October, 1974): 435–50.

Nixon, Rob. *Slow Violence and the Environmentalism of the Poor*. Cambridge, MA: Harvard University Press, 2011.

Oakland, John. "Virginia Woolf's 'Kew Gardens." *English Studies*. 68.3 (June 1987), 264–73.

Oppermann, Serpil. "Ecological Imperialism in British Colonial Fiction." *Edebiyat Fakültesi Dergisi / Journal of Faculty of Letters*. Cilt/Vol. 24, Sayi/ Number 1 (Haziran/June 2007). 179–94.

"From Ecological Postmodernism to Material Ecocriticism: Creative Materiality and Narrative Agency." Eds. Serenella Iovino and Serpil Oppermann. *Material Ecocriticism*. Bloomington: Indiana UP, 2014. 21–36.

"Material Ecocriticism and the Creativity of Storied Matter." *Frame*. 26.2 (November) 2013: 55–69.

Paltin, Judith. "'An Infected Carrier of the Past': Modernist Nature as the Ground for Anti-Realism." *Interdisciplinary Studies in Literature and the Environment*. 20.4 (Autumn 2013): 778–94.

Parham, John. *Green Man Hopkins: Poetry and the Victorian Ecological Imagination*. New York: Rodopi, 2010.

Parry, Benita. "Materiality and Mystification in A Passage to India." *Novel: A Forum on Fiction*. 31.2 (1998): 174–94.

Peppis, Paul. "Forster and England." In *The Cambridge Companion to E.M. Forster*. Ed. David Bradshaw. New York: Cambridge University Press, 2007. 47–61.

"Schools, Movements, Manifestos." In *The Cambridge Companion to Modernist Poetry*. Eds. Alex Davis and Lee M. Jenkins. New York: Cambridge University Press, 2007. 28–50.

Sciences of Modernism: Ethnography, Sexology, and Psychology. New York: Cambridge University Press, 2014.

Phillips, Dana. *The Truth of Ecology: Nature, Culture, and Literature in America*. New York: Oxford University Press, 2003.

Picasso, Pablo. "Picasso Speaks." *The Arts*, New York, May 1923. Available at www.learn.columbia.edu/monographs/picmon/pdf/art_hum_reading_49.pdf (accessed October 14, 2015).

Pound, Ezra. "Canto LXXXI." *The Cantos of Ezra Pound*. 1954. London: Faber, 1986.

—— *Make It New: Essays By Ezra Pound*. New Haven: Yale University Press, 1935.

Rasula, Jed. *This Compost: Ecological Imperatives in American Poetry*. Athens: University of Georgia Press, 2003.

Rohman, Carrie. *Stalking the Subject: Modernism and the Animal*. New York: Columbia University Press, 2009.

Roos, Bonnie and Alex Hunt. "Systems and Secrecy: Postcolonial Ecocriticism and Ghosh's The Calcutta Chromosome." In *The Cambridge Companion to Literature and the Environment*. Ed. Louise Westling. Cambridge University Press: New York, 2014. 184–97.

Ryan, Derek. *Virginia Woolf and the Materiality of Theory: Sex, Animal, Life*. Edinburgh: Edinburgh University Press, 2013.

Sackville-West, Vita. *Country Notes*. London: M. Joseph, 1939.

Said, Edward. *Culture and Imperialism*. New York: Knopf, 1993.

Schama, Simon. *Landscape and Memory*. New York: Vintage, 1995.

Scott, Bonnie Kime. *In the Hollow of the Wave: Virginia Woolf and the Modernist Uses of Nature*. Charlottesville: University of Virginia Press, 2012.

Sharpe, Tony. *W.H. Auden*. New York: Routledge, 2007.

Sheehan, Paul. *Modernism, Narrative, and Humanism*. New York: Cambridge University Press, 2002.

Shwarz, Daniel. *Reading the Modern British and Irish Novel: 1890–1930*. Malden, MA: Blackwell, 2005.

Smith, Craig. "Across the Widest Gulf: Nonhuman Subjectivity in Virginia Woolf's Flush." *Twentieth Century Literature: A Scholarly and Critical Journal*. 48.3 (September, 2002): 348–62.

Snaith, Anna. "Of Fanciers, Footnotes, and Fascism: Virginia Woolf's *Flush*." *Modern Fiction Studies*. 48.3 (2002): 614–36.

Stallworthy, Jon. *Wilfred Owen*. Oxford: Oxford University Press, 1998.

Stape, J.H. *An E.M. Forster Chronology*. London: MacMillan, 1993.

Staveley, Alice. "Conversations at Kew: Reading Woolf's Feminist Narratology." *Trespassing Boundaries: Virginia Woolf's Short Fiction*. Eds. Kathryn N. Benzel and Ruth Hoberman. New York: Palgrave, 2004. 39–62.

Stevenson, Randall. "Forster and Modernism." In *The Cambridge Companion to E.M. Forster*. Ed. David Bradshaw. New York: Cambridge University Press, 2007. 209–22.

Stone, Wilfred. H. "Forster: the Environmentalist." In *Seeing Double: Revisioning Edwardian and Modernist Literature*. Eds. Carola M. Kaplan and Anne B. Simpson. New York: St. Martin's, 1996. 171–92.

Suleri, Sara. "The Geography of *A Passage to India*." In *Literature in the Modern World Critical Essays and Documents*. Ed. Dennis Walder. New York City: Oxford University Press, 1990. 245–50.

Summers, Claude. "The Flesh Educating the Spirit: *Maurice.*" In *Critical Essays on E.M. Forster.* Ed. Alan Wilde. Boston: G.K. Hall, 1985. 95–112.

Theocritus. *The Poems of Theocritus.* Trans. and Intros. Anna Rist. Chapel Hill: University North Carolina Press, 1978.

Thoreau, Henry D. "Walking." In *Wild Apples and Other Natural History Essays.* Ed. William Rossi. Athens: University Georgia Press, 2002. 59–92.

Turner, Henry S. "Empires of Objects: Accumulation and Entropy in Howards End." *Twentieth Century Literature: A Scholarly and Critical Journal.* 26.3. (Fall 2000): 328–45.

Virgil. *The Eclogues of Virgil.* Trans. David Ferry. New York: Farrar, 1999.

Wasley, Aidan. "Ideas of America." *W.H. Auden in Context.* Tony Sharpe, Ed. New York: Cambridge University Press, 2013. 47–55.

Watson, Robert. *Back to Nature: The Green and the Real in Late Renaissance Literature.* Philadelphia: University of Pennsylvania Press, 2007.

Westling, Louise. "Literature and Ecology." In *Teaching Ecocriticism and Green Cultural Studies.* Ed. Greg Garrard. London: Palgrave Macmillan, 2012. 75–89.

The Logos of the Living World: Merleau-Ponty, Animals, and Language. Fordham University Press: New York, 2014.

"Virginia Woolf and the Flesh of the World." In *New Literary History.* 30.4 (Autumn 1999): 855–75.

Wheeler, Wendy. *The Whole Creature: Complexity, Biosemiotics and the Evolution of Culture.* London: Lawrence & Wishart, 2006.

Williams, Raymond. *The Country and the City.* New York: Oxford University Press, 1973.

Wolfe, Cary. *Animal Rites: American Culture, the Discourse of Species, and Posthumanist Theory.* Chicago: University of Chicago Press, 2003.

"Introduction." In *Zoontologies: The Question of the Animal.* Ed. Cary Wolfe. Minneapolis: University of Minnesota Press, 2003.

Woolf, Virginia. *Between the Acts.* 1941. London: Penguin, 1992.

"The Countess of Pembroke's Arcadia." In *The Second Common Reader.* 1932. New York: Harcourt, 1932. 32–41.

"Death of the Moth." In *The Death of the Moth and Other Essays.* New York: Harcourt, 1970. 3–6.

The Diary of Virginia Woolf. Vols. I–V. Ed. Anne Olivier Bell. New York: Harcourt, 1982.

Flush. London: Hogarth Press, 1933.

"How It Strikes A Contemporary." In *The Common Reader.* 1925. New York: Harcourt, 1984. 231–41.

"Kew Gardens." 1919. In *The Complete Shorter Fiction of Virginia Woolf.* Ed. Susan Dick. New York: Harcourt, 1989. 90–5.

"Outlines." In *The Common Reader.* 1925. Ed. Andrew McNeillie. New York: Harcourt, 1984. 183–205.

"Modern Fiction." In *The Common Reader.* 1925. Ed. Andrew McNeillie. New York: Harcourt, 1984. 146–54.

Mrs. Dalloway. 1925. Ed. Mark Hussey. New York: Harcourt, 2005.

"The Novels of E.M. Forster." In *The Death of the Moth and Other Essays*. 1942. San Diego: Harcourt, 1970. 161–75.

"The Novels of Thomas Hardy." In *The Second Common Reader*. 1933. New York: Harcourt, 1932. 222–32.

A Passionate Apprentice. Ed. Michael E. Leaska. London: Pimlico, 2004.

"The Pastons and Chaucer." In *The Common Reader*. 1925. Ed. Andrew McNeillie. New York: Harcourt, 1984. 3–22.

"Poets' Letters." In *The Essays of Virginia Woolf*. Vol. I. Ed. Andrew McNeillie. New York: Harcourt, 1986. 101–5.

"A Sketch of the Past." 1939. In *Moments of Being: Unpublished Autobiographical Writings*. Ed. Jeanne Schulkind. New York: Harcourt, 1976. 64–137.

Three Guineas. New York: Harcourt, 1938.

"Thunder at Wembley." 1924. In *The Essays of Virginia Woolf*. Vol. 3. Ed. Andrew McNeillie. New York: Harcourt, 1986. 410–14.

To the Lighthouse. Ed. Mark Hussey. New York: Harcourt, 2005.

The Waves. 1931. New York: Harcourt, 1978.

Wylie, Dan. "The Anthropomorphic Ethic: Fiction and the Animal Mind in Virginia Woolf's Flush and Barbara Gowdy's The White Bone." *ISLE: Interdisciplinary Studies in Literature and Environment*. 9.2 (2002): 115–31.

Zapf, Hubert. "Creative Matter and Creative Mind." In *Material Ecocriticism*. Eds. Serenella Iovino and Serpil Oppermann. Bloomington: Indiana University Press, 2014. 51–66.

Index